Aimee Semple McPherson

Aimee Semple McPherson

The Story of My Life

WORD BOOKS, Publisher
Waco, Texas

Contents

INTRODUCTION

Before her passing in September, 1944, Aimee Semple Mc-Pherson had commenced writing a new autobiography. Her previous volumes of this nature, *This Is That* and *In the Service of the King,* ended with the opening of Angelus Temple and the vindication after the kidnapping, respectively. Thus, the last seventeen years of her life has not been published in book form.

The manuscript which forms the basis for this book remained unnoticed among the archives for more than two decades. When its presence was called to the attention of the Heritage Committee of the International Church of the Foursquare Gospel, the chairman of that committee, Rev. Charles Duarte, was authorized to contact the present writer with a view to completing the manuscript. His letter of February 24, 1969, stated, "We need someone who will complete the story in her style of writing, someone who personally knew her."

The plan was to finish the autobiography using Sister McPherson's own accounts of the episodes of her life, as contained in sermons, articles, and documents both published and unpublished which were at hand. At the time the assignment was accepted, I had no idea of the enormous extent of research materials—thousands and thousands of pages and millions of words—which were available to read. It was necessary to go through the complete files of Sister's publications from 1917 and accumulated reams of photocopies and clippings pertaining to her life. Several secretaries spent weeks in photocopying every personal reference found in the stenographically reported sermons on file in the offices of the International Church of the Foursquare Gospel. Many sets of sermon notes with personal incidents outlined were consulted, besides scores of pertinent documents, many of which were supplied personally by Dr. Rolf K. McPherson.

The story, as it appears here, is Sister's story—in her very own words, as much as possible, gleaned from the many sources relating her experiences beyond the period covered in the manuscript which was not finished at the time of her death. There is much material which could have been added, relating interesting incidents and details, but such inclusion would have lengthened

7

the book unduly, and in the case of describing revival meetings would have been largely repetitious.

In recent years there have appeared many distorted portrayals of Aimee Semple McPherson, researched almost entirely from unfavorable press publicity and the testimony of people who opposed her. Because of this I requested permission to insert in this introduction a quotation from a letter written by Dr. Rolf McPherson, her son, commenting on a statement in a proposed publication to the effect that his mother had a "high-strung temperament" and was given to "flying into uncontrollable fits of temper." Dr. McPherson wrote:

> I am at a loss to understand where anyone originally gained this impression, for surely those who knew her were greatly impressed by her even temperament and ability to deal calmly with any situation. I have never in all my life seen her lose her temper in any manner, and in the rearing of us children she was always able to deal with us diplomatically rather than through any means of punishment. I just do not believe that there is one witness who could be found to say that he saw her have an "uncontrollable fit of temper." Never once in her ministry did she lash back at those who were critical of her.

The secret of Sister McPherson's ministry was her unique ability, under the anointing of the Holy Spirit, to make Jesus real to her audiences—to make him so real that congregations recognized his wonderful presence in their midst, not just in theory but in actual fellowship. Her overwhelming desire was to lift up Christ that all men might be drawn unto him. With the prayer that this story of her life will likewise tend to glorify Jesus Christ, by showing what he can do through a humble handmaiden, it is offered to the reading public.

RAYMOND L. COX

1

Childhood Kaleidoscope

"Do you want to kill her?"

"Of course not!"

"Well, mark my words, if you take that child out into the cold, she'll die of pneumonia!"

"She'll be as warm as a bug in a rug."

"Take a look at that window!"

"I have been for anxious hours."

"It's zero weather, and snow is in the air."

As she answered the older woman, there were splashes of crimson in the young mother's cheeks, deep hued as the peonies that had lately bloomed in the garden. A light of high resolve glowed in her dark brown eyes. She closed the oven door softly and gathered up a pile of blankets that had been warming over a chair. Approaching the red-checkered tablecloth, she began spreading them out carefully, the heaviest on the bottom, and then a mountainous, graduating heap that ended in a soft, small square of pink.

The kitchen was cheerful and cozy under the mellow light of the hanging kerosene lamp. But outside large snowflakes danced merrily and came to flatten themselves like inquisitive white stars against the windowpane. "It's only five miles," she said, placing a tiny, squirming babe on the table and beginning to wrap her up in layer after layer.

"Land sakes! She's only three weeks old! What good can a church service do her yet?"

"The Bible says, 'Train up a child in the way he should go, and when he is old he will not depart from it,' and I feel that the training cannot begin too soon. I want her to be accustomed to the singing, the music, and general revival atmosphere from earliest infancy."

Flossie was unfastened from her hitching post, the rubber

9

sheet taken from her steaming back and carefully spread over
the lap robes. The lines unwound from the whip by the light
which Maria held were cuddled up in the mother's right hand,
and the young daughter clasped securely in her left arm.

We reached the meeting house where the lights were shining
bravely through the bleak barrack windows. The crude, wooden
benches held a smattering of humble, earnest folk. A bebraided
band was playing. I was carried down the aisle to the front seat
where glowing embers crackled merrily in the reddened brass
burner. Tambourines were jingling. I wakened and joined
heartily in the refrain.

Of course, I remember none of this, but on good authority
I am told that back in the farmhouse that night an anxious
household was proudly assured, "Why, anyone can tell that
she is going to be an evangelist! You should have seen the way
in which she contributed to the interest and music of the
evening!"

Thus it came about that when six weeks old, I was dedicated
to Christian service in a solemnly impressive ceremony wherein
the most grave questions were asked and answered. And from
my earliest recollection, I was rocked to sleep with Bible stories.
The result was that before I was four years old I could stand on
a chair in a meeting or on a drumhead on the corner and recite
almost every story as easily as the neighbor's young ones could
lisp, "Mistress Mary, quite contrary, how does your garden
grow?"

Sunday school was the most exciting social event of my baby
years. One Sabbath morning a huge eye had been drawn upon
the blackboard beneath the printed word: "Thou God seest me."
That eye made me vaguely uncomfortable. Wherever I moved,
it followed me with baleful insistence. It filled me with vague
alarm to know that my slightest thought and deed was thus
followed and weighed.

"Mother," I ventured as we jogged along the country road
behind the sorrel mare, "can God see me now?"

"Yes, dear. Why?"

"Even through the top of the buggy?"

"Um-hum!"

"Can he see me now?" I called later from beneath the reser-
voir of the steel kitchen range.

"Anywhere and everywhere, darling."

"Thanks," I said in a subdued tone and went down into the cellar to cut new potato sprouts for the spring planting. I worked with religious industry, for was not the Great Eye still following me?

The day before election, I was five years old. All but father and I had gone to town. "Aimee," he called.

"Yes, daddy."

"The mayor of Ingersoll and some of the councilmen are to visit me this afternoon. I'd like to look my very best. Do you think you are old enough to wash my hair?"

"I'm almost five!" I flamed.

"All right! All right!" he soothed, "Get busy!"

For soft water, I melted snow in a kettle. For a rinse, I filled a pitcher from the cistern and skimmed the polliwogs out. To protect his eyes, I gave him a towel, saying, "Bend over and hold it tight."

For long minutes I lathered and rubbed the curly head and beard I loved so well. "What a pity folk's hair gets yellow before it turns real white," I mourned.

"'Twill be white soon enough!" he sputtered through the suds.

"I know, but this is a 'portant day!"

Just then I had a bright idea. I had seen Aunt Elizabeth put bluing in yellow clothes to make them snowy. Why would it not have the same effect on my father's hair? Running to the kitchen cabinet, I climbed upon a high enamel stool and took down the large bottle labeled Indigo Blue, removed the cork, and poured half its contents over the down-bent head.

I would have used it all, but the queer color it evolved frightened me. Recorking the container, I set it down and went back to furious soaping. But horror of horrors, it wouldn't come out! Down through his curls, down through his beard, all through his mustache ran the liquid dye.

Poor dad! He looked exactly like Bluebeard in the picture book he had smuggled to my room. Trying to keep my voice steady, I said, "Watch out for the soap!"

"I am."

"Keep your eyes shut!"

"Yep!"

I worked for dear life. After the fourth or fifth soaping, dad straightened his back, still holding the towel to his eyes, and roared, "Say, young woman, just how dirty do you think I am?"

"Just a jiffy!" I wheedled. But still the stubborn hue would not budge. At that moment the mayor arrived.

"I say, Jim, are you in?" called a voice from the driveway.

"Let me loose!" cried my father, jumping up and throwing the cloth from his eyes. "Here, give me that dry towel—quick!" Rubbing vigorously, he shouted, "Be right out!" He ran his unsuspecting fingers through his blue locks, smoothed his turquoise beard, and hurried out.

Electrified by fear, I ran to the mirror and turned it to the wall. Just then a "w-h-o-o-p!??!" came from the yard. Regaining my corner, I stood there petrified. The door opened, dad burst in, walked to the looking-glass, turned it around, staggered back, and came toward me.

From this point on, the story is too painful to relate! Suffice it to say that that afternoon he went to town, had a barber shave off his hair, beard, and mustache. But even then there remained an indigo tip to the bristling stubble. The Methodist choir was without a leader for the ensuing month, and I was in disgrace.

The incident left such an indelible impression upon my mind that I have used it throughout my later years to assure hopeless men, "Though no power on earth can remove the stains left by carelessness and sin, the fountain opened in the house of David can wash them whiter than the driven snow."

Sometimes I meet youngsters who are flirting with temptation. "I am a mere spectator, not a participant!" they explain. For ammunition I delve into my years of adolescence.

Aunt Elizabeth had baked scads of cookies. After giving me six, she had retired for an afternoon nap, saying, "No more for you until suppertime!"

For a few moments I had sat upon the back porch, playing with the thirteen kittens my wild protestations had saved from drowning. Finally they grew sleepy. I was awake. "U-m-m-m! But those cakes were good!" I rhapsodized. "I'll go into the pantry and have a look at the great tin which contains them."

They were on the very topmost shelf. I decided to climb up and have a look at them, the better to visualize the treat that lay in store. Past large pans of rich milk, over baskets of eggs, cans of flour, sugar, baking powder, corn meal, butter, lard, preserves, currants, raisins, cheese, marshmallows, and flavorings, I made my ascending way. Balancing myself with wide-spread feet amidst the soap chips and vinegar, I secured a grip on the board beneath the maple-sugar patties and lifted the lid of the cookie-filled spectacle.

"Why not hold one in your hand a moment?" whispered the Tempter. "You don't need to eat it."

"Guess I will," I decided.

Just as I reached in, something terrible happened! The nails must have pulled out of the cleats which supported the shelves. At any rate, down came cookies, cheese, sugar, flour, oatmeal, cream of wheat, hominy, bacon, milk pans, eggs, and girl! Amid the frightful din, I picked myself up and sat holding my poor head. My father entered with a birch switch and went to work. I have never seen anyone beat up the batter of a cake so quickly. He had all the ingredients close at hand!

Like all other restless youngsters, I was constantly getting into dilemmas and difficulties. After similar outrages to the dignity of my household, I would be banished to my room and told that in exactly one-half an hour I would be spanked. I was thoroughly familiar with those whippings. They were no gentle love pats, and my parents never stopped till I was a thoroughly chastised girl.

The time of waiting for the footsteps on the stair, the opening of the door, and the descending palm was the worst of all. On one such occasion I stood looking wildly about for a way out of the dilemma. No earthly recourse was nigh. Taught as I was about heavenly intervention, I thought of prayer. Dropping to my knees by the side of my bed, I began to pray, loudly, earnestly, "Oh, God, don't let mama whip me! Oh, God, dear, kind, sweet God, don't let mama spank me!"

At this moment the door opened. I knew that my mother stood framed in the portal, the very analogy of justice. Even yet the skies might send an answer to my petition. I kept my eyes shut tightly and with firm-clasped hands continued my wail, "Oh, God, don't let mama whip me!"

Poor soul! She was probably in a quandary. Doubtless I needed chastisement, but on the other hand would not the punishment destroy my faith in prayer? "Oh, God . . ."

I heard a chuckle of irrepressible laughter behind me and opened my eyes. "Your father has just brought up a white owl from the woods," she said. "It's down in the kitchen on the back of a chair. Perhaps you'd better go down and look at it."

"Thank you, God!" I breathed and dashed out to slide down the banister. The lesson taught me that the worst sinner might find mercy upon his knees in fervent prayer.

School Days

"Ready?" called my father up the stovepipe hole which led into my room. It was the occasion of my first day at school.

"Ready," I answered from the square of the stairway.

"Do you know your letters, young lady?" he asked as Flossie jogged along.

"No."

"You should learn at least the first three."

"Tell me."

"Letter rip, letter tear, and letter fly."

"I wonder whether I can remember them?"

"Better say them over a few times."

"Letter rip, letter tear, letter fly. Letter rip, letter tear, letter fly. Letter rip, letter tear, letter fly."

In due time I stood before the austere English master amid the long line of new recruits.

"And what's your name, little girl?"

"Aimee Elizabeth."

"How much do you know?"

"The first three letters of the alphabet."

"May I hear them?"

"Certainly. Letter rip, letter tear, letter fly."

The roar which rocked the schoolhouse left me sitting discomfited on a high stool behind a red-clothed tabletop, wearing a high, pointed dunce cap, wondering what it was all about. But at recess I redeemed myself.

"Salvation Army! Salvation Army!" chanted a taunting group.

"Have you ever played it?" I asked.

"No!" scoffed the boys.

"Bring that cheese box for a drum, a piece of wood for a stick, and that fishing pole for a flagstaff," I ordered. "I'll go get the red tablecloth for a banner." Fatty Peck carried the standard. I beat the drum and led out in "Hold the fort, for I am coming . . ."

The parade was a great success. 'Round the school, the woodshed, and the horse stable we went singing, "Glory be, we've got him on the run, shot the devil with the gospel gun." For a time the girls stood scornfully at one side, but they finally swung into line at the rear, beating shingles for tambourines and using mufflers for bonnets.

High school, even in a town of five thousand, had its complexities for the country girl. Alternately riding horseback, bicycle, buggy, or cutter, one moved up from grade to grade.

"See what I have here," I called to my father one evening, "a handsomely engraved formal invitation to a collegiate ball!"

"But, my dear, you cannot go," mother interjected.

"Why?"

"Because you are a Methodist, and Methodists don't go to dances." (Of course, all this happened years ago. Methods and standards have changed perceptibly since then.)

"Everyone else is permitting their children to go!" I wailed. "May I?"

"No," my father spoke up.

"Don't be old fashioned," I told them.

"Again, I say *no!*"

But in the end my parents relented. They usually did if I stuck to my text long enough. Attired in a brand-new dress and dancing slippers, I pirouetted gaily before the mirror and set forth. Radiantly happy on the surface, I was secretly troubled within, for I surmised that at that moment a prayer meeting was being held in my behalf at home. But after the first waltz I forgot all about my qualms. Dancing must be all right. My partner was

exceptionally good, and he was none other than the young
Presbyterian minister.

Thereafter life became a busy little round of dances, skating
rinks, novels, and ragtime music. Elinor Glynn was at the top
of the pile of books, and the Bible was at the bottom. "Mandy
Lee" and other hit tunes were at the foreground of the new
piano. The hymnal was pushed farther and farther to the rear.

In the upper class a new book was introduced. It was labeled,
High School Physical Geography, but it rocked the foundations
of my early faith. So-called science was arraigned against the
Word of God, evolution against Genesis, and mundane chance
against the miraculous. Aghast at its heresy, I cornered a pro-
fessor in his laboratory den. "May I speak to you, sir?"

"Yes, little girl."

"I have been brought up to believe that my Bible is infallible."

"Yes. Go on."

"I find my new textbook diametrically opposed to its teachings. Would you please tell me which to believe?"

Looking down from his superior years of height and wisdom,
he smiled tolerantly. "Your Bible is a wonderful classic of litera-
ture. As such, it is worthy of your notice and study. But as to
its scientific value and early history of the human race, it is
woefully bigoted and misinformed. Ancient superstitions have
been superseded by biological research, faith by nebular hypothesis, and the mud man of the Pentateuch by the amoeba of
Darwin."

"Then, the school book . . . ?" I quavered.

"Is correct!" he snapped.

"And . . . the Bible is filled with falsehoods?"

"With errors," he amended.

I had a feeling that the ground had opened up and swallowed
me. I was falling down, down, down, down into a black coal
chute where leering specters jeered, "There is no God! There is
no heaven! There is no hell! If the Scriptures tell one lie, they
must leak like a sieve! Now where's your faith? Now where's
your faith?"

"C-could you tell me more of your proofs?" I stammered.

Something about my blanched face must have stricken his
heart, for the teacher gathered up his papers and exclaimed
hastily, "I'm due in my class, but here are some library references," and he went out.

I stood staring at the titles of the suggested books and was soon in the town library reading Voltaire, Ingersoll, Paine, and others. If they were true, then religion was a travesty and a farce. Church bells were a hollow mockery. Fox's martyrs had died in a vain cause. Missionaries were misguided souls. Prayer was a useless superstitious repetition.

With my head buzzing like an overturned beehive, I went home to the farm and met my father at the top door of the cellar as he ascended with a broad pan of cream for the churning. "How do you know there is a God?" I demanded through stiff lips.

"Aimee! What do you mean?" he roared, almost falling down the cellar, milk and all.

"I mean just what I say," I stood my ground. "All my life you have spoken with assurance of an all-seeing, all-knowing Father. But what proof have you of his actual existence? Have you ever seen him? Did your father or his parent see him? How do you know that it is not all a myth?"

"Have you gone mad?" he cried.

"Don't be like that! I have to know."

"Who made the constellations of suns, moons, stars, and satellites?"

"The schoolbooks explain all that, daddy," I replied out of my immature research. "These bodies once consisted of molecules which were drawn together by the law of gravity. They acquired a whirling motion and became a whirling gaseous mass. The lunar bodies, including the earth, were thrown into stellar space. The sun flew off, the moon flew off, the stars flew off," said I, emphasizing the oration with wide-swung book bag. "Then the earth flew off, and here we are!"

"Yes, here we are. But who was the Lawgiver back of the laws of gravitation?"

"The schoolbooks do not explain that."

"If there is no Creator, who made man?"

"Oh, they do account for that!"

"Yes?"

"He just happened."

"Providentially or accidentally?"

"Accidentally. The lavalike ball of earth grew cool on the outer surface, caved in in spots, and salty oceans formed."

"And then?"

"Our great, great, great, great grandmother appeared."

"Her name?"

"The amoeba. You have probably never heard of her, but she is a very important personage in the textbooks of today."

"Of what did her family tree consist?"

"On that point, too, the writers seem a bit hazy. She may have ridden to earth on a fiery comet, but I gather that spontaneous generation is the most popular hypothesis."

"That's a new word in this household."

"Which?"

"Hypothesis."

"We use it every day."

"Can you define it?"

"Not exactly."

"Then bring down the dictionary."

Webster was taken from his frequently invaded shelf, and I read, "A state of things assumed as a basis of argument; a theory which may or may not prove to be true; supposition, conjecture."

"Go on," said my father coldly, "tell me more of this conjectured antecedent."

"She is the oldest, simplest, and lowest form of cell life and began in the ocean. Her size is so diminutive that fifty thousand could pass through the eye of a needle without crowding."

"And she set the clock of life ticking which later evolved all the greater mammals?"

"So we are taught."

"Hmm! Someone should turn the old nursery rhyme to

> Poor little amoeba,
> Don't you cry,
> You'll be an elephant
> By and by."

"Dad! Be serious!"

"I was never more serious in my life. How did the old girl first get the spark of life?"

"I've told you—spontaneous generation."

"Do your professors claim that they can evoke something out of nothing today?"

"No, but they expect their experiments soon to yield results. Voltaire spent some thirty years watching one cell of water, hoping to see life spring forth, but was unrewarded."

"Men used to claim that because a piece of meat left exposed gave rise to maggots, that this was a sustaining proof," he said. "But I understand that Pasteur has thoroughly discredited all that by the vacuum and by hermetic sealing."

"At any rate, we are still teaching it. And it's bidding fair to turn out a goodly number of agnostics, if not atheists."

"There'll be no agnostics in this family," came the grim rejoinder. "You are going to a revival meeting with us tomorrow night."

"Impossible!" I cried. "Tomorrow night is the fancy dress carnival at the skating rink. I have my costume and am scheduled to lead the first ice waltz."

"Then call for your mother and me at the church as soon as it is over. Be there at nine sharp."

"Yes, sir."

The carnival was a gala one. Clowns and kings, snow queens and tumblers, bands and gaiety, laughter and spills, all were replete. Regretfully, I slipped out, removed my skates, and drove Fritzie among the jingle of cutter bells and the song of frosted sled runners to the door of the church. It was crowded, and I stood with my back to the wall as the evangelist was giving the altar call.

"Come on! Come on!" he called. "Make your decision tonight. This may be your last opportunity. Come while all of life lies before you. Hesitate no longer. Christ is awaiting your answer. Come! Come!"

With the strains of the ice-rink band still ringing in my ears, the call left me unmoved. Revivals were not new to me. But the last tune played at the carnival was. I hummed it over as I waited my parents' exit.

"There'll come a day of reckoning!" said the preacher, "a day when sinners will be obliged to pay for their neglect."

His eyes seemed to search me out. I stood at attention. "This is ridiculous," I reassured myself. "He can't mean me!"

"My dear, are you a Christian?"

I started as the hand of a young woman about my own age was laid upon my shoulder. I recognized her as the daughter of the evangelist. Drawing myself to my full height, I answered haughtily, "No! I go to high school!"

"What has that to do with it?"

"I study evolution."

"So do I," she acknowledged, "but while I pass my examinations by writing, 'The monkey is my cousin,' my mind repudiates the preposterous theory and assures me that God and not the ape is my Father."

"It is all too complicated for me," I protested.

"But—these Christians—how happy they are!"

"They are not real Christians!"

"Why, what do you mean?"

"With one hand they pay money to build churches and convert us; with the other they pay taxes to make us atheists."

"You poor dear! Wait here till I go get my mother."

"I'll wait," I answered. "My parents are down in front."

The youthful zealot disappeared and soon returned. A sweet-faced woman followed in her wake. She talked to me earnestly for a few moments, then worried, "Stay here till I fetch my husband."

Nervously I stood my ground, shifting from one foot to the other. The snow was flurrying outside, and I could hear Fritzie's impatient whinnyings. Why didn't my parents come along? Revival songs filled the air:

> Why do you wait, dear brother?
> Oh, why do you tarry so long?
> Your Savior is waiting to give you
> A place in that sanctified throng.

The evangelist, fortified by his wife and daughter, approached. "What's this I hear about evolution?" he asked.

A little crowd was gathering. My cheeks grew hot as I was singled out for attack. My father and mother stood on the edge of the crowd. Their cheeks were as red as my own. Valiantly I stood my ground, but to no avail. At best it seems the adherent of evolution stands in slippery places. I was soon beaten back to my last remaining trench.

"Well," said I, "if the Bible is true, why do our neighbors pay good tax money to tear down our faith?"

"That I cannot answer," said my inquisitor.

That night there was a strange and pregnant silence in the cutter. Only the snow-muffled trit-trot of the horses' feet and the deep-throated melody of the sleighbells broke the stillness. I stole a sidewise glance at the face of my mother. It was decidedly grave, her lips set in an unaccustomed straight line. I turned toward my father and was fascinated by a slow procession of tears that trickled down his face, landed in his beard, and froze there like salted diamonds.

Somehow I did not feel very proud of the scene I had made in the back of the meeting hall. I had committed the most heinous sin in my category—I had hurt someone deeply. Hurt myself? Oh, yes, I might do that with impunity. That was my business. But hurt others? To me that was the crime unforgivable.

In silence we topped the last hill. In silence I dismounted and swung wide the broad gate. In silence I lighted the lantern and helped dad unhitch Fritzie and close the barn doors. Wordlessly we lighted our lamps, wound the clock, fed the cats and the dog, locked the door, and went to our respective rooms. One might have thought that this was the crack of doom. I turned the key of my door softly, went to my window, threw it wide, and without stopping to remove my coat or hat, kneeled down and looked out.

Moon magic melted the misty hills. The entire landscape lay under a coverlet of sparkling snow. Ice coating enveloped the apple trees. I could almost reach out my hands and touch their shining limbs. The roof of the barn lay deep under its blanket of white. I'd have to get a shovel and help my father clear it off in the morning or it might weaken the rafters.

The entire atmosphere seemed stretched taut in the clear, cold air, like the strings of an overstrained violin. The very stars were singing in a high-pitched tremolo. Up the gem-arched Milky Way the radiant moon was gliding lazily. Venus winked at Saturn. The Big Dipper ladled out stardust in the bowl of its smaller sister. The Dog Star swung warily away from the Big Bear.

How magnificent they were . . . those lofty, luminous bodies that topped our tiny earth! How precisely they moved and swung and sang! It was as though a Master Musician beat exacting time with a directing baton and the orchestra of the universe moved and played, chimed and swayed in unison. Surely there must be a Divine Hand back of so much precision, order, and splendor!

Kneeling there in the great white silence, my spirit was caught up in the wonder of it. I shivered slightly beneath the scintillating galaxy of glory. My breath turned to frost crystals on the frozen air. Suddenly, without realizing what I was doing, I stretched my arms through the window, and, looking past the stars, cried, "O God . . . if there be a God . . . reveal thyself to me!"

Born Again

"Oh, God . . . if there be a God . . . reveal thyself to me!" I presume that the Heavenly Father answers that prayer for every earthling who sincerely sends his desperate petition wafting to the skies. At least he answered mine before the next midnight.

High school closed for the day. I had several hours for leisure before rehearsal in the Town Hall for a coming Christmas play. Four hours weighed heavily on my hands. How to spend them was the question. I had thoroughly memorized "Paddy and His Pigs," "The Porcupine in the Bed," and "The Fireside Fiasco" skit. What next? Walking the ice-sheeted streets with my father, I noted a sign over a Mission Hall which read:

REVIVAL MEETING
Robert Semple, Irish Evangelist
All Welcome

"Let's go in," dad suggested.

"Righto!" I replied carelessly. Little did I realize that this was to be the turning point in my life. News of this revival had reached my ears. Curiosity drew me, but interest stayed my restless steps. The song service moved with gusto. The milkman lifted his hands as he sang. So did the dry cleaner, and I giggled with amusement.

I sobered suddenly. The evangelist entered with a Bible under his arm. He stood some six feet and two inches in stature, had a shock of chestnut-brown curly hair, one lock of which he was continually brushing back from his blue Irish eyes.

One might laugh *with* him, for his message effervesced with sheer, clean humor, but one did not laugh *at* him. That was out of the question. "Let us turn to Acts 2:38–39," he said and read: ". . . Repent and be baptized every one of you in the name of Jesus Christ for the remission of sins, and ye shall receive the gift of the Holy Ghost. For the promise is unto you and to your children, and to all that are afar off, even as many as the Lord our God shall call."

Then he started to preach. Cold shivers ran up and down my back. I had never heard such a sermon. Using his Bible as a sword, he cleft the whole world in two. On one side he placed the Christian; on the other, the sinner. According to his gospel, everyone was bound either for heaven or hell. There was no middle ground. Why, to listen to him preach one would gather that there was some visible difference between the sinner and the church member! I had never noticed much. They both smoked the same cigars, played the same game of poker, and read the same novels.

"You must be born again!" he cried. "Come out from among them and be ye separate, touch not the unclean thing. If the love of this world is in you, the love of the Father is not there. In Christ all things have become new, so that the things I once loved I now hate, and the things which I once hated I now love. Call upon him while he is near and seek him while he may be found."

Then the speaker began to talk of the baptism of the Holy Ghost. As he described the living, vital power which he declared had been poured out upon thousands in this latter day, his face glowed as though an electric light had been turned on from within. Then, suddenly, in the midst of his sermon the evangelist closed his eyes and with radiant face began to speak in a language that was not his own. To me this Spirit-prompted utterance was like the voice of God thundering into my soul awful words of conviction and condemnation. Though the message was spoken in tongues, it seemed that God was saying to me, "You are a poor, lost, miserable, hell-deserving sinner!"

No one had ever spoken to me like this before. I had been

coddled, loved, and perhaps a little spoiled. I had been told how smart and good I was. But thank God that he tells the truth. He does not varnish us or pat us on the back or give us little sugar-coated pills. He shows us just where we stand, vile, sinful, and undone outside of Jesus and his precious blood.

The evangelist resumed his preaching in English, but all I could remember was my interpretation of his utterance in other tongues. Invisible hands had reached out and were shaking my soul. Old-fashioned conviction settled upon me. I knew then that there was a God and that I was a lost sinner. In blind panic I rose and fled the place. But it was too late. The gospel hook of the Fisher of Men had caught me firmly. I do not remember how I got through the rehearsal at the Town Hall that night, but I do know that for three days I sought to laugh it off, skate it away, and drown my misery in ragtime music, to no avail. The third day, while driving home in the cutter on that December afternoon in 1907, I could hold out no longer. It seemed that the heavens of brass would fall upon me and that in another moment it would be too late.

"God, be merciful to me, a sinner!" I cried, and the woodland to the left rang with my voice. The sun burst through the clouds. A great peace fell over me. It was as though the warm crimson blood of Calvary was pouring over my being. Great tears were splashing down upon my gloved hands as I held the reins.

As I entered the house, I felt the Unseen One close beside me. My parents were in the barn at the moment, and I was glad to be alone. The whole place seemed flooded with golden glory. Lifting the lid from the sheet-iron stove in the dining room, I burned my dance slippers, ragtime music, and novels.

"Where's the fire!" shouted my father.

"Here," I answered softly.

"Do you want to set the chimney aflame!"

"No."

"Then, what's the idea?"

"I've been converted and have no use for these things any longer!"

My dad looked at me quizzically. "I'll pay a wager that it will not last any longer than two weeks," he asserted. "Where and how did it all happen?"

I told him, and he reiterated his prophecy. But it did last—lasted through all these years and promises to continue throughout eternity. The next day I revisited the mission and told the evangelist of the change which had transformed me.

For a week I was supremely happy . . . walking, riding, singing in a dream. I, who had never known a brother or sister, had an Elder Brother with whom I could talk. I took to him my every problem, and he shared my every joy. Not a moment of the long miles to and from school but he was right beside me. Closer was he than hands or feet, nearer than thought or breathing.

"Oh, never leave me! Let me never grieve thee!" I would murmur. Recess time and noon hours I spent with my Bible, hidden away in a corner of the basement. When I prayed, I talked to Christ. When I read his Word, he talked to me. Then one day the calm of my serenity was broken. A frown puckered my brow, and I became increasingly uneasy. "The whole thing is too one-sided!" I cried. "You are doing all the giving; I all the receiving. Selfishness is an abhorrent trait. Lord, what can I do in return for thee?"

Running to my Bible for his answer, as was my custom, I found words like, "He that winneth souls is wise, and shall shine as the stars forever and ever." It was as though a great voice had spoken in trumpet tones, "Now that you, yourself, have been saved—go, help rescue others!"

Kneeling by my bed in the little upstairs room, I closed my eyes very tightly and concentrated upon the problem. In fancy I saw a wide, black, swift river rushing past. Millions of men, women, and children were being swept to destruction in it and, flinging up their hands appealingly, were dashed over the raging falls to a fearful fate.

"Even as I have been lifted," I sobbed, "I should in turn stretch out my hand to all whom I can reach and draw them to solid ground. I should be willing to cross the continent upon my knees to say to one poor sinner, 'Jesus loves you.' "

A sense of futility rolled over me. "How can I, a daughter of the farm, five miles from the nearest town, ever hope to be a soul winner? Besides, only men are allowed to preach."

"Mother, do women ever preach the gospel?" I asked one evening over the ironing board.

"No, dear."

"Why?"

"Oh, you and your whys! Well, Eve, the mother of all living, was the first transgressor."

"But if a woman was the first to bring sin into the world, why should she not be the first to take it out again?"

The busy housewife rubbed the beeswax over the iron and slid it smoothly to and fro over pillow cases and sheets before vouchsafing a reply. "I don't know."

"Do skirts and trousers make so vast a difference?"

"Seemingly. Women can instruct their children, teach Sunday school, go to heathen lands as missionaries . . ."

"But," I interrupted, "at what age must the schooling stop? And if they preach in foreign lands, just where and why is the color line drawn? If they are good enough to exhort the black, the brown, and the yellow man, why not the white?"

"Why not do your homework?" mother questioned.

Gathering up my algebra, trigonometry, and physiology books, I retired to my room and got out my Bible and concordance. "Women . . . women . . . women," I queried aloud. "Why are they prevented from Christianizing the world?" I found that Deborah, a woman, led forth her gleaming armies beneath flaming banners under the sunshine of God's smile. The woman at the well preached the first salvation sermon and led an entire city to Christ, having chosen as her text, "Come, see the man that told me all I ever did." Moreover, a woman had delivered the first Easter message and none other than the Master had so commissioned her.

"Why wasn't a man dispatched with that first all-important message?" I mused audibly.

"Because the men were all in bed and sound asleep, I presume," replied my father, who had appeared unexpectedly in the doorway.

Sheepishly, I leaped up and faced him. "How long have you been standing there?"

"Just a moment. Why?"

"Why are there no women preachers, dad?" I demanded.

"There's Evangeline Booth."

"But her work is mostly that of a commander. She doesn't pastor a church."

"But Paul was taught by a man and his wife, Priscilla and Aquila. He tells of one man who had seven daughters and another who had nine that prophesied."

"Prophesied? What does that mean?"

"Judge for yourself. Turn to 1 Corinthians 14:3. 'He that prophesieth speaketh unto men to edification, and exhortation, and comfort.' "

"But what of that verse, 'Let your women keep silence in the churches,' that mother quoted just now?"

"Read it."

"You mean that it does not mean just that?" I exclaimed eagerly, flipping the pages of the Good Book.

"Of course not! It has no reference to the teacher but to the ignorant and the untutored. Here it is: 'Let your women keep silence in the churches; and if they would know anything let them ask their husbands at home.' "

"You mean . . ."

"In the old world few ladies were taught to read or write. They were usually seated in the balcony or upon one side of the church. Naturally, Paul objected to their calling out to their mates, 'What does he mean, John?', and he besought them to ask their questions within the sanctity of their own home."

"But where, where's the door to service!" I asked myself again and again. "How does a person become a soul winner? How can one so lowly and so isolated appeal to the world of mankind?" During the following days I spent much time in Bible study. It was, I found, the baptism of the Holy Ghost that galvanized the mediocre and transformed them into evangelists of power. Peter had not been a farmer, but as a fisherman he had sprung from as humble an origin. Matthew was originally a tax collector, and Luke, a small-town physician.

Peter had failed in all five of the cardinal points of a successful, international soul winner. Yet something supernatural, dynamic, and all-transforming possessed and filled him and changed him into a whirlwind of eloquence, fire, logic, and fearlessness. I found that this "something" was nothing more or less than the baptism of the Holy Ghost on the memorable day of Pentecost.

"Is this selfsame power for men and women of today?" I queried.

"The promise is unto you, and to your children, and to all that are afar off, even as many as the Lord our God shall call," answered Acts 2:39.

Earnestly I began to seek this power. Returning to the mission, I requested the bright-faced devotee to mark my Bible at Acts 2:4, Acts 10:45–46, Acts 11:17, Acts 19:6, . . . and went home to study some more. Rising in the middle of the wintry night I would plead, "Lord, vouchsafe to even me this wonderful power that I may lead sinners to thee."

Meanwhile the evangelist, Robert Semple, had gone to Stratford, Ontario, to conduct a campaign. The follow-up meetings were conducted in cottage prayer meetings. I skipped school at every possible opportunity to attend the afternoon sessions.

"How radiant are the countenances of these people," I thought. The milkman, with whom I would not have thought of associating previously, became a saint upon an unreachable pedestal. The dry cleaner and his wife were spiritually lofty beyond my grasp. I felt that I would be willing to black the shoes of these, God's elect, in order to receive that which they possessed.

"Here is a letter which I would like you to take home to your parents," said the high-school superintendent one afternoon. Innocently, I placed the document in my mother's hands. I stood abashed before the Methodist minister as mother read solemnly: "Madam: Your daughter, who came second to winning the scholarship last year, is missing so many periods at present that unless the time is made up in homework, she shall doubtless fail her next examination."

"Just where have you been, my lady?" inquired my mother. It was as though dark clouds were thundering.

"At prayer meeting," I replied miserably.

"These people with whom you are associating are in all likelihood rank fanatics," said the preacher. "What warrant have you that in seeking this so-called power you may not become possessed with an evil spirit?"

I fled to my room and fell on my knees before my open Bible. "Oh, Lord," I wept, "you couldn't—you wouldn't—when I am seeking thine anointing so ardently?"

My Bible fell open to Luke 11:9–13: "Ask, and it shall be given you; seek, and ye shall find; knock, and it shall be opened unto you. For every one that asketh receiveth; and he that seeketh findeth; and to him that knocketh it shall be opened. If a son shall ask bread of any of you that is a father, will he give him a stone? or if he ask a fish, will he for a fish give him a serpent? Or if he shall ask an egg, will he offer him a scorpion? If ye then, being evil, know how to give good gifts unto your children: how much more shall your heavenly Father give the Holy Spirit to them that ask him?" That settled the matter for me. I would seek for this enduement of power from on high.

The next Monday morning snow flurries were in the air, and a blizzard was in the offing.. But with fur rugs piled about me, Fritzie and I set out for the mile-away station. The north wind whipped the high, white drifts to a fury. They cascaded over each canyon like a spuming waterfall. The cutter tipped over twice, but at last I got on the train. Snow plows were attached to the engine. Finally we reached the main street and jogged along past churches and homes, stores, and post office.

My route to school led past the house in which the prayer meetings were being held. The last words of my mother as I left the farmhouse rang in my ears. "If you skip school and attend another of these services, I shall insist upon your remaining at home entirely!" I looked longingly at the house, then gave reign to the horse. If this were my last visit, I might as well make it an early one. My tug of the bell resounded through the sparsely furnished hall. The drift-drowned door opened.

"What's the matter, dear?" asked the busy mother whose many children clung to her skirts.

"This is my last opportunity to visit your meetings," I replied. "It is now or never."

As I spoke, the blizzard descended in full fury. Telephone wires snapped. Shovelers of snow fled to their respective dugouts.

"Would you mind if I came in to pray until the afternoon meeting?" I asked timidly. A half-dozen youngsters peered out from behind her skirts as she replied, "Come in out of the snow. There's a fire in the parlor. I'll close the door."

From morning until noon I prayed. What a new world! Earth was receding, heaven drawing near. At 12:30 the door opened. "I've nothing but potato soup to offer you," ventured my hostess. "Do you like it?"

"Love it!" I replied. "Let me help you."

"No—no. With six children, a husband, and so many visitors, I simply add a new cup of water for each extra guest."

"Never," said I, sitting down at the table, "never has potato soup tasted so good."

From Monday morning until Saturday I prayed. Rising at any hour I wakened, I would slip out of bed, wrap the covers about me, and kneel, beseeching the Power above me to empty me of self and fill me with the Power promised from above. On that last morning the air was still frosty. The baseburner had not yet been shaken down. Water was frozen in the pitcher and wash basin. The blizzard had continued throughout the entire week. Drifts were piled so high about the doors that even the sound of snow shovels had ceased until the frost-nipping, ear-piercing winds would die down. Trains had ceased to run. Snow plows could not get through. Even telephone wires were down.

Shivering, but determined, I bowed my knees beside the big leather Morris chair and stormed the gates of prayer. I felt as though I had been battering my way through a thick stone wall that was now as thin as tissue paper. "Lord," I cried, "I'll never eat or sleep again until you fill me with this promised Spirit of power!"

"I am more willing to give than you are to receive," said my open Bible.

"Forgive me!" I murmured. "The waiting is on my part, not on thine." And then the glory fell. My tightly closed eyes envisioned the Man of Galilee, bleeding, dying, thorn-crowned on Golgotha's Tree. Tears streamed down my face. I found my trembling lips singing:

> Let me love Thee, Savior,
> Take my life forever,
> Nothing but Thy service,
> My soul shall satisfy.

"Glory, glory to Jesus!" I repeated over and over. Then my lips began to quiver and I began to speak in other tongues like those of the ancient Upper Room. Ripples, waves, billows, oceans, cloudbursts of blessing flooded my being. My form slipped to the floor and lay there submerged beneath the downpour. A little puddle of tears wet the carpet. I shook as though I were holding the negative and positive handles of the electric battery in the school laboratory.

"This settles it," I declared. "From this moment on my life is thine and thine alone. Honor or dishonor, weal or woe, pain or pleasure—naught shall move or change me from the sunshine of thy love and the footstep of thy service."

As wholeheartedly as the tempest had descended, it rolled up its great clouds and was gone. The sun came up and shone upon myriad crystal snowflakes and immense roof frescoes of silvery icicles. Snow shovels sounded again in the streets, and a persistent scrunch-scrunch of snowshoes was heard as men went to work.

"My dear! My dear!" exclaimed my hostess upon descending the stairs and entering the room. "I can see by the shine upon your face that you have found that for which you have sought! I'm glad! Glad! You shall be the winner of countless souls."

"But—how can I?" I questioned. "Where is the door to service?"

"It opens by itself at the end of the road of consecration," she replied. "Come. We have oatmeal and milk for breakfast."

The telephone wires were repaired. My mother got in touch with friends, who notified her as to my whereabouts. She drove to town for me over a wilderness of billowing snow. I told her of my experience.

"The day of miracles is past," she affirmed. "It ended with the death of the apostles."

"I shall never give up that which I have received," I replied. "But if you can find any Scriptures to prove your statement, I promise that I shall not go back to the meetings, ever."

"Good girl. I know that I can trust you to keep your word. Go along to school now, and when you return, I shall have found the passages and references from the Bible to support the truth."

When I returned that night, I found her seated at the table, just where I had left her, surrounded by commentaries, concordances, and the Bible. The breakfast dishes were unwashed. The lamps were uncleaned. The floor was unswept and the beds unmade—an unheard-of state of affairs in our home.

"Wh-what did you find?" I queried softly.

"My dear, I have discovered that God's gifts have never been withdrawn. The promise is unto as many as the Lord our God shall call. And in the last days he has promised to pour his Spirit upon all flesh. The servants and the handmaidens shall prophesy. I too shall seek the fullness of his Spirit."

4

Just Married

Spring broke over the countryside. One night, while sitting up in a neighboring house with two children who had been struck by typhoid fever, the door opened, and Robert Semple, the evangelist, stood revealed in the lamplight. Tall, dark, and smiling, he appeared with the rain shimmering on his shoulders. He was like some knight in armor.

A surge of gladness swept through me, but I said, "I—I thought that you were in Stratford—preaching!"

"I was. But I am here now."

"So I see."

"I heard that the children were sick and came to sit up with them."

"But I'm attending them at present."

"Then they have two nurses tonight," he replied and entered, depositing his coat, hat, and muffler on a nearby chair. "What all have you been doing? Your replies to my letters have been so very brief, with the exception of the fact that you have received the baptism of the Holy Spirit." His large blue eyes were fixed upon me as I tried to put into words my desire to be a winner of souls.

"Let's not talk about my uneventful little humdrum life," I faltered. "Tell me about yourself and your meetings."

There followed a graphic description of crowded halls, evangelistic meetings, sermons, and altar calls. As he talked, I could see lines of eager men and women pressing forward in answer to fervent invitations to kneel at the altar and accept Christ.

"Oh, Mr. Semple!" I sighed. "I would give the world for such a life!"

"There is no thrill or joy so great on earth as that which comes to the evangelist when seekers come pouring down the aisles to the mourner's bench."

32

The soft, rosy light from the shaded kerosene lamp which graced the narrow damask-covered table which separated us fell upon my scattered schoolbooks. Picking up the geography book, the young minister flipped its pages to the yellow map of the Orient. "Here it is—here!" he exclaimed softly, almost as though talking to himself.

"What is it? Where is it?" I puzzled, leaning closer to follow his slowly moving index finger.

"China," he smiled. "China, with her mighty millions offering a continual challenge to Christianity. And here—this busy little island of Macao—this is my destination and point of attack."

A sea of yellow faces rose before my young, impressionable mind. I imagined myself standing before such a throng who had never heard the blessed Word. In fancy I stood on a platform just above their heads and spoke eloquent words from a full heart. I saw them come surging en masse to embrace the Savior. "How wonderful!" I breathed. "I wish that I could devote my life to such a cause!"

"That is just what I came to talk to you about," the voice of the man who had won me to Christ broke through my reverie. "I know that you are only seventeen, but I love you with all my heart. You will soon be eighteen. Will you become my wife and go with me to China?"

I stared, amazed. The earnest face with the blue eyes, crowned by the chestnut curls, swam before me. I was speechless. But inexpressible longing to help him rose within my heart. I knew that I loved him deeply, loved his ministry, his Christ, his teaching, his message. But to save myself, words would not come to my lips.

"Don't try to answer yet," he said as his hand groped over the tablecloth and covered mine. "Let us pray about it."

He dropped to his knee by the shabby sofa, and I kneeled beside him, my hand still in his. Robert prayed, but I could not utter a syllable for the lump in my throat. I did close my eyes very hard. Through the tears that welled through my lids, I saw what appeared to be a long, shining road stretching up and away toward the Heavenly City. Robert and I were going up an angel-bordered highway that led to the Throne of God— together.

Startled, I gazed about me. There was no road—only the flowered wallpaper, a bit faded in spots. I closed my eyes again, and there was the road, only this time I was walking up the path alone. Without realizing the full import of that which I had seen, I rose and said yes to God and yes to Robert. Had I known that within two years I would be a widow, penniless and alone in China, and, after that, a mother, my answer would still have been in the affirmative, for the two most heart-happy years of my life lay just ahead. He was my theological seminary, my spiritual mentor, and my tender, patient, unfailing lover.

Shortly thereafter, on August 12, 1908, there was a wedding at the old farmhouse. The straightforward manner in which Robert had gone to my mother and father for consent, coupled with the dealings of the Lord in their own hearts, had won consent upon the subject, though my mother declared that all the sunshine, music, and laughter would be taken away from the homestead.

My father walked about the place a bit disconsolately. A worried frown puckered his brow. "What's wrong, dear?" I asked, perching on his knee.

"We'll miss you!" he grunted gruffly. "Who's going to gather the eggs, milk the cows, and do the chores now?"

"Now! Now! The new hired man can do that. What is really on your mind?" And then it all came out.

"This man you are marrying, Aimee—he seems wonderful, but has he any money?"

"Shame on you, dad! Of course not! He's a preacher."

"Has he a salary?" he persisted.

"No, he is an evangelist and trusts the Lord and the people he serves."

"W-well, I hope it will turn out all right."

"A-ha!" I teased, plucking a long hair from his head. "Ah-ha! The Scotch blood of your distant ancestors is showing up at last!"

"Scotch blood is the finest in the world!" he flamed. "It's not stingy; it's just practical. Who's going to buy clothes and food?"

"I'll pray about it," I answered comfortingly.

"I think I would," he advised cryptically as I disappeared up the stairs.

"Oh, Lord, who is to provide for me?" I prayed, kneeling in the same old well-worn spot.

My unfailing Bible opened to the words, "Take no thought for what you shall eat or what you shall put on. The Lord knows you have need of these things."

"The Lord will," I said to my father later over the steaming milk pails.

"How did you get your answer?"

"My Bible fell open at the passage," I replied and quoted the words of the promise.

"I do not doubt but that will be very true in your case," he smiled.

The next morning an air of mystery pervaded the place. Festoons and garlands of flowers were everywhere. Carriages arrived, and many hands tapped at the front door.

Robert was waiting for me, under the flower-trimmed arch on the lawn, very tall and solemn in his faultless black. . . .

"Do you, Robert James . . . ?"

"I do."

"Do you, Aimee Elizabeth . . . ?"

"I do."

At last it was over. Attired in my blue traveling dress with my husband at my side, a broad gold wedding ring upon my finger and white ribbons fluttering from the buggy whip, we set out for town. Old shoes and a dishpan rattled from the rear of the carriage, and a "Just Married" sign advertised our happiness to all. Robert stopped the horse and got out to remove those encumbrances after we were out of sight.

"Did you like the wedding, Robert? And all the guests and the wedding presents?"

"I didn't notice them much, darling," was his somewhat disconcerting reply.

"Did you like my wedding dress?"

"I didn't see that either."

"Why—why, your eyes were wide open!"

"All I could see was you," he said in a soft Irish brogue.

"Did you ever kiss the Blarney Stone?" I laughed.

"No, that was in the South of Ireland, and I lived in the North at Magherafelt, near Belfast."

"I'm sorry it's not a fine place I'm bringing you home to," said Robert as we climbed the rear flight of steps to the little three-room apartment above a small store.

My eyes roved over the unpretentious furnishings. A table with a patched checkered cloth, three kitchen chairs, a stove with a broken fire-box door, curtains that had seen less grimy days, a living room which was converted into a place for sleep by letting down a folding bed, a cracked mirror that made it look like an ancient wardrobe by day, a couple of leather chairs, and a tiny cubicle for dressing that we called our third room.

"It will be heaven," I gulped bravely, "heaven with you and him whom we serve."

The air was stale and heavy. "Spoken as a brave soldier," praised the tall man who gathered me in his arms. "Here, let me open a window or two."

As the sash went up, a billow of smoke stirred the faded cretonne curtains. "The foundries are close by," he explained.

"The foundries?"

"Yes, where railway engines are repaired. I go to work in the boiler factory tomorrow so that I may earn some money for our daily bread," he added gaily.

"You—you are a minister!" I faltered.

"Yes, but the church here is small, and I do not wish to add to its struggle for existence. Even Paul, the greatest apostle, worked at tent-making, you know."

"But in the old country you and your father owned a splendid department store. And you have held such splendid positions."

"We're in the field now, darling. Nothing matters but the cause of Christ."

"What will you have to do in this boiler factory?"

"Pretend I'm a worm and wriggle inside long tubes, scraping off whatever deposits may have lodged there."

I could not quite reconcile the picture of my six-feet-two-and-a-half-inches tall husband in his immaculate wedding suit performing this feat. But I changed the subject. "I love you so!"

"Not a millionth as much as I love you, for my heart is much bigger than yours," he affirmed.

Monday morning I was up early and had hung my carefully tubbed and boiled washing on the line. "The proof of the good housewife is the snowiness of her laundry and the lightness of her biscuits," a farmer wife had advised me on my wedding day. I was not so sure about the biscuits, but that the washing was drift-white I made certain by rubbing my knuckles until they bled and bending my back until it ached. A lazy wind was blowing, and the clothes should be dry in an hour, I reckoned.

Accordingly, I heated up my charcoal iron, took my clothes basket and went to gather them in.

To my horror, the tablecloths, napkins, sheets, and pillow cases were as black as my husband's face when he had returned from work. Emptying the iron of its fuel, I did my first work over again and once more pinned my washing on the line. In an hour it was as black as ever. Great billows of smoke surged over the high board fence, and I was reduced to tears of vexation.

"Dry it in the house," advised a woman from the floor below who came up and helped me string a clothesline from stovepipe to the window. That night Robert and I ate a supper of frankfurters and cabbage salad under the dripping edges of smudgy linen.

"Don't you be minding at all," he soothed as we dressed for church. "It's a grand meeting we'll be having this evening. The hall is filled already. Get your hymn book and see that you play well." The service was a glorious one, and the altar was lined with converts.

Days brightened. Robert was called to London, Ontario, and then to Chicago. He worked tirelessly for God, and I did the smaller tasks, keeping house, playing the piano, and praying with the converts.

"We're leaving for China in six weeks," Robert announced one night. "It's yellow pearls we should be gathering for the crown we lay at the Savior's feet."

"Do we go under some mission board?" I inquired.

"No, we go by faith and trust in the Lord!"

The problem of support did not seem to bother Robert. But I was haunted with anxiety. "Darling, doesn't it cost a lot to go to China?" I ventured to ask when my husband had bidden farewell to all but one of the local churches in which he had spoken.

"Yes, sweet."

"Have we the money on hand?"

"Not yet."

"Do you think you should say good-by to the last congregation that you shall address in America until we have our fare?" I timidly asked.

"My dear," he said, "have you never learned the lesson of faith?"

"What do you mean?"

"I mean that if God has truly called a person to a certain place he will provide the means of getting him there. One might be tested. He might even get to the dock without having his passage, but someone will come up and place the money in his hands before the gangplank is pulled up."

"Forgive me for my unbelief," I apologized. "I'll try to trust more implicitly."

That night after an inspired address delivered in the Italian church, Robert said good-by to the crowded audience. Our transportation need was not mentioned. "May we not all pass by and shake hands with you and your wife?" someone asked.

"We should be most happy," we agreed.

The audience formed itself into a seemingly endless line up one aisle and down another. Robert stood on the platform. I stood midway of the corridors. Arms were thrown about Robert's shoulders. Hands patted him on the back. Money was pressed into his hands. My own cheeks were showered with fervent Italian kisses as ample-bosomed women shook hands and left checks and bills in my palm. Shortly my purse was filled, then my hat, and gold and silver was spilling over onto the floor. "Good-by, dear Sister," they would say, "and God bless you."

When we arrived home, we counted the offerings they had given—pockets full of bills and checks which amounted to our boat fare and a little more. "God had a man on the end of the dock all right," I commented. "You were right about having faith when in the center of God's will."

My husband chose to sail from St. Johns, New Brunswick. Accordingly, we returned to Canada where he preached and farewelled in the church wherein he had ministered before coming to Ingersoll. We visited my old hometown briefly and parted from my parents on the bleak little railway station platform. They could hardly restrain their tears.

"I don't suppose we will ever see you again in this world," rumbled dad tactlessly.

"Remember the day when we dedicated her to God?" murmured mother, striving to keep her trembling chin up.

"Of course."

"Well, he is claiming our pledge."

"It didn't seem so bad when she was in the country, but who's going to play that locked piano now? Who's to . . . ?"

"Sh-h-h! Smile, can't you?"

"Sure! I'm smiling! I'm s-smiling."

A screech of the whistle, a hiss of released air brakes, and we were off. The disconsolate little group on the platform faded to a flutter of handkerchiefs and was lost around a bend of the icy February River Thames. Funny little stream! How often I had flown around its curves on gleaming skates. Now I was to see its mother in London, England, as it whirled past the lovely houses of Parliament.

At St. Johns I bundled up and leaned far out of the window. I had never before seen an ocean. A thousand times I had tried to envision it back on the sleepy farm as a child. And now I was to see and cross the mighty Atlantic. Suddenly there it lay, stretching away and away, as far as the eye could see. In the distance its ships looked small as ten-cent toys in a bathtub. Streamers of smoke flowed like funeral crepe from a hearse in each spumy wake.

"Why so pensive, mavourneen?" Robert asked as he looked up from the copy of *Pilgrim's Progress* which he had been reading, holding my hand and using my cold fingers to turn each page.

"I was wondering what she would look like."

"Oh, like a busy little world all in herself, white and tall, with gold trimmings and a voice so big and gruff it makes folks jump out of their boots. She'll eat nothing but black coal and devour it so fast that it will take an army of men to feed her."

My face was growing more and more pale, and my hand trembled a little in Robert's.

"It will take a dozen men all day long every day to keep putting a new white dress on her, and she'll have a funny little tail at the back that goes, 'B-r-r! Bur-r-r-h! B-r-r-rh!' "

"Oh, Robert!" I cried, aghast.

"Honey! Don't cry! You are talking about the good ship *Empress* of Ireland, aren't you?"

"N-no!" I sobbed. "I'm talking about our baby."

"Mavourneen!" he cried, gathering me into his arms. "You don't mean . . . why didn't you tell me?"

"Wanted to surprise you."

"You did!" he rejoiced, almost speechless with pride.

"And she won't be that large and she won't have a voice that makes folks jump out of their boots!" I wept, ashamed of myself for weeping at so small a misunderstanding.

"Sure an' faith, an' it's small and dainty as a pixie she'll be, with a voice as soft as the fairies that dance in the moonlight!" he cried. "But why do you say 'she'?" he asked suddenly, holding me farther from him as he wiped my eyes carefully with his handkerchief.

"Because I'm sure. That's what I've been praying for."

"Here! That window is too cold for the likes of you!" he said solicitously. "Let me put it down this minute. But it will be springtime in Ireland when we visit the old folks there before sailing away to China. The robin redbreasts will be singing above the shamrocks. I say—let's call her Robin for the time being—shall we?"

Away to the Mission Field

A high wind whistled through the riggings as the *Empress* nosed out to sea. The ocean became a roaring madhouse. Frightened whitecaps whipped the portholes. Sea gulls scurried for shore. The prow of the vessel lifted and bowed before the gale. The ship creaked and cried like a human soul. Coats hung on the wall swayed steeply from one wall to the other. Chairs slid from bunk to bunk. Glasses crashed to the floor and lay in a thousand bits. Sailors buttoned their sou'westers firmly and ran to lash everything moveable. Great combers pounded on the forecastle. We were in for it.

As the boat rolled in a trough, I lost my balance and collided sharply against Robert. "You'll have to get your sea-legs, little landlubber," he exclaimed, setting me back on my feet.

The storm intensified. Icebergs floated by as the dinner gong sounded. "Ro-Robert!"

"Yes, my darling."

"I-feel a—bit—queer, right here," I gulped with my hand on my stomach.

"Seasick," he ventured. "Best go to bed right away."

With his help I did and remained there a full week. The ship rode out a storm which has gone down in history, a storm which swept away the bridge and which emptied more than the dining room of its passengers. Lying in my bed where Robert had placed me, I listened to the struggling ship as she sobbed, sighed, screamed, sank, shook herself, and scrambled up the storm-scarred sea-stairs only to be seized a second later by sloshing, slaughter-bent waves. Again and again we climbed, till I felt our spars pierce the low-clinging clouds, and ever we sank, sank till I waited for our keel to grind and crush her life out against some rocky ocean bed.

I was surprised that nothing of the sort happened. Always at the last second we began that sickening climb again. I knew that I was going to die! But somehow I didn't. Merciful oblivion came at last only to be interrupted by successive days and nights of pounding, battering rams.

Seated at the tables of various seasoned commanders on later voyages en route to visit our missions, I sometimes referred to my first sea voyage. Invariably captains shiver as they recall the storm of 1910.

"Let's see!" they would muse. "That was the storm that swept the wheelhouse from the *Lusitania,* wasn't it?"

"H-m!" they continued as the soothing, all-concealed orchestra graced the meal. "She landed several days late, as I remember."

I had never indulged in the luxury of fainting but I made up for lost time on that voyage according to Robert and the ship's surgeon. "She's coming 'round," I heard one day as I slowly came up from the swirling seas of seasickness. Something acrid and burning was being forced down my tortured throat.

"P-please d-don't! I'm all right!" I choked.

"In her condition," I heard Robert say in a faraway voice as another wave hit us.

"Buck up!" began the doctor as he lurched for the cabin door. "We should make it in three more days."

"If ever I reach terra firma," I gritted after the latchet clicked,

"I'll never ask anything of life but a 'bonnie green hill where I can lay me doon and dee.' "

"Good night, mavourneen," Robert's voice came from far away.

"How far away is Ireland and your Shamrock hills?" Still no answer. Blackness veiled my little sky. The next thing that I remembered was Robert's voice. "It's all right now, mavourneen. We're passing the breakwater. We'll be in Liverpool shortly and we're all packed. There is land ahead."

"Land!" I brightened. "Just let me look at it once more and I'll never cross the sea again even to America!"

"There, there, dear! It's all over now! Listen!" A strange sound surged through the porthole. "See! We're slowing up!"

The next few hours are rather hazy in my mind, but gradually I became conscious that I was in a wide bed in a Liverpool hotel recuperating from my near visit to Davy Jones's Locker. Robert was bending over me solicitously. Life began to look differently. I sat up, a bit wobbly. "Where are we, Robert?"

"In Liverpool, darling. Tonight we sail for Belfast. We'll be there before ye know it, and your new parents are awaiting."

That night we sailed and slept on a calm sea. In Belfast I was introduced to Robert's kind father, mother, two sisters, and two brothers and found them all most charming.

We all set out by car for Magherafelt, a quaint town lying twenty miles distant among emerald hills, bottomless lakes, and winding roads. My husband's home adjoined the general store of his father's where everything from boots and shoes to granite dippers and outing flannel for baby garments was sold.

I fell in love with my father- and mother-in-law, and, never having had a brother or sister, Sam, Will, Marion, and Maggie were a constant delight. I was treated as one of the family in that quaint, glorious stone house among the shamrocks.

One day a bolt of outing flannel was presented me by Mother Semple with the goodly advice that I apply myself to the making of baby clothes while I still resided in a healthful, civilized world. "I'll be back in an hour," Mrs. Semple smiled encouragingly, "to offer any needed help."

The door closed behind her very trim taffeta back, and I was left alone with my squares of outing flannel, my needles, thread, and thimble. "I should have told her that I have never learned to sew," I mourned. But screwing up my eyes and folding over the edges of the cloth as I had been so recently instructed, I

began the solemn task of running my threaded needle in and
out. I soon dispensed with the thimble, and growing tired of my
task, looked out the window. Finally, however, finishing the
third side, I started down the homestretch of the fourth.

Suddenly the door opened and Mother Semple stood by my
side. Examining what I had thought to be neat, wee stitches, she
threw me into consternation by exclaiming, "Wirra-wirra! Dear,
and why did you go to the bother of basting it first?"

She had mistaken my earnest first efforts at needlecraft for
basting! I looked down at the zig-zag trail my thread had woven,
glanced at the high unfinished pile of diapers, and threw up my
hands in despair.

"Now you'd just be better giving them to me," she comforted.
"Sure and Maggie and I will have them finished in no time."

"Oh, thank you!" I breathed, as she gathered the whole
bundle up in her arms.

"I wonder what he will look like?" she murmured, laying her
cheek softly upon the fluffy cotton.

"Would you be so disappointed if it were not a he?" I whispered. "I have ordered a she."

"Bless you, she would be just as welcome. But oh, I wish you
and Robert could stay in Ireland until she is born. Can't ye be
after persuading him?"

"Mother dear, he insists upon sailing at once—says the hours
are few and that millions are dying without Christ."

"Then I suppose I must be content," she said with a brave
show of resignation. "Ever since he was a wee bairn he has
given the most of his time to prayer that he might be a soul
winner. He would always be out in the loft of the barn crying to
God to use him."

"M-mother, tell me more about his early years . . . everything!"

"Come out with me and I'll show you the place," she offered.
With reverent awe I followed her, and the small back yard immediately became a shrine. "Now you be running along and
rest. I'll be in shortly."

Reluctantly I left the scene of Robert's early travail before
God and looked back over my shoulder at the sad little silkclad
figure drooping at the fence. "Oh, God," she groaned, "must ye
be after taking him? I know that I shall never see him again . . .
never!"

Guiltily as though I had been an unwelcome eavesdropper, I tiptoed into the house and closed the door. Mother Semple spent an increasing number of hours thus in the days that followed. Always, however, she emerged from her particular Gethsemane with the laurel of peace resting serenely upon her brow. Who, I wondered, was the greater martyr . . . the missionary who plunged into the torrid heat and pestilential sordidness of heathendom, or the missionary's mother who stayed at home and kept tearful vigil at the altar of her son?

While in the north of Ireland, Robert was asked to preach in Belfast. The meeting was a glorious success, and the altars of the great hall were crowded. We received an invitation from the lord mayor to visit him at the city hall and were presented with the key to the city. I was awed with his pompous robes, golden chains, and gleaming medals. Robert stood very straight and tall among the crowd that had gathered on the marble steps for the ceremony.

Came the day of sailing to England, the counting of luggage, and last-minute tearful good-bys. Came the deep-throated voice of the whistle, the creak of anchor chains, the groan of pulled-up gangways that had joined Robert to his native Emerald Isle, the watery plop of cast-off mooring ropes, the fading song, "God be with you till we meet again," and the blurring form of Robert's weeping mother. She looked very frail and forlorn as she leaned upon the arms of her husband and elder son, William.

"If you don't like China, hurry back to Ireland," called Sam as he ran along the pier with nimble feet.

"Shure an' faith we will," laughed Robert with forced gaiety. Sam's reply was swallowed up by the widening distance, and we were gone. All that remained of the shore was the flutter of waving handkerchiefs and the toylike outlines of the city set against a deep green hill.

"Now don't forget to go to London before you sail and call upon Cecil Polhill, the well-known Christian millionaire," our Canadian friends advised. "Perhaps he will give you a thousand dollars or so. He would never miss it, and he is so friendly toward missionaries."

"Have you kept your letters of introduction, Robert?" I asked as our train pulled into London.

"Yes'm, and Mr. Polhill has asked us to stay at his mansion

in the city. I'm after thinking we'd better drive up to his house in a taxi."

"Oh, but we shouldn't! We should be saving every penny."

"No, we'll arrive in grand style."

A gold-braided doorman received us and attended to the luggage. An elegantly uniformed butler with an impressive John Bull tummy greeted us as I stood overawed in the vastness of the marble reception hall. Mr. Polhill received us graciously at the desk of his well-stocked library, and we were shown to our room.

Standing in the middle of the softly carpeted floor, I looked about me curiously. Such gorgeous furniture and such a massive fourposter I had never before seen. "You are looking weary, my lady," said Robert, gathering me up in his arms and placing me on the golden counterpane. "It's a good sleep you should be having while I go to the meeting house and preach."

He kissed me tenderly and departed. I lay for a long time staring up at the impressive canopy over my head. How rich Mr. Polhill must be! What did it feel like to be entrusted by God with so much wealth? How he must love being able to gladden the hearts of struggling missionaries and ease the anxiety with which they faced their field of foreign labor! Would he really give us a thousand dollars? Or perhaps a thousand pounds? Mm-m-m! Then we could have a comfortable little house in China. What would China be like? In what sort of home would we rear our baby? Would it be a boy or a girl? Oh, well, that was a good six months away! So musing, I fell asleep.

"My car is at your disposal today, and my personal secretary will show you about the city," said Mr. Polhill over the gleaming silver of his laden breakfast table the next morning.

London Bridge, London Tower, Big Ben, the Houses of Parliament, Madam Tussaud's, the British Museum, Westminster Abbey, St. Paul's Cathedral may be an old story to many, but to me they afforded a wonderland.

A week slipped by, and the time of our sailing was at hand, but nothing had been said yet about money. "Don't ever hint for it or he'll shut up like a clam," our American friends had warned. "Most likely he will hand you an envelope full of bills as you say good-by."

The afternoon before we embarked my host surprised me by suggesting that I bring the message at the meeting that night.

I was caught squarely upon the horns of a dilemma. If I told him that I was no preacher, he might think me a poor prospect for the mission field. If I agreed and did poorly, I might be even more disgraced. Seeing my hesitation, he evidently put it down to false modesty and urged, "Oh, come along! Everyone will be jolly pleased to hear you."

"Th-thank you, sir."

"Right, the car will call for you at seven o'clock."

"But, Mr. Polhill . . ."

The door closed after his neatly tailored back. I was in for it. He hadn't even heard me. All day I prayed and ruffled the pages of my Bible to no avail. No text or subject suggested itself. In desperation I dressed and turned to the Good Book once more. A hand tapped at the door, and the butler's apologetic, "Hurrumph!" sounded. "Beggin' your pardon, ma'am, but you are fifteen minutes late. The car is at the door."

"Right down," I promised and clung to the security of the long, curving banister as I descended to my fate. If only Robert were there! But he had been in meeting all day. Maybe he could give me a last-minute suggestion when I reached the hall.

I had a moment's misgiving when we arrived at the building. It covered an entire city square. Oh, well, probably some small inner room would be used for the service. "Hurry, Sister," urged the driver, steering me through the stage door. Before I realized it, I was ushered onto a huge, crowded rostrum. Gasping, I gave one petrified glance over the vast audience which rose in tiers to the very top of the fifth balcony of the auditorium. Some fifteen thousand were assembled in convention, and many speakers were lined up ready to deliver their messages.

The minister in charge turned toward me and said, "Ah! Our lady missionary is a few minutes late, but she has now arrived and will speak immediately." With this he bowed politely and sat down.

Wildly I looked about me. If only someone would start a chorus, I might sit down a moment and thumb through the pages of my Bible in a last-moment flurry. But the minister had seated himself in the last empty chair, and there I was.

Closing my eyes, I prayed through chattering teeth, "O L-l-l— lord, if you ever h-helped me in my l-i-f-e, h-h-help me n-n-now!"

My Bible fell open at Joel 1:4, and the verse seemed to stand out in boldfaced type. Feeling much like a swimmer beginning a high dive, I commenced. "That which the palmerworm hath left hath the locust eaten; and that which the locust hath left hath the cankerworm eaten; and that which the cankerworm hath left hath the caterpillar eaten."

Palmerworms, locusts, cankerworms, and caterpillars! God bless me! What a text for a beginner! I knew that I was about to faint. But suddenly something happened. The power of the Holy Spirit fell upon me till I trembled like a leaf. Then the Lord took possession of my tongue even as he had on that memorable day when he had baptized me with Pentecostal fire, only this time it was in English. The words seemed to flow forth without conscious volition or self-will. It seemed as though I was caught away by the oratory of another. The people were leaning forward in their crimson, velvet-covered chairs. Now and then a volley of amens and hallelujahs thundered through the huge hall. At other times the applause sounded like hail on a tin roof.

As quickly as the flow of words had started, they were turned off. The power that had galvanized me into a tornado of utterance ceased as though someone had pulled a switch. I was as deflated as a balloon when the air is let out. Dimly I wondered why so many ministers were shaking my hands up and down. The sea of people were clapping and wiping their eyes. Robert threw his arm over my shoulder and helped me into the car.

"I say! How did you ever do it? I didn't know we had a second preacher in the family! You'll be after doing the work from now on." Robert's praise was comforting in my ears. "How long did it take you to work that sermon out?"

"Oh, Robert," I burst into tears, "I didn't do it at all. It was just like speaking in tongues, only it came in English."

"Good morning, mavourneen," Robert's voice came softly from up somewhere in the vicinity of the canopy. "An' how's the preacher lady, this foine mornin'?"

"M-m-m," I murmured sleepily. "Good morning . . . why, you are all dressed!"

"We sail for China today, young woman."

"Of course! I should be up and packing!"

"Dinna ye worry now! We are living in a millionaire's home, and the maids have attended to all that. The butler has fastened the last strap, and the chauffeur is loading everything into an extra car now."

"Such style!"

"Enjoy it while you may. It may be your last opportunity, dear."

"Have you seen Mr. Polhill? Did he think I did all right in yesterday's sermon?"

"Said he was never more thrilled in his life!"

"Oh, but I'm glad! Did he—did he give you an envelope yet?"

"Not yet, but let us keep our eyes upon God, the Master Treasurer."

"Yes, of course," I answered, dressing hastily, "but that thousand pounds would mean everything to us just now." I had quite made up my mind that it was to be five thousand dollars.

Robert opened his mouth to say something, but just at that moment came a soft tap upon the door. "Mr. Polhill is waiting to say farewell," came the muffled voice of the butler.

"Coming."

I cast one lingering look over the haven of our gorgeous room, then joined him in skimming lightly down the broad circle of the magnificent stair.

"Permit me to congratulate you upon your triumph of yesterday! You will make a splendid ambassador for Christ in the Orient. It has been a benediction to have you both in our home, and I trust you will receive this modest gift with my blessing." Sure enough, there was the prayed-for envelope . . . a long, slim businesslike envelope, which he placed in Robert's hand.

Robert thanked him sincerely, and soon we started for Southampton. We were alone at last and racing for the steamer. My husband sat looking abstractedly out of the window, as though his thoughts were far, far away. He turned the sealed envelope over and over in his hands. Thinking of China, I supposed.

"Robert!" I burst out finally, "if you don't open that envelope soon I'll . . . I'll . . ."

"Oh, yes, of course, of course, darling!"

There came a faint tearing of papers through the purring of the motors. Then, before my fascinated eyes, three small, crisp bank notes fluttered out. Each bore the denomination of one pound sterling. "Fifteen dollars!" I choked, "Fifteen . . ." A tempest of tears followed the sudden letdown.

"Are our hopes built upon earthly or heavenly foundations, mavourneen?" he soothed, holding me close. I thought that there was a tinge of reproof in his voice.

"Oh, God, of course! Besides . . ." I hastened, "come to think of it, it was wonderful of Mr. Polhill to entertain us so lavishly. We may be most thankful for this fifteen dollars some day."

My thoughts were diverted from money matters to dread of returning seasickness as we mounted the steep gangway of the trim white China-bound steamer. Black billows of smoke rolled from her funnels, and she tugged at her moorings, like a white stallion at his reins. Then a deep, pea-soup fog descended, obliterating the wharves and streets. Traffic slowed, and as the fog increased, a patient conductor lighted his lantern and stepped out in front of his tram-car to guide the motorman. Ships' whistles blew. Motors churned. Good-by, dear, cloud-shrouded England.

By the time the steamer began to toss her foaming mane amid the weltering waves of the English Channel, Robert and I were unpacked and had our luggage stored away, thanks to his foresight. "Better get to bed, m'lady," he cautioned, suiting his action to his words. "Creep into your berth and lie very still before you become seasick."

"Darling, last voyage I took your remedy and was ill all of the way. Would you mind if I work out a plan of my own this time? I would like to stay on my feet this trip, walk right up to that old lion called Mal-de-mer, and snap my fingers in his face."

Just then the vessel took a nasty lurch, spilling tooth brushes, the contents of a vanity case, and sundry other small belongings all over the cabin. I hastened to gather up the wreckage. "I've always been told . . . oh, darling . . . do as you like!" he groaned and turned over among the pillows of the upper berth.

Robert kept to his bed, according to his prearranged plan, but I trotted about the deck and answered the dinner gong religiously. The tables became more and more sparsely attended as foghorns vied with foam-flecked breakers. One particularly rough morning, my courage almost failed. As I dressed in our cabin, the floor came up to meet me. The clothing, hung on the door, swayed like a pendulum left, right, left, right. The glasses and decanters rattled in their receptacles. Suitcases slithered about on the floor like curling irons on a Canadian ice rink. But, adhering to my policy, I determined to go up to breakfast.

"Good morning, ma'am," smiled the waiter, looking a bit green about the gills. "You are almost the only one up this morning!"

"Good morning," I replied. "One oatmeal, one glass of orange

juice, one breakfast steak, and one cinnamon toast, if you
please."

"Good, madam."

Deliberately, as though defying the fates, I sipped my orange
juice and downed my oatmeal. With every successive swallow I
felt an ever-increasing lump gathering in my throat. Desperately,
I remembered the advice of a fellow passenger, "If you eat and
eat and then are unable to retain your food, just eat some more
and you will never be seasick again."

"Your breakfast steak will be here in a moment," gasped the
waiter as an especially audacious wave swept the dining salon
windows, bathing all with a sea-green light.

"Keep it hot," I instructed. "I'll be back in a moment!" Wildly,
I dashed down the deserted passageway. What happened at the
horseshoe bend I omit, except to say that I had plenty of room
for the rest of my breakfast when I was again seated at the table.

"Will you be wanting the steak now, madam?" asked the
waiter, glancing doubtfully at my greenish complexion. Grimly
I set myself to the task of eating, as though this was the one sure
cure of seasickness. Maybe it is at that . . . for I never felt a
trace of the malady again throughout the long voyage.

The trip was one of absorbing interest. Gibraltar, the Island
of Malta, and then the cosmopolitan port of Suez. Aden rose
fiery red beneath the burning copper sky. No river, spring, or
water hole dotted this rocky gateway to the Red Sea. Speaking
of the Red Sea, I spent many a long hour leaning over the railing
and trying to figure out just where Moses and the children of
Israel crossed.

Then the days became almost insufferably hot and muggy.
There was not one good lungful of air to be had anywhere.
Babies became fretful, and almost everyone slept out on deck.
The water was as calm as glass. Every cloud and scurrying alba-
tross was mirrored perfectly. The brooding sea lay like a pool
of black oil. "What a marvelously calm passage!" I smiled
damply one afternoon, mopping my steaming brow.

"Have you taken a look at the barometer today?" inquired
Robert, glancing up from a thick, illustrated volume of Bunyan's
Pilgrim's Progress.

"Why, no!"

"It's falling like a plummet, and the captain says that we may
look out for a typhoon."

And sure enough, clear into sight of Manila we were blown before the monsoon spent her fury. Then suddenly, all was calm again, and we steamed into the harbor of Hong Kong. Presently, a glorious, cloud-wreathed mountain detached itself from the shoreline. I gasped at the sheer, green wonder of the steep hill.

"I am going to adore China!" I whispered happily to myself. In a cloud of spray the swift motorboat of our pilot swung alongside. As I leaned far over the shipside to watch the unfoldment of the changing panorama, a strong pair of arms encircled me, and a soft Irish brogue laughed in my ears, "The top-o'-the-mornin' to ye, mavourneen! I've been a-lookin' for ye everywhere! Don't ye ever sleep?"

"I'm sorry!" I repented, conscience stricken.

"Dinna ye be worrying at all! What are ye after, thinkin' of your new home?"

"Robert, it's divine," I enthused, looking up from my five-foot-three to his six-foot-two. "See those teeming thousands on the streets of Hong Kong and Kowloon? There should be enough lost souls there to occupy the balance of your natural life! Where do you think we will live, dear?"

"Shure an' faith! It's to a foine big palace I should be takin' you an' the wee one! An' here I am with nary a salary!" Robert worried.

"Why, you're a fine one to be scolding me about lack of faith!" I chuckled, glad to be able to even the old score. "What was that you told me in England, about a man on the end of the dock with an envelope in his hand?"

"I'm not worried about myself . . . it's you and the wee bairn that should be havin' a home!"

"But I *do* have a home, one that I'll possess as long as I live. Open the door, Robert." Smilingly he played the old game of which we never tired. Opening his arms, he waited till I walked into them and cuddled up close to the white linen of his immaculate tropical suit.

"Now close the door," I commanded, laughing up into the Irish blue eyes that shone down from the green-lined brim of his white cork helmet. Instantly I was pressed tightly to his breast. "Lock it tightly, dearest," I called.

"It is locked."

"Then, you see, I have all the home I'll ever need, and I can carry it right around with me."

My heart was very young and gay as I looked out from my secure shelter upon the colorful, weird life of Kowloon Harbor.

China

"Hello, up there!" "Welcome to China!" So called the little group of white-clad missionaries who stood on the docks, waving parasols and sun helmets.

"There is a strange and wonderful fellowship among foreign missionaries," explained Robert, after he had waved and called back a greeting. "At home they are enclosed in Presbyterian, Episcopal, Methodist, and other shells. But out here they are just Christians and join hands as one working band."

"Maybe they are driven together by the necessity of companionship and encouragement," I reasoned. And I was right. These self-exiled crusaders for God fairly ate us up with pathetic questions as to conditions at home, the welfare of loved ones, whether or not there were revival fires ablaze here and there, whether friends had sent them a message, and a score of other queries.

We were taken for temporary shelter to a large mission home and initiated into the manner and means of beginning our work. Together we prayed, sang, attended services, and stood in a long cue before post-office windows every time a ship came in. Together we rejoiced or stood crestfallen according to whether or not the anticipated letters arrived. I have always thought that if only people at home could see the eager faces at the grilled window, they would be more prompt and consistent in writing these lonely, courageous souls.

"Now as soon as you have located a house, the next thing to do is hire a cook and a teacher of the Cantonese language."

"Oh, I am quite able to do the cooking and housework!" I exclaimed, thinking of our dwindling dollars. "Besides, we never employed a servant in our lives and we have not come here to put on airs before the poor Chinese."

"But this is not America!" they explained. "You would instantly 'lose face' before the natives and nullify your work."

"But can we afford it?" I demurred.

"A houseboy who will do the cooking can be had for about two cents a day. Wage prices are far different here. You must have an amah too."

"An amah? What's that?"

"An amah is a nurse or house attendant. She can be had at a similar rate."

"I took your husband to the native markets today," said a male missionary one afternoon. "I'm afraid his stomach is not very strong."

"Oh, I may get used to it after a while," replied Robert, looking rather pale around the gills.

"Were they beautiful?" I queried.

"The foreign markets, yes. Such fruit and flowers as you have never visioned. But the native section—ugh! Stale meats, dried rats, dogs, greasy geese, and worms—"

"Worms?!"

"Yes, buckets of them! The Chinese buy them for one sen [one-tenth of a cent] and eat them alive. I saw one fellow at it. He purchased one such long creature. It had a brown back and a pink tummy, and its edges were delicately scalloped," he added, striving hard to maintain his Irish humor. "Then poising the thing aloft, he tipped back his head, opened his mouth, and deliberately dropped the worm down his throat. It gave a last despairing wiggle and disappeared."

"Oh, Robert!" I shuddered.

"Sorry, dear," he repented. "But that's just what happened."

Immediately upon our arrival, Robert started to preach the gospel through an interpreter, and I set about the task of house hunting. This proved to be bewilderingly difficult; available residences were either too poor or too expensive. But at last I discovered a whole street of empty flats on the road that led to the cemetery. They were astonishingly reasonable. I looked them all over and chose the one next door to the Hindu temple, where priests constantly thumped their tom-toms and swayed in a seemingly never dying chant.

We soon learned that the reason the street was deserted was that the houses were haunted. I cannot explain it, but there really were the strangest noises, tappings, footsteps, and happenings I ever heard tell of. "Was it imagination?" you ask. "Was it the demon hosts worshiped in the adjacent Hindu temple?" I do not know. But certainly the powers of hell seemed to hover over that heathen land whose flaming sky burned like the lid of a burnished copper cauldron.

Robert slung a hammock for me on the piazza, and I spent much time there overlooking the great masses of people who surged past. Especially fascinating were the numberless funeral processions. There were military funerals that lumbered past with the tramp of steel-shod heels, dragging a gun carriage with a flag-covered corpse, attended by brass bands. Chinese burials tripped by with the tinkle of many glass windbells, with banners, with great loads of chickens, rice, roast pigs, and other tempting edibles to be placed upon the grave of the deceased, that the spirit might rise at pleasure and eat.

One day I saw one of our most prominent Chinese Christians wending his way to the cemetery, laden with similar foodstuffs for his ancestors. "When are you going to cease this nonsensical heathen rite?" I asked. "You know that the dead cannot rise and eat."

"When you Christians cease placing flowers upon the graves of your departed," he replied, unruffled. "Can the dead rise and smell them? That is yours . . . this is our custom."

Dealing with the Chinese unbelievers proved a different problem than I had imagined. "Are you a Christian?" I asked my Cantonese teacher one morning.

"Indeed not!" he sniffed.

"You sound bitter," I told him.

"Why shouldn't I be?" he stormed. "You Christians came to China in ships and at the point of the cannon forced opium and Bibles upon us from the same vessel. Chinese never forget."

"How long will it take me to master Cantonese?" I hastily changed the subject.

"May take as long as twenty years and then make many errors," he comforted. "But come . . . get to your lessons."

Day and night the heat pounded down upon us like a merciless battering ram. "Robert," I would scold, "you should not be out preaching at noon."

"But I wore my cork sun helmet and carried the green-lined white parasol."

"I don't care. You are going to be struck down with prostration . . . the older missionaries say so. Please, dearest."

"But I do love them so, and I feel one life is too short to give."

"But isn't it better to conserve that life and prolong it?" I would argue.

"Come now, mavourneen, get your wrap and let us go out and spread it on the lawn of the cemetery. There's a wee breath of air there."

Lying on the greensward among the tombstones, I would try to forget the flaming torridity and watch the gorgeous, bright-plumed night birds returning to their nests and the great dinner-plate-sized magnolias on the trees above us.

My husband would cradle his head on my knees and sing the air of "Bringing in the Sheaves" in that peculiar tuneless way of his:

> Bringing in Chinese,
> Bringing in Chinese,
> We shall come rejoicing,
> Bringing in Chinese.

"Robert, you surely do love these poor natives!" I would murmur. "Don't you?"

"Why, of course I do, or I would not be here!" he would answer in surprise. "This is my place. And do you know, darling, I have a peculiar feeling that when the Lord comes back again, I shall rise to meet him from Chinese soil, bringing with me the souls that I have won."

At home I would hear him praying in the next room, "Oh, Lord, save China! Lord, send a revival to China!"

When he would come out to the piazza later, I would inquire, "My dear, were you not afraid to kneel in there with all those huge rats scampering about?"

"I didn't even hear them," he would reply. "What are you doing sitting with your feet curled up under you in the hammock? Not afraid of mice, are you?"

"Mice? Why, Robert, those rats are as large as puppy dogs, and they look at one in the boldest and most ferociously fearless manner, as though they challenged possession of the house. And the centipedes! Have you seen them crawling over the walls? They have a thousand legs, and just one bite is sure death!"

"Not sorry you came, are you, sweet?"

"Of course not!" I said indignantly. And I meant it.

One day, as I sat on the piazza while Robert was out preaching, a Hindu funeral procession passed. Tall, black-bearded men clad in white from their huge, tightly wound turban to the hems of their long flowing robes carried an open bier on which reposed their uncoffined dead. His shrouded form was completely covered with flowers. The seemingly endless group turned into the neighboring temple. "I suppose they will place his body in a coffin there," I mused.

Shortly the tom-toms began beating wildly, and a chant which sounded like "Ala be Ala be A-a-ah" rose in a steadily mounting monotonous crescendo. Unable to bear the ever-recurrent pounding and singing, I went into the house and busied myself with a letter to my parents. Presently I became conscious of the pungent odor of burning meat or eggs. The acrid smoke poured through the rooms from the direction of the kitchen.

"That cook again!" I fumed. "I have told him again and again not to fry those rotten eggs or stew his favorite stale meats. I'll tell him!" Hurrying into the kitchen, I called his name, but he was nowhere to be seen. The stove was quite empty. The billows of offensive smoke were rolling through the open windows. Fearing the house was on fire, I rushed to the opening and looked out. The sight which met my eyes froze me with horror.

The body of the Hindu had been placed upon a high, stone altarlike funeral pyre. Much wood had been placed beneath and above his corpse. Indian friends were seated in circles at a distance from him, rocking to and fro chanting their ceremonial intonations. Attendants were pouring kerosene upon fires which leaped and played about the central fire. That which curdled my blood was the fact that the deceased acted like no ordinary dead man! He drew up his knees, sat up, and acted as though he were actually alive. It did not occur to my uninformed mind that these were the contortions caused by burning sinew and muscles.

Hysteria seized me. Making a valiant effort not to scream, I closed the windows, ran to my bedroom, and moaningly cast myself on the bed. "Control yourself! Remember the baby! Suppose she should be marked or born dead through this!" I sternly commanded myself. But to save me I could not stop my convulsive trembling or curb the ever-growing feeling that I must shriek aloud.

At that moment Robert mounted the stair. "Darling! Darling! What's the matter?" he cried.

"Those Hindus!" I gasped. "They . . . they're burning a man alive in the back yard!" Then I added unreasonably, "Don't touch me! Don't touch me or I'll scream."

My husband did the natural thing, came over and gathered me up in his arms. For no reason at all, his sympathetic caress touched the match to the pent-up powder keg of my emotions, and immediately I was in the grasp of violent hysterics. It seemed as I listened to the high-pitched wails and wild laughter that came from my heart that those screams came from another person entirely. Catching up a corner of the counterpane, I stuffed it into my mouth to deaden those piercing, soul-rending sounds.

"Oh, Robert, I . . . I'm so sorry!" I managed finally.

"There! There! Dinna weep! It is because of the wee one that's comin' ye are crying so!"

"No-no! They are really burning a man out there!"

"Hush, dear, he is dead and knows nothin' of it."

"But I tell you, I saw him sit up and raise his arm!"

"I'm so sorry you saw it, mavourneen, but that is just the effect of the flame on human bodies."

I knew I would never live through the ordeal. But somehow I did. Lived to come down with a fine case of tropical malaria. Malaria—have you ever had it? Aside from being very ill, I found it quite interesting. For a solid month, night and day, I lay beneath the mosquito-netting canopy of my hot, sticky bed and watched the clock. Every hour, on the hour, I would be tossed high over the crater of a volcanic fever. Up, up, up it would go, till thoughts and words became a muddled blur. Then down, down, down I would plunge into the fathomless depths of an icy sea.

"Poor, poor darling" would come the voices of ministering missionaries as a new chill gripped my form and I danced a prostrate tattoo upon the moist blankets.

"Oh, I don't mind . . . but will the 'bambino' be all right?"

"I—I hope so!" they would reply, and then I would again ascend the skyrocket of consuming fever. At times I would emerge for a short rational period. Then I would hear the measured tread of missionary funerals. White-faced men and women trudged behind the tiny caskets of their young who, like fragile flowers unable to bear the withering blast of China's noonday furnace, had folded their petals and gone to sleep.

Then came the day when Robert took to his bed. He had been ailing for some time but had passed the matter over lightly. "It is nothing," he smiled wanly.

"It is the horror of the East," visiting ministers declared gravely.

"What is the horror of the East?" I roused myself to ask.

"Dysentery," they replied significantly. "Better keep him in bed and give him a light diet."

"I did not come here to lie abed!" Robert declared, struggling up and into his white-starched suit. "My wife is somewhat better, and we have made all arrangements to go to Macao, the Portuguese settlement on the neighboring island. Besides, the island is said to be much cooler, and we will both be well shortly in the sea breezes."

And so we sailed. Macao was truly beautiful in its topography. But I, because of my illness, remember very little of it except its strange mixture of races, its steeply slanting streets, and the dark, dank, dismal, upstairs tenement in which we lived.

Robert, for the first few days, made valiant, intermittent efforts to continue his preaching, through an interpreter. But his ailment grew more serious. He spent more and more time in bed. I was already bedfast again with my chills and fever. If I had thought myself acquainted with malaria before, that acquaintance was a most sketchy one. Besides, here, there were no kindly visiting missionaries to care for me.

The days that followed were a nightmare! Between my seizures of burning and shivering, I would stagger over to Robert's cot and try to care for him. When my fever was at its height, he would toss aside his covers and weave his wavering steps toward me with a change of cooling towels.

His pain and bleeding increased with every hour. Finally, I made our houseboy understand that he was to telephone Hong Kong for aid. He, in turn, informed me that a nurse and doctor were on their way.

The return trip is a fevered blur in my memory. Robert had to be carried out and onto the ship in a canvas hammock suspended on a bamboo pole and slung between the shoulders of two trotting coolies. I was able to sit up, with my head on the nurse's shoulder, both on the boat and up the steep inclined railway of the Hong Kong peak that led to Matilda Hospital. But Robert's recumbent form forbade similar transportation.

"Where is my husband?" I inquired dizzily.

"There, there! He is all right. Put your head down again and keep still," the nurse replied.

"Where is he?" I persisted.

"Over there. Look through the trees . . . the coolies are carrying him up the mountain in his hammock. He is too ill to sit up."

I leaned out the window of the tram-car and was able to distinguish his swaying body slung from a pole as the fleet-footed runners ascended the winding rocky trail. Just then, the fever gripped me again, and I remember little more till I awoke in a cool white bed in a large ward of Matilda Hospital.

Through a mist, I discerned two long rows of beds wherein a score of other patients slept, read, tossed, or moaned. White-clad figures were approaching. They bent over me, parting the canopy of mosquito netting. "Here you are, little lady, hold this," intoned a calm, assured doctor.

My teeth rattled against a thermometer. "H-m-m!" he remarked noncommittally, "keep her chart for twenty-four hours, nurse."

"Yes, doctor," she replied, and they were gone.

The aforementioned chart was hung in such a position that I could see the ominous red lines that soared up and up with my fever, till they looked like the rocky steeps of the mountain whereon I was housed. Then they dropped down like the abysmal craters of the surrounding canyons.

"There, child, don't worry! This is the last attack you will suffer," said the doctor the next day. "Open your mouth. That's right, take this."

Gratefully I swallowed the bitter potion of quinine he administered. Every few hours came a new dose of the medicine, and my malaria stubbornly relinquished its malignant embrace. I slept, only to be awakened by the whirr of a stout wooden slipper slithering overhead and crashing against the wall behind my bed.

"It is nothing," informed a nurse, "just an amah killing a large centipede."

"Where is my husband? How is he?" I replied, struggling up.

"Now! Now! Lie still!"

"How is he?" I insisted.

The face of the doctor loomed between the bed curtains. "Take it easy," he enjoined. "That is just what I have come to talk to you about! His condition is grave. What have you been giving him to eat?"

"Principally a vegetable diet," I stammered. "Celery, lettuce, tomatoes, peas, potatoes, and similar market produce. But recently he has been unable to retain his food."

"Who did your marketing?"

"The Chinese cook."

"H-m-m! Just what I feared! Did no one ever warn you against partaking of the local, home-grown foodstuffs?"

"W-why, no!"

"Do you not know how Chinese fields are fertilized?"

"N-no, sir," I whispered, awed by his deepening frown. "How?"

"The places in which you have lived have no sewerage, of course, and all the human refuse of the unclean natives is dumped upon the gardens to enrich the soil."

"U-ugh!" I shuddered. A mental picture of the leprous beggars, the victims of smallpox, and of unnameable diseases shuttled before my eyes. Were their diseases imparted to the plants they grew?

"Where is he? Will he soon be all right?"

"He is in the men's ward. We are doing everything possible."

"May I go to see him?"

"This is not visiting day. Besides, you had better get well enough to sit up before you try walking."

"Doctor—"

"Yes, my dear?"

"Did Mr. Semple explain to you that we have no money? How can we ever pay you?"

"That's the least of your worries, child! If you had a million pounds, you would be unable to spend a penny of them here. This hospital is absolutely free to missionaries."

"God bless you," I whispered, after his retreating form. "And God bless the good Matilda, after whom this institution is named."

A day or two passed. "Feeling stronger?" inquired the physician.

"Yes, thank you. Is this—is this visiting day?"

"No. But I have arranged for you to go to your husband immediately."

"Oh, how kind of you!" I exclaimed, little realizing just why he was so kind. On the arm of the nurse I navigated seemingly endless connecting corridors that led to the men's ward. Down the avenue between the long rows of beds we made our way. Robert was at the farther end.

I hardly recognized the dear face that smiled at me in welcome. His large blue eyes burned feverishly above sunken cheeks. His lips were bloodless; his hands skeleton thin. His Bible was open at his side.

"See that you do not tire him, dear," said the nurse and withdrew. Then she turned to whisper, "Be very cheerful."

I held his hand and tried to talk cheerfully, but Robert interrupted me, "Darling, promise me, if the wee one should be born tonight, have her brought in to me, no matter what hour it is."

"Certainly. But she will not arrive for almost a month."

"That's all right, but promise me."

"Of course!"

"Mavourneen, what would ye be after doin' if anything should happen to me?"

"Don't talk like that, dear! Nothing will happen to you. We are here for life."

"You are so far from home," he continued as though he had not heard me. "You have no money. The baby is coming. What . . . would . . . you . . . do?"

Suddenly his face contorted with tears of agony. The nurse came swiftly to his side. "You must go now," she said to me. "See, you are tiring him."

"I'm so sorry. Good-by for now, Robert."

As I stood a moment, clinging to the white enamel rail at the foot of his bed, I saw the look of anguish disappear and his face become as tranquil as a lake after a summer storm has passed. His voice was quite steady as he said, "Good night, dear, I'll see you . . . in . . . the . . . morning."

The words rang out strangely, hauntingly, ominously in my ears, as I returned to my bed. Unable to sleep, I sat up and watched the swift night spread her black blanket over the restless sea and hill. The wind began to howl dismally, thunder rolled, and jagged forks of lightning began to lick the mountain with snakelike tongues.

I sat up on the side of the bed, staring out the window that opened upon the court between the men's and women's ward. I could see the light burning steadily over Robert's head, though all the rest of the wing was in darkness. What was happening? Was he worse? The patient next to me stirred, turned over on her pillow, and remarked, "Typhoon's coming; the storm signals have been up all day, and the ships are scurrying to harbor. There'll be many a man lost tonight."

As though her words were a sign, the fury of the gale broke over the peak. Closed doors and windows rattled. Iron lanterns groaned eerily as they rubbed against outer stone walls. Buffeted trees screamed as though in mortal pain. It seemed like the building would be lifted from its foundation.

"The doctor got caught out in a typhoon once," my informant continued, "and he had to crawl back to the hospital on his hands and knees so as not to be blown away."

At two o'clock I was still wide awake, listening to the warring elements and watching the light over my husband's bed. It never went out. Now and then a shadow would be cast upon the distant inner wall as the forms moved about him. A choking hand seemed to grip my throat. My heart hammered. The night light went on at the nurse's desk, and she moved toward me. "Are you asleep?" she queried.

"No."

"Then get up quickly, put on your kimono and slippers."

I was off the bed in a second and donning attire. Shaking like a leaf, I asked through chattering teeth, "My husband . . . he . . . he's not dying?"

"Don't stop to talk now . . . just hurry."

I stumbled after her as she led the way down the dim hallway. Lurid flashes of lightning caused the curtained beds to leap out like ghosts, then disappear. My limbs were shaking so violently that I wondered whether I would ever reach my goal.

The doctor, a nurse, and a white-clad intern were bending over Robert's bed. The former was just drawing a hypodermic needle of adrenalin from the patient. Robert was smiling . . . not at me, for his eyes were closed . . . it must have been that he was looking at Jesus.

Something went wrong with my knees. They just wouldn't stay up. I fell in a little heap by my husband's side, pressed my lips to his hand, and wailed,. "Oh, Robert! Don't leave . . . you can't leave me now!"

The nurse who was drawing the white-sheeted screens about the bed touched me on the shoulder and said, "Quiet, dear, you will awaken the other patients."

"He's gone," said the doctor quietly.

"No! No!" I cried, looking up quickly. But it was true.

Somehow, I knew that I was going to scream . . . yet I must not! Just at that moment the strong arms of my Savior closed about me, and I found myself whispering through stiff lips, "The Lord gave, and the Lord taketh away. Blessed be the name of the Lord!"

"I'll take you back to your bed now," said the nurse kindly, lifting me to my feet.

"May I kiss him?" I managed.

"No! No!" cautioned the physician, "remember the baby and be brave."

Brave? I wanted to be, but the blow had left me stunned. Maybe they would let me see him tomorrow, I reasoned, as I was led away. The storm was screaming now, like maddened demons. Where was Robert's spirit? Was he winging his upward way through that fearful blast? Did he see me? Would he ever be able to look upon the face of his child from somewhere up there in the clouds? What was that he said about feeling he would rise to meet Jesus from Chinese soil, taking the souls of those who had been converted through his ministry with him? Then he really wished to be buried here! What would I do? Where would I go?

"Five dollars, five dollars and thirty cents," I kept repeating to myself as I paced the floor. "Nurse, how much does a coffin cost in China?"

"Why, I don't know, dear. Why?"

"How much does a grave cost in Happy Valley?"

"I don't know that either. Have you no funds?"

"Only five dollars and thirty cents. I've just counted it."

"But the mission board who sent you out . . . won't they?"

"We are not under any board. We came by faith."

Just then I remembered Robert's words, "Don't worry, darling, there'll be a man on the end of the dock." And there was.

Outside my window stood a small stone icehouse. I sat by the window, gazing at it fixedly. The body of my husband lay cold and stiff therein. After the custom of the East, which must bury their dead at dawn, funeral plans were necessarily urgent. It all seemed so cruelly sudden that, despite the intense heat, I had pleaded with the doctor to keep the body for at least a day before interment.

Nurses moved about behind me. A mother crooned to her newborn babe. Tourists laughed and chatted . . . as though the end of the world had not come! Their gaiety irritated me strangely. I felt that I could never smile again. It seemed as though the wheels of eternity should have been stopped and the doors of normal living sealed when Robert died. But in that empty universe of mine, life moved on—babies were born and lovers held the hands of their sweethearts in lingering caresses. The dawn threw back the sable crepe of night. The skies were as placid and sunny again as though nothing had happened, as though the moon and the stars would shine again and yet again.

"Could I go to Robert?" I questioned a passing intern. "Should he not have a blanket?"

"He's dead, m'lady!" came the cockney voice. "He feels neither cold nor heat now. Have you ordered his coffin yet? Or do we bury him in a sheet?"

The world spun dizzily about me. Out of the whirl, a mailman came into view. "Letter for you, Mrs. Semple," he called.

"Are you the man on the end of the dock?" I whispered, as memory sped on swift wings and events both remote and current seemed to telescope.

"No, I'm the man on the top of the mountain," he laughed. "Here you are."

With listless fingers I opened the envelope, thinking only of the sheeted form within the ice house yonder and wondering how I would be able to inter my beloved. Automatically I shook the white paper rectangle held negligently in my hands. A shower of American currency fluttered out and landed in my lap. Dazedly

I counted the bills. They amounted to sixty-five dollars. "Enough for a coffin," I whispered, "and maybe for a grave."

The letter bore a Chicago postmark. I read its contents over and over again. It read as follows:

> My dear Sister in Christ:
> Greetings in the precious name of Jesus! What is wrong? The Lord wakened my sister and me in the middle of the night and bade us send you this money. At first we demurred, thinking to rise in the morning and secure a money-order, but he assured us of its safe arrival. I dressed hurriedly and will make my way to the nearest mailbox. But please do tell us why this urgent need.
> Hastily and lovingly,
> Mrs. Blank

Lifting tear-blurred eyes to the blazing skies, I gave thanks to the God who sees the sparrows fall and never forgets the one lone sheep.

Early the next morning I heard heavy, muffled footsteps slithering over the outer graveled walk between the ice house and the top of the steel incline path. I ran to the window. Two coolies were passing. They carried a loosely swinging burden suspended from a swaying bamboo pole. The long slim outlines I knew were those of my husband. Uncontrollable sobs shook my body. A nurse led me back to bed.

"May I attend his funeral?" I asked the hastily summoned doctor.

"Impossible!" he decreed. "Your good missionary friends are taking splendid care of all that. You must think not of the dead but of the living. Concern yourself with the new Robert, soon to be born."

Somehow day followed night, and night followed day. Missionaries visited me with homemade candies and flowers. They told me details of the ceremony in Happy Valley, the songs sung, the message delivered, and the satin-lined casket.

A month passed. Autumn was in the air as one day I stood leaning over the stone balustrade of the garden precipice and peered into the shadowed ravine below. The cemetery shrouded in mist lay just over yonder hill. The fog was closing in—in! I was enveloped within its folds.

That night the angel of life and death spread his wings over the peak of Hong Kong. At 9 A.M., September 17, 1910, our child was born.

"It's a girl. What shall we name her?" came the voice of the nurse from out the ether fog of a strange, private room.

"I would like to name her after Robert," I whispered wanely.

"How about Roberta?"

"Lovely!"

"And what of her middle name?"

"Star," I replied, "for she is to be my star of hope in the blackness of an Oriental night."

"Roberta Star Semple. That's a glorious name," enthused the nurse, changing my sweat-damp pillow for a cool, fresh one. Gently she wheeled a baby basinette into the room and placed my priceless treasure in it. My dream-laden eyes never left that precious spot till I lay shrouded in the slumber of exhaustion.

Came hours of terror when I considered my penniless, husbandless future amid the dark, unknown labyrinths of China. Came moments of heavenly bliss when my daughter was cradled upon my breast. Came the day when I was able to leave the hospital.

"You must have a Chinese basket," admonished my nurse. "On your return trip to America you can use one-half of this telescoping valise as a bed for your baby and the other half for her clothes."

"R-return t-trip," I stammered. "Robert came here to evangelize China."

"But he's gone now. Your first duty is to your baby, and, without adequate means of support, Southern China is no place to rear a child."

For six weeks, I thought this over. Recalling Robert's words, "What will you do? Where would you go, if anything happened to me?" I was in a quandary.

More money arrived. I cabled my mother and Robert's of his death and Roberta's birth. Mother cabled back and sent a lovely baby layette, including a long baby dress adorned with a hundred tucks and inserts. The price of my return ticket soon accumulated.

"Robert!" I whispered through the long tropic nights, "Robert, where shall I go? What shall I do? Shall I stay in China to carry on? Or shall I go back to America?" But my beloved did not answer.

Hospital attachés were most kind to us. At last the American-bound ship entered harbor. I gathered my babe in my arms, and, accompanied by missionary friends, made my descent by the steep tramway down the mountainside.

"What would you do? Where would you go?" My husband's question still rang in my ears as I entered the wide portals of the American burial grounds of Happy Valley.

"We will wait at the gates," murmured the tearful little group that accompanied me on my first, lone vigil to the new tomb. "Perhaps you will want to be alone."

"God bless you!" I breathed, "God bless you."

"Shall we mind the baby?"

"No, Robert said that I should bring her to him as soon as possible."

With shoulders erect and chin held high, I clutched the tiny, throbbing, warm bundle within my arms tighter and wended my way in and out of the forest of headstones and wide-winged angel statues beneath which Robert and I had so often sat in repose. The city of the dead was not a strange or unfamiliar place. Here Robert had called me "mavourneen"; here he had spoken of rising from Chinese soil.

A cemetery attendant led me to the moist mound of soil that served as Robert's last earthly covering, then silently slipped away. Laying my pink-blanketed baby upon a neighboring grassy sward, I ran to the grave of my husband and, kneeling down, called, "Robert—Robert, can you hear me? Robert, what do you want me to do? Where do you want me to go? Shall I stay here in China and carry on your work? Or shall I go home to America and take care of our baby? My loved one—please speak to me!"

But, no answer was forthcoming. The mound that hid my beloved from view was as strangely silent as the slumbering Sphinx.

"Robert . . . Robert, please speak to me!" I called. Still no answer. Just then, a bird of paradise sailed overhead, lighted in an overhanging magnolia tree, and sat pruning her feathers. Simultaneously, Roberta began to cry, pitifully, helplessly, pleadingly.

I had my answer. My first duty was to take my child to a place of healthful safety. Robert's work was done. Mine was but begun. He dwelt among the birds of paradise. Mine was the grim task of carrying on.

"Wh-o-o! W-h-o-o!" squalled the steamer in the Kowloon

Harbor. "Wh-o-o! W-h-o-o!" Her tone was commanding, imperious. Gathering my wailing babe into my arms, I wended my way back to the missionaries, who placed us safely within waiting rickshaws and directed them toward the wharf.

On the Shelf

Through misted eyes I waved to the missionaries on the dock. Sampans, junks, and smoky tugs were weaving patterns on the blue sea all about us! But I paid them small heed. My eyes were fixed upon a distant, cloud-wreathed valley where stood a simple wooden cross, identified only by a regulation number. Someday I would have money enough to buy a granite monument for that beloved resting place, I vowed.

Slowly, surely, with gathering speed the *Empress* pulled away from the coastline of China. I stood alone on the upper deck, clasping Roberta Star close to my heart. My heart? It seemed as though I had left the greater half of it back there in the purple shadow of Happy Valley! "M-m-wha! M-m-wha!" wailed the small bundle in my arms.

Robert Semple. . . . Roberta Star. . . . He was gone. She was living! I must think first of her! Reluctantly I withdrew my gaze from the far-distant fading lights, tucked Roberta under my cloak, and groped my tear-blinded way to our stateroom.

In New York my mother instantly fell in love with Roberta, welcomed us to share her little furnished apartment, and then went out to continue her arduous task, leaving us alone in the heart of the roaring city.

The turmoil of the streets was surpassed only by that within my heart and mind. I found the Glad Tidings Mission of Rev. Robert Brown in the heart of New York City and was not only welcomed there but invited to come to the rostrum and give my testimony. This proved a difficult task. Twice while I was speaking Roberta, who lay wrapped in her little pink blanket on the front seat, awoke and began to cry. Excusing myself, I went down, adjusted her bottle, and returned to the pulpit. Yet my one solace in these bewildered days was the mission.

Everyone was sympathetic, concerned but remote, as laughing and chatting they returned arm in arm with their loved ones to their cozy homes, and I went back to the folding wall-bed in my mother's apartment. I felt as alone as the sole survivor of a shipwreck on a small, barren isle, while the teeming billows of the mighty metropolitan sea surged and swirled about me. Somehow marriage had changed my feelings concerning maternal financial support. I had the feeling that I was a visitor who should soon be excusing herself of her hostess and returning to her own home. But where was my abode?

"Mother, dear," I said one day, "I feel embarrassed every time you give me a dollar of your hard-earned money. You have to walk so many miles to earn it that your poor feet are all blistered!"

"You must not feel that way, darling," she replied, counting out the nickels, dimes, and quarters that she had collected between Columbus Circle and the Battery.

"But what am I to do eventually?"

"Maybe when the baby is a little older, you too can solicit for the Salvation Army. They allow me to retain 50 percent of what I take in, and I might be able to work out the same arrangement for you."

I looked down at the tiny face of my doll-like slumbering infant and remembered how I had seen my mother that evening jingling her tambourine before the door of first one theater and then another, smiling bravely up into the faces of the shivering, fur-clad revelers who every now and then tossed in a coin.

Roberta looked as frail as a tropic magnolia that I must guard against New York's wintry blasts. "She is only thirteen weeks old," I sighed. "Besides, I have a persistent feeling that my only happiness lies in the carrying on of my husband's work of soul-saving campaigns."

"But how?"

"I don't know."

Restlessly I thought about Chicago and the warm friends Robert had made through his ministry there. Possibly, I thought, I might be able to become oriented to my new life there. One day the pastor of Glad Tidings Mission pressed an offering into my hands, and this, coupled with mother's aid, enabled me to reach that middle western city.

Kind friends received me, wept over my bereavement, and caused me many a poignant pang by musing, "I wonder whether Brother Semple was really in the will of God, seeing that he succumbed so soon after reaching Southern China?" They found me a dim little furnished room and then returned to their daily round.

Elevated railways thundered overhead, subways rumbled beneath, streetcars clanged and clattered, crowds milled and hurried, automobiles grazed the hem of my black dress as I attempted to cross busy thoroughfares with my baby in my arms. I felt increasingly sad and sentimental.

Whenever some tall, smiling man would take his lady's arm and help her across the street, whenever I would pause to gaze into a window upon the characteristic picture of a proud, solicitous father bending over the bed of his pale-faced wife in whose arms snuggled a newborn babe, the tears would course down my cheeks, and I would hastily lower my black chiffon veil.

I was as a chip tossed aimlessly in a maelstrom of a definite, classified, well-ordered life. "Where shall I go? What shall I do?" I whispered to the pillow at night as I lay wide-eyed staring through the murky darkness at the grimy street lamp that shone in my window or as I turned in utter desolation to kiss my own shoulder a lonely good night.

I tried to help out in some of the local churches in which Robert had preached. But I was soon obliged to abandon this effort as Roberta became more and more frail. Her complexion was like transparent wax. I could find no food that agreed with her.

One day a sister in the Lord gave me some money when she discovered me counting over my dwindling hoard of pennies. That night, while stirring the baby food and sterilizing a nursing bottle over the blue flicker of canned sterno, purchased at a local ten-cent store, I made up my mind to go home to the farm and keep my daughter away from the smoke and the noise of the city until she was stronger.

I wrote my father, and like a storm-buffeted bird lost from its mate, flew back to the practically deserted nest. Dad, who proved to be almost as lonely as I, stood shivering over the unpolished kitchen range stirring oatmeal. He was almost pathetically glad to see us. The house was bitterly cold, the dishes unwashed, the beds unmade, the coal-oil lamps sooty, and the kitchen linoleum unscrubbed.

Propping Roberta's basket on a chair by the open oven door, matters were somewhat remedied. I swept, dusted, filled and cleaned the lamps, washed sheets and pillowcases, and made the beds, then shoveled and converted the dazzling tips of snowdrifts into a warm bath for the baby.

"My! My! It begins to look like home!" praised father, returning from the barn with a bucket of warm, frothy milk in each hand and some fine flecks of hay in his snow-white locks. "But, I say, I'm as worried as you are over the health of the little one. See if she can keep some of this fresh Jersey milk on her tummy."

But her system was still upset. My elderly parent would go to the bookcase, hunt out the family doctor book, search for his spectacles, adjust them, and then the two of us would pore over baby foods and remedies. But still with no results.

Finally a neighbor lady came plowing through the snowdrifts and suggested an old stand-by of her grandmother's day. I thanked her, and she went her way. The food seemed to give temporary aid, and I busied myself helping my father with the milking and the stable chores. One day as we were both wielding snow shovels, clearing a path from the door to the front gate, he inquired wistfully, "How long do you think your mother will stay in New York? Did she say anything about returning to the farm?"

"No, dad. She says that all the money in the world could not induce her to bury herself out here again and that she merely put up with it as long as she did for my sake. When I married, it set her free to go. She loves the city and really seems a part of it."

"Maybe if I get a neighbor to look after the stock, I could go to her . . ."

"No, darling. I'm afraid you would get run over in the rush."

"Young lady, I'll have you know I'm as spry as the next one!" he stormed, straightening himself up to his full six feet. "I'm going to visit her, and that is final."

"Yes, sir," I apologized, admiring his straight form and but slightly enfeebled limbs. Then, changing the subject, I asked whether he remembered the time I had gotten a big hole in my stocking and he had fixed it by blacking my leg with shoe polish.

Poor dad! He did go to the big city for a visit but only stayed a short time before returning to the farm. There, some years later, he died alone in a neighboring hospital, and I returned for the funeral. Later I visited the quiet little country burial grounds and purchased a granite headstone, which is set up in his memory.

Try as I would to accept the situation through that first long winter, my heart continually yearned for the work of the Lord and to take up Robert's task of evangelism where his hands had laid it down. Roberta was somewhat stronger by spring, and I returned to Chicago to make another attempt at helping in the missions and churches. But again, my little daughter became ill, and in my penniless widowhood I did not know where to turn. A doctor examined the baby and said, "Sister Semple, you cannot expect her to get well in these furnished rooms or by traveling about constantly from one place to another. You must get her a good home with plenty of fresh air, warmth, and care. She needs all of your time."

I knew that he was right, but his advice was easier to give than to follow. About this time Harold McPherson, a young man just six months older than myself whom I had met almost immediately after my return from China, asked me to become his wife and allow him to take care of Roberta and me. He declared that if my daughter were his own, he could love her no more than he did. It seemed good to have someone to carry my little one in one arm and my grips in the other. The prospect of his home sounded cozy and inviting. Roberta seemed so fragile and I so all alone that I said yes. Before the marriage took place, however, I made one stipulation, telling Mr. McPherson that all my heart and soul were really in the work of the Lord, and that if at any time in my life he should call me back into active ministry, no matter where or when, I must obey God first of all. To this he agreed, and we were married on February 28, 1912, under these conditions.

After spending a period of time in a furnished apartment there in Chicago, my husband's mother invited us to come and live with her in Rhode Island. Our home in Providence was lovely. The sky-blue waves of Narragansett Bay broke in a sheen of silver spray over moss-covered rocks and fell back again to be swirled out once more into a dazzling sea of gold and turquoise. Mr. McPherson's mother proved to be a most excellent New England housekeeper. His father was a fellow Canadian from New Brunswick, inordinately fond of deep-sea fishing, a hard worker, and a conscientious provider for his household. By all the laws of domestic arrangement, I should have been happy. Roberta was beloved, petted to her heart's content, and made strong and healthy.

When Harold's money ran short, I went to New York and accepted my mother's offer to join her as a solicitor for the Salvation Army. Dutifully I walked the beat between Columbus Circle and the Battery. Likewise I stood before theaters at intermission and closing hours, wearing a Salvation Army bonnet and uniform, and jingling a tambourine which my mother procured for me. Restaurants and bars where tipsy men gave liberally became my hourly haunt.

While soaking my blistered feet, I counted the receipts of the day, and mother carefully divided this sum fifty-fifty with the army, permitting me to take my half home to help with household expenses. I continued this means by augmenting our livelihood until shortly before my son, Rolf McPherson, was born.

But through all these strenuous days and that of the comparative quiet of our Providence home, a voice kept hammering at the doorway of my heart. It shouted, "Preach the Word! Do the work of an evangelist!"

"Impossible, Lord!" I would protest. "Impossible!"

"I have called thee, and ordained thee, a prophet unto the nations," echoed the Voice.

"No, Lord, I cannot go!" I would reiterate. Then would come a paralyzing silence when all communication with heaven was shut off as completely as that blank which ensues when a telephone is disconnected. Returning to the privacy of my own room, I weepingly sobbed, "Oh, Jesus! Jesus! Jesus!"

Observing my unhappy and melancholy state, my mother-in-law sought to comfort me, saying, "Why can't you be like other folks? Attend shows or movies. Play bridge, take up dancing."

"But he's calling me!" I replied.

"Who?"

"Our Lord, Jesus."

"Calling you to do what?"

"To preach the everlasting gospel."

"Nonsense! You are pining your life away! You should devote your entire time to your home. In a few days you will be welcoming your second child. Exercise is what you need."

"Yes, dear," I replied, endeavoring to shake myself from my despondent inertia.

"You can see that it is impossible to preach now!" I reasoned with my heart. "Think less about yourself and more of these Axminister and Wilton rugs, these highly varnished oaken floors, this mahogany parlor furniture, and the polishable brass beds in yonder! Think of caring for the fine bathroom, done in blue and white, the finishing of your baby's pretty crib with its fluff and ribbons. It would be perfectly absurd to even think of entering the evangelistic field now! If it was difficult for you to manage with one baby, how would it be with two?"

"Are you not glad to have so lovely a home for your little ones?" asked Mrs. McPherson, sagely.

"Of course," I agreed, attacking the rugs with broom and carpet beater and vacuum cleaner. Such a fever of restlessness came upon me that it is a wonder I did not wear off the polish from the highly varnished floors with my dust mop.

But my domesticity was short-lived. Ever and ever would return to me the Divine Command, "Preach the Word! I have called thee, and ordained thee!"

"You will feel differently after the baby comes," soothed my hard-pressed mother-in-law comfortingly.

In due time Rolf was born. From the moment of his birth he has been an unfailing comfort. My husband, showing no partiality between the two, trotted about the house and garden bearing one baby on each shoulder.

But I was a constant problem. The call of God was upon my soul, and I could not get away from it. My nerves became so seriously affected that I could not bear even the singing of the teakettle. The voices of my littles ones must be subdued to whispers, and even the sunshine was an unbearable torment, so I lived behind closed shutters and drawn blinds. My health broke, and I was taken to the hospital, where I underwent a serious major operation. Instead of improving, I grew steadily worse. Even under ether I could hear the Voice bidding me keep my early pledge to preach the Word.

Finally my condition became critical, and I was taken in to a separate room to die. A nurse sat by me in the early hours of the morning, watching my flickering pulse. Through the death silence which was broken only by my own painful breathing came the Voice of the Lord in trumpet tones, "NOW WILL YOU GO?"

Lying there face to face with the Grim Reaper, I realized that I was either going into the grave or out into the field with the gospel. I made my decision and gasped out the words, "Yes—Lord—I'll—go!"

Instantly, new life and warmth surged through my being. I was healed and turned over upon my side, much to the consternation of the nurse. In a few days I was up and about.

An interesting thing about my healing was that, whereas children of the Lord had prayed for me to no avail when I had been unwilling to heed the Divine call, my slightest cry, made with an obedient heart, was accorded an instant hearing in heaven, and I was at once made whole.

8

Can a Woman Preach?

"Yes, Lord, I'll go!" Over and over I kept repeating the words of the promise I had made to God and under the terms of which my life had been spared, that I might serve him.

"Yes, Lord, I'll go!" I did not know how or where I was to go, but I intended to start anyhow. Like Jonah heading back toward

Nineveh, like Moses stepping forth to cross the Red Sea, I went with all haste.

Not feeling myself strong enough to enter into another argument with Mr. McPherson or his mother as to the futility or impracticality of such a venture, I telephoned for a taxi at eleven o'clock at night. With my infant son, Rolf, clasped in one arm and Roberta sleeping in the other, I instructed the driver to pile our suitcases on top of the car and climbed inside.

I ordered him to drive to the railway depot and set out for the Canadian farm. Somehow it seemed the most natural thing in the world to go back to the original starting point again and begin my second effort from there. When the morning express pulled into Ingersoll, my father and my mother (who had returned for a brief visit to the farm) were there to greet me. I learned that a Pentecostal camp meeting was on in Kitchener, Ontario (then called Berlin), and my parents urged me to attend.

"But . . . the children . . . would I be able?" I stammered.

"Go along now! We've got the best Jersey milk in the country to make the boy grow like a weed. Roberta is out in the flower gardens already." The matter was settled. I would go. But before departing the next morning I telegraphed this message to my husband: "I have tried to walk your way and failed. Won't you come now and walk my way. I am sure we will be happy."

So it happened that, lean in my soul but determined to obey God's call, I sat on the edge of my seat under the big canvas top, waiting for the minister to finish his sermon and give the altar call. I was the first one down at the mourner's bench. Brokenly I began to sob, "Oh, Jesus, forgive me! For—"

Before I could finish the words it seemed as though the Lord had placed his hand over my trembling lips, saying, "There, there, my child. Say no more about it."

Again I tried to apologize to God and again I was stopped. The suddenness and magnitude of this hearty reception broke my heart. I fell under the power at his gracious feet, wailing, "Dear Lamb of God, let me be as one of thy hired servants. I feel unworthy to testify or preach, but just let me love thee and dwell in thy house, Oh, Savior!"

But almost before I knew it, I was up and praying for others who knelt beside me. The old-time anointing of the Spirit was burning in my soul. Those upon whom I laid my hands received the baptism of the Holy Ghost, right and left.

Service over, I stood before the raised platform and beckoned to the preacher, to whom I was a stranger. "Is there anything I can do for Jesus?" I asked.

He looked at me rather unseeingly and murmured abstractedly, "Why, I'm sure I don't know."

"Well, if there is, be sure to let me know."

Making my way out of the tent, I saw a woman who appeared to be one of the workers. "Is there anything that I can do to help?" I queried.

"Nothing that I know of now, dear," she replied unpromisingly.

"Is there anything that I can do to help you?" I halted others as I made my way through a long line of sleeping tents that bordered either side of the improvised street.

"Is there anything that I can do for Jesus?" I finally quizzed an aproned man who sat before the kitchen tent at the end of the street, peeling potatoes. He smiled down on me from beneath his tall, white cook's cap.

"Why, sure there is!" he answered.

"Then tell me quickly! I am desperately anxious to get into the work of the Lord. What can I do?"

"Can you wash dishes?"

"Why, why certainly, I can wash dishes. Every woman can do that."

"Then here you are," he said enthusiastically and, suiting his action to his words, lifted a flap of the tent and revealed two washtubs filled with dirty cups, saucers, plates, and cutlery. "The hot water is over on the stove. The towels are in that trunk."

Now if there is any task I dislike above another, it is washing other people's dirty chinaware. But I found myself completely happy as, setting about my task, I took the plates out of the cold greasy water, emptied out the tubs, and set to work with scalding water and soap. In fact, I found myself actually whistling as my fingers flew. Glory to God! I was in the work of the Lord! What matter that mine was the simple task of a kitchen maid? Was I not a part of the glorious whole that goes to make up a soul-saving constituency?

I was particularly careful to wipe the handles of the cups and tureens carefully and polish all dishes without leaving finger marks. Somehow I felt that if I was faithful in that which was least, the Lord would make me ruler over that which was more exalted.

Dishes done, I continued my round of pestering questions, "Is there anything more that I can do? What is next on the program?"

"Can you wait tables?" I was asked.

"Yes, sir!"

"Then hurry up and get your trays going. We are serving chicken dinner to scores of ministers in the dining tent."

I fairly flew between the kitchen range and the ministerial tables. It was a tedious task. If you have ever tried to fill up even one preacher on chicken, you can imagine the job of filling up scores and scores of them! But I was in a good place to ply my constant, plaintive, eager questions at every opportunity, "Do you know of anything that I can do for Jesus?"

"Can you play a piano?" asked one man through a mouthful of chicken.

"Hymns? Yes, sir."

"Then take the piano for the evening service."

Happy? It seemed as though I hit every key from top to bottom that night. What I may have lost in technique, I made up for in enthusiasm.

"Can you lead a choir? Our director is ill," asked an evangelist the next day.

"Oh, yes, sir!" I assented eagerly.

"Where did you lead your last one?" he smiled.

"Why, I never directed one yet, sir; but you asked if I *could!* I can do all things for Christ!" My eagerness won the day, and the task was mine. Joyously I ran between my duties, washing dishes, setting tables, making beds, beating time for the singers, praying at the altars till after midnight. It was heaven! *Heaven!*

At last the major camp meeting was over. The groups of ministers had returned to their own pastorates, leaving the one local preacher to carry on over the closing weekend. It developed that he had lost his voice. And, when next I asked him, "Isn't there something else that I can do?"

"Can—you—preach?" he managed in a cracked whisper.

"Y-yes, sir, I'll try!" I stuttered.

"Well, upon my word! It seems that that is the only thing left around here for you to try!"

And thus it was that I preached my first sermon as an independent evangelist. I do not remember the text of the message. But I do recall that some eleven souls made their way to the altar to accept the Lord. As I saw them coming down the aisles, such a wave of exultation swept over me that I was weak and dizzy from the sheer joy and glory of it. Many thrilling things have happened in my life. I have been 'way up in a balloon, flown in a Zeppelin, skimmed over the Alps in an airplane, been submerged in a submarine, looked down into the actual boiling crater of Mt. Vesuvius, preached to thousands of men from the keel of the Titanic as she lay in the shipyards of Belfast, received keys from mayors of several cities, opened the Senate and Congress, spoken over national radio hook-ups, climbed the pyramids, walked the streets of the Holy Land, ridden on camels in the heart of Algiers, sailed blue Galilee, packed the Royal Albert Hall in London, filled the Boston Gardens. But for sheer, breathtaking, 1000 percent thrills, there is still none to me like that known by the soul winner when sinners burst into tears of penitence and run down the aisles to fall at the altar of the Almighty!

Standing there and looking down through swimming eyes at those first eleven converts, I did not know that they were but the advance guard for hundreds of thousands who would follow in their steps throughout the years of my life-long ministry. But I do know that to this very day I am still as thrilled over the sight as upon that first occasion. I still want to laugh and cry, dance and shout all at once.

While still standing there, carried away by emotion, I looked down to find a woman tugging at my skirts. She said, "You are just the one I have been looking for."

"Yes?" I said politely.

"I live in Mount Forest," she continued. "It is a small little town where very few persons go to church. My mission hall is a tiny affair, holding but some fifty chairs. Even these are empty most of the time, and I don't dare ask a really good preacher to come. I thought maybe you would come."

"I'll be glad to go!" I told her. "But first I must run home to Ingersoll to see to my babies, then on to the neighboring city of London, where I have promised to help for ten days in the camp meeting. I could be ready in about two weeks' time."

"Then it is settled. But remember, I told you that it is a hard and difficult field. We have had no real revival there as far as the present generation can remember."

"Then it will afford a good school of experience," I reasoned, "and I shall do my very best. With God all things are possible."

At the close of the London meeting I collected my children and
left for Mount Forest and my first small mission. As the train
thundered through ripened Canadian wheatfields, bearing Rolf,
Roberta, and me to Mount Forest, I felt like Ruth, the gleaner
of old, going forth with the shining sickle of God's Word.

My hostess, Mrs. Sharpe, met us at the depot, and we set out
for her home. As we walked the main street of the little farming
town, we passed the characteristic general store, barber shop,
quaint little bank, and grocery. "Now you must not expect too
much," Mrs. Sharpe warned. "You know our place is very small."

"I cannot wait to see the mission hall where I am to preach."

"You won't have to—there it is now, just across the street."

Yes, there it was, under a little sign bearing its name, Victory
Mission. I hurried in, made my way down the center aisle between some four dozen chairs, and stepped up on the tiny platform to look around the empty place. "A doll's church," I
whispered to the baby in my arms.

At the opening service I was shocked to find the place practically empty except for two men and a boy who came in that
night. Still, I preached to them as earnestly as I have ever addressed the large audiences of from eighteen to thirty thousand
people in later years. But the next night the same handful of
persons were there again, also the next night and the next. Sunday morning and evening the attendance was no better. It began
to wear upon my nerves. Why waste so much energy on so few?
I determined to have a frank talk with Mrs. Sharpe. "Sister," I
began, "w-where is your congregation?"

"Why, this is the congregation!"

"How long have you been preaching to them?"

"Oh, almost two years."

"Well," I opined, "I think they are all preached up. Let's go
out and hunt a real crowd."

"I'm afraid that is impossible. I warned you when you were
invited to come that the people of Mount Forest are not great
churchgoers and that this is a small town."

"Everyone goes to a fire," I reasoned. "Let's get out and ring
the alarm."

"What do you mean?" she asked.

"How about street meetings?"

"No use. We have tried them, but no one stops to listen. You
can only pray and trust the Lord to melt this town's heart."

"Well," I replied, "I am going to help him. Faith without works is dead, you know. I am going out to get a crowd, right now!" Down the main street I wended my way with a chair. No one stopped to look at me curiously as I stopped at the chief corner. I surveyed the scene and sought to lay my plans for a siege of souls. The sleepy little town lazed in the sunset.

How could I gain their attention? I remembered Robert Semple's slogan: "When in doubt, pray." So, I started in. Setting my chair down firmly just outside the curb, I mounted the tiny rostrum, lifted my hands high to heaven, closed my eyes, and just stood there lifting my heart to God without speaking a single word aloud. Minutes passed. Nothing happened, but I never moved, never spoke, never lowered my arms. Then a wave of interest and excitement stirred the populace.

Footsteps hurried from all directions until a sizable crowd had gathered, but I never moved. I was afraid to by now. One would not have realized that there were so many people on the street!

I opened my eyes and looked wildly around. Then I began to tremble. But, though I tried to speak, not a word would come. My mouth merely opened and closed several times. Then, with desperation, I shouted, "People—follow me quick!" Jumping down off the chair, I hooked my arm through its back and ran off up the street toward the mission. The crowd ran after me.

I never stopped till I reached the door. I ran in, and they ran in too. Racing to the little platform, I cried to the doorkeeper, "Lock that door! And keep it locked till I get through!" Having gotten the people, I was fearful lest I could not hold their interest. But they showed no inclination to leave. That practically settled the crowd problem. I have never had to seriously worry over it since that eventful day. If you are annoyed over attendance, why not try the chair-and-prayer method at some busy intersection? I can heartily recommend it and practically guarantee that it will work. Anyway, I preached to those people for forty minutes. The next night there were as many outside the tiny hall as were able to get into it.

"It is a lovely evening. Why not try preaching outside on the lawn?" someone suggested.

The crowd trooped out and sat on the grass while I preached on the piazza. The piano was hastily trundled out, and some farmers removed the lanterns from their wagons and tied them in the trees. And so I had a great church after all. My dome was the starry heavens. For music, the wind whispered through the pines. For pews, we had the soft green velvet of the lawn. For parishioners, there were men in denim overalls and women in alpaca housedresses. For a penitent form, we utilized the crumbling edge of the piazza. It was all very thrilling! Great broad-shouldered farmers came down to the improvised altar and gave their hearts to the Lord. All that week I preached out of doors, and scores wept their way into the Kingdom. The crowd grew in numbers till we had more than five hundred. They arrived on horseback, on bicycles, buggies, and in wagons. They arrived on foot and in new horseless carriages.

A woman preacher was a novelty. At the time when I began my ministry, women were well in the background of life in Canada and the United States. Women in business life and before the public eye were the exception to the rule. Men largely monopolized activities outside the home. Still, they reasoned, "If the Lord chooses a woman to attract those to himself who otherwise might not have come, who among us should question the wisdom of God? We get saved just the same way, whether the preacher is a man or a woman."

Orthodox ministers, many of whom disapproved even of men evangelists such as Moody, Spurgeon, Sunday, and the rest chiefly because they used novel evangelistic methods rather than the conventional and formal modes of orthodoxy, disapproved all the more of a woman minister. Especially was this true when my meetings departed from the funereal, sepulchrelike ritual of appointed Sundays and swept the country with the paeans of joyous and fervent every-day-in-the-week revivalism.

Yet right at the first there was borne in upon me the realization that the popular methods of that day were too archaic, too sedate, too lifeless to capture the interest of the throngs. Times had moved forward; the gospel was ever fresh and up to date; but the musty modes of presentation were antiquated. The people wanted to hear not only of the Christ of 1900 years ago, but of the living, vitalizing, empowering Christ of today!

"Lady, you ain't no regular preacher!"

I looked up into the face of the speaker, a bewhiskered, weather-seamed old farmer with corded muscles rippling in his brawny bare arms. "I'm only a beginner," I apologized. "But why do you say that? You—you are laughing at me!"

"Why," he replied mirthfully, "you have been here a whole week and have never taken up a single collection. What kind of a preacher is that?"

"It was an oversight. I hadn't even thought of it!"

"I'll help you remedy matters right now." He took a large, broad-rimmed straw hat and moved industriously among the crowd. If anyone hesitated to give, he would just stand before the victim, holding out his improvised collection plate and say, "Come on now, Bill, you old tightwad! Loosen up," or "Cough up, Williams. Dip deep in your jeans, Spud!" Flushed but triumphant, he returned with his headgear filled to the brim with coins and bills.

After the meeting I counted the treasure. It amounted to some sixty-five dollars. So proud was I of this offering that I sat up almost all night watching it. "That is your money. You worked hard for it. The people gave it willingly. There are no strings attached to it. Place it in the bank for a rainy day," said self.

"It is the Lord's money. It should be invested in the work. Seek first the Kingdom of God, and all else shall be added unto you," whispered the Spirit.

The following morning, hearing of a man in a neighboring town who had a tent for sale, I boarded the train and went to see him.

"Yep, lady," said the man, "right up these steps to the store-room. The tent originally cost me five hundred dollars, but I'll let you have it for one hundred and fifteen."

"I can pay no more than sixty-five," I faltered.

"That's ridiculous! Why, it should hold five hundred people!"

"I am so disappointed! What shall I do? Fall rains will be coming on soon, and I have a glorious revival started in Mount Forest. C-couldn't you—"

"Well, lady," he compromised, "I'll tell you what I'll do for you. Seein' as how yer a preacher, I'll let you have it for sixty-five, on one condition."

"Oh, yes, sir, anything." I opened my purse and held the bills temptingly before him.

"The tent is heavy and bulky. If you do not put me to the trouble of spreading it out . . . in other words, if you will buy it in the bag, it is yours."

"Done! Why, I would not dream of putting you to so much trouble. God bless you, sir. Please load it on the train for me."

Back on the meeting grounds, I excitedly called Mrs. Sharpe and all the neighbors, "Come, come quickly! Come and help me get my canvas cathedral out of the bag."

Painstakingly and laboriously we dragged the big top from its hiding place and stretched it out upon the lawn. Friends, take my advice: Never buy a tent in a bag! From one end to the other my purchased meeting house was full as a sieve of rips and tears, and mildew and moths had completed the ruin. Nevertheless, we sewed and patched and got it up. It was the old push-pole type, and all my ingenuity was necessary to hoist the heavy poles into position. Even then if I made it taut in one place, it sagged in half a dozen others.

But with perspiration-damp hair straggling down my cheeks, skirts bedraggled with dirt and dust, and with calloused, broken-finger-nailed hands, I stuck to my task, driving in tent stakes with a sledge hammer and making the guy ropes secure. When it was up and decorated with mottoes and garlands of smilax, it looked fairly well. I walked around it as proudly as the archbishop of Canterbury treading the aisles of his cathedral.

The following morning was Sunday. I now had a place to shelter the people. The tent was already filled to capacity when I mounted happily to the pulpit. The streets were lined in all directions with all types of vehicles. The tent flaps swayed merrily in the stiffening breeze.

As I looked out over the hundreds of persons seated comfortably upon the long rows of benches I had borrowed, my joy overflowed. This was something like it! I preached as one inspired. The words fairly poured forth in a stream.

Just then the wind bore down heavily upon my end of the tent. The canvas sighed, and then, with a despairing cry, shrilly shrieked, "Eek-squeek—r-r-rip!" The breath oozed right out of the tent and out of me too. A wide tear appeared about the pole directly over my head. Then the whole tent began to slide sickeningly down. I lost the interest of the crowd. Their eyes were raised to the billowing folds that were collapsing over us.

In those early days of evangelistic enthusiasm everything was either the Lord or the Devil to me. I believed that Satan was trying to break up my meeting. Scarcely realizing what I was about to do, in my excitement I lifted up my arm to the tent top and cried, "In the name of Jesus, I command you to stop right where you are till this day's meetings are over!" And believe it or not, a roped seam caught on a protruding nail and stayed up. Moreover, the wind died, and the meeting was successfully completed.

"O-ho!" you say, "that was not God, Sister, that was the nail." Perhaps. Just the same, I give the Lord credit. People who advance the other explanation seem somehow to me very much like the little boy who was slipping down the roof of the barn. Poor little fellow—he was falling faster every moment. "Oh-oh-oh! Lord, help me," he cried in a frantic prayer. "Lord, help me. I am falling—I am falling off the roof!" At that moment his trousers caught on a shingle nail, and his sliding stopped. Securely held where he was, he again lifted his voice to heaven and said, "Never mind, Lord, I've caught on a nail now."

So many of us are like that little boy—we pray when some trouble arises, and when the darkness is past, we begin to reason with ourselves, "Now possibly that was not God who delivered me after all!"

After the meeting was over, we took the tent down and spread it on the ground. The next day I again took the big needle, got a lot of women from the congregation to help me, and worked all morning and all the afternoon sewing yards and yards of canvas, dozens of bolt topes, spreaders, and guys all over the tent. By dark the tent looked like an inner tube all covered with patches— so many patches that there seemed to be very little left of the original tent. Then we got it erected again, this time to stay.

When we had finished, every muscle in my body was weary. I was so tired that I ached, too fatigued to preach, too exhausted to do anything. Surely nobody would expect me to preach after such a day as this. So I determined to rest that night and pinned a little note on the tent postponing the meeting till the morrow.

"No meeting tonight," the note read. "The evangelist is too tired after mending the tent all day."

But I did preach that night. And the next night. And the night after that. Preparatory to going to bed instead of preaching, I took my Bible and knelt down to pray. The Bible somehow fell from the bed to the floor, and there it opened of its own accord. "He that saveth his life shall lose it, but he that loseth his life for my sake and the gospels, the same shall save it," were the lines staring me in the face.

Yes, I preached that night. And though I was dead tired as I stepped to the platform, when we stood for the first hymn all my weariness dropped from me like a cloak unclasped. It has been like this since that night. No matter what labor or troubles the day brings, no matter how physically or mentally fatigued they leave me, I am always completely refreshed the instant I stand in the pulpit. As my day, so is my strength—the more I have to do, the more strength I seem to have with which to do it. And when the message comes, I feel the infusion of power just as does a copper wire when the electric current reaches it. I am revitalized, remade alive.

Many souls were saved that night simply because, after I had mended and erected the tent, God showed me that he would provide strength sufficient for my every need. Never since, in any emergency or throughout any long-drawn siege, has that strength left me. The current is sent through this human cord, and the light flares its hallowed beacon throughout the world.

At that particular service which I had so nearly foregone, eighteen of those big, broad-shouldered farmers were converted. They came down to the rough altar, and their huge shoulders shook with inward sobs. When at last they rose from their knees, their faces were shining. The meeting went along gloriously, continually increasing in power, in numbers, and in results at the altars, where the lives of men and women were transformed from darkness into light.

From the greatest to the least, they came, from city officials and the best families to the most hopeless sinner, who in this instance seemed to be the town bell ringer. He was a novel character and seemed to be the football of everyone in his drunkenness, kicked out of saloons, earning his pittance by ringing his bell up and down the street. "Hear ye! He-a-r ye!" and along he would go to announce an auction sale, a football game, or whatnot. After he was converted, he told me that I was the first person who had ever called him Mr. Connor. Others had always called him Monkey Abe. A marvelous transformation was wrought. Sobered and dressed in a freshly cleaned and mended suit, he proudly strode up and down the streets ringing his bell more loudly than ever. "Hear ye! Hear ye! I have given my heart to Christ. Come down to the revival tonight and hear Sister McPherson preach the Christ who saved even me."

For the two years immediately following that night, in summer and in winter, north or south, I worked by day and dreamed by night in the shadows of the tent. I watched my tents as a mother watches her only child; I could not bear to be out of sight of them. They were the entire world wherein I lived, breathed, and had my being. I slept on a soldier's canvas cot in a little tent beside the big one—myself and the two children—and as I slept, I sometimes stroked the side of the cot and felt that I too was a soldier upon the battleground of the Lord.

In the midst of the Mount Forest meeting I received several telegrams from Harold McPherson asking me to come home and "wash the dishes." I wired back that I was now an evangelist with growing success in soul winning and could never leave the field. Mr. McPherson then came to Mount Forest and, after hearing me speak, said, "Darling, I had no idea you could preach like that. You must never stop."

Along the Atlantic Seaboard

One day, as I knelt in prayer, there came to me over and over the word "Corona! Corona! Corona!" So dependent was I upon the Lord for my daily needs that I cried out, "Bless God, he has heard my prayer and is sending me the Corona typewriter for which I have been praying!"

Still upon my knees, I turned to open a pile of mail that I had dropped upon the floor. Imagine my surprise when I opened a letter on the top of the pile of invitations and read the postmark, "Corona, Long Island." Up to this time I had not been aware that such a place existed. The handwriting was barely legible and had evidently been written laboriously by some good and prayerful old saint. It read:

Dear Sister McPherson:
    For two years I have been lying upon my face before God, be-
seeching him to send a revival to Corona.
    He has now revealed to me that a mighty city-sweeping revival
is to be sent through your ministry. Souls shall be converted in
great numbers, saints receive the Pentecostal baptism of the Holy
Ghost, and miracles of healing be wrought here at your hands.
    My home is open to you. Your room is all prepared. Come im-
mediately, expecting great things of the Lord.

The Spirit immediately witnessed to my heart, and, finding that
Corona was just outside New York City, I set out for the place.
I experienced some difficulty in locating the address and walked
many blocks with a heavy suitcase in my hand. But finally someone located the street on a city map. It was in the colored district.
Wonderingly, I approached the place and tapped upon the door.
    The door opened wide. My eyes flew open with astonishment.
A beaming-faced coal-black mammy almost filled the aperture.
"Oh, I beg your pardon," I said. "I am looking for the lady who
wrote me to come to Corona to hold a revival campaign. I
thought—I thought that this was the correct address—"
    "Is yo' all Sistah McPherson dat's been preachin' in a big
tent?"
    "Yes."
    "Why, bless yo' heart, chile! Come in dis bery minute! I'se
been alookin' fo' you all day. Come in! Come in!"
    Two great black arms went around me, and I was pressed to
her ample bosom before I could realize that this child of God was
the author of the letter.
    "I had a friend word it for me," she explained as she led me
up and up a narrow staircase to a tiny attic bedroom. Removing
the travel stains, I descended to find a carefully set luncheon
spread upon the parlor table. As I ate, my hostess talked, and the
shock of surprise gradually began to wear away.
    "Ef eber dar was a town dat needed a Holy Ghost revival, dis
am it!" she exclaimed earnestly, as she spread thick blackberry
jam upon a slice of bread and laid it on my plate.
    "Y-yes?" I stammered, somewhat regaining my powers of
speech. "In what church or building is the campaign to be held?"
    "It's to be held right heah in Corona, ob course."
    "But what is the name of the hall or building in which it is to
be conducted?"

"Why bless yo' heart, honey, ah don't know nuffin 'bout dat. Ah thought yo' all'd arrange 'bout dem things when yo' all arrived. Yo' know more 'bout dem things than ah do!"

"But, mammy, who is supporting and sponsoring the meeting? Have you a group of people—a company of believers who will assist me?"

"No, chile, ah couldn't seem to get them interested in a revival," she sighed. "Ah reckon I'se 'bout de onliest one yo' all can depend on right now; but dere will be plenty mo' when de meetin's get started."

"M-m-m, yes—" I murmured, and tried to wash down with a swallow of milk the lump in my throat. "Then, there really are not any—any real preparations for the campaign—yet?"

"Preparation! Preparations!" she burst out. "Deed dere is preparations, chile! Preparations aplenty. Didn't ah tell yo' I'se been aprayin' fo' dis heah meeting for mor'n two years? Ah's got it all prayed through now. De clouds ob glory are jes ready to burst 'pon dis town when yo' all begins to preach de Word."

After the humble repast, at mammy's suggestion we had a season of prayer. No one could hear that rich, full, earnest voice upraised to God without knowing that here was one who communed with the Master as friend communed with friend. She looked like a radiant black angel, and her heart was of pure gold.

Rising, I prepared myself for action, saying, "I think we had better go out and look for a meeting hall right now. I am a stranger and do not know where to go first."

"Ef ah was younger, ah would go with you, chile, but ah knows de Lawd has a prepared place awaitin' somewhere. Yo' all run along and ah'll stay home an' ask de Lawd to guide yo'."

Mustering up my courage, I set forth in search of an auditorium but met with scant encouragement. No town hall, no empty theater, no vacant lodge rooms were available. The only room offered came in response to an inquiry put to a saloon keeper.

"Well, lady," he said kindly, "I doubt whether you will find a place for a meeting house. But if the parlor back of my saloon will do—it would seat a couple hundred—you may have it."

Thanking him kindly, I declined the offer and passed on. The next day and the next, the search continued without avail. Tired, footsore, weary, I returned to my room and, after bathing my hot face, flung myself disconsolately into a chair.

"What a peculiar situation," I gasped. "Is it possible that I am here out of the will of God? What was the meaning of that strange insistent word *Corona! Corona!* that I heard in prayer?"

The city's desperate need of a Holy Ghost revival, its coldness and formality were laid bare before my search was ended. But was the dear old colored mammy right in positively declaring this was God's time and that he had called me to conduct a campaign at this moment? I leaned back wearily in the chair and closed my eyes. A perplexed frown puckered my brow.

A footstep was heard coming up the walk below. Rap! Rap! Rap! A hand was knocking at the door. Perhaps it was someone coming with news about the auditorium, for I had flung out inquiries in all directions. Leaning over the banister, I listened and was astonished at the words of the big voice that came booming up the little hall.

"I understand there is an evangelist lady here."

"Yes, suh. Sistah McPherson am here to conduct a revival."

"Well, I am the pastor of the Swedish Methodist Episcopal Church down the street, and I wonder whether she'd have time to come down and conduct some meetings for us?"

"Jes' a minute, suh, I'll call her an' yo' ask her yo'self. S-i-s-t-a-h!"

"Yes, mammy."

I almost stumbled down the stairs in my eagerness and stood breathless, looking up at the minister who had come like a messenger from the sky at this perplexing moment.

That night I found the church half filled with people, and they spread the story throughout the town. The next afternoon the church was full, and that night it was overflowing to the streets, though church members had been warned by their ministers to keep away from the Pentecostal people and have nothing to do with those folks who talked in tongues. Just one week from the day meetings were opened, the break came. A Sunday school teacher from one of the large churches, a man whose sound Christian standing had been known for years, was the first to receive the baptism. The wife of a leading citizen was the second, and when the altar call was given, scores from the audience, which was made up entirely of church members, gathered about the altar.

Never having seen a Pentecostal meeting, they were very stiff and did not know how really to get hold of and seek the Lord.

Knowing that their ministers had warned them that this was all hypnotism, however, I was very careful not to lay hands on or speak to the seekers. But I earnestly prayed by my own chair, "Oh, Lord, send the power. Lord, honor your Word just now."

Then it was that Mrs. John Lake, who had risen from the altar and taken her seat in the audience again, suddenly fell under the power, with her head upon her husband's shoulder. In alarm the people said, "She has fainted. Run and get some water." But I knew she hadn't fainted and kept on praying, "Lord, send the power. Baptize her just now."

Quite a crowd had gathered round her, but before they could get back with the water, praise the Lord, the Holy Ghost had descended and filled her. She broke out speaking with other tongues, to the amazement and delight of all. On and on she spoke in a clear, beautiful language, her face shining with the glory of the Lord. One said to another, "What do you think of it?" Another exclaimed, "Oh, isn't it wonderful, marvelous! How I wish I had the same experience!"

The news of this well-known sister's baptism quickly spread through the town. The next night three were slain under the power and came through speaking in tongues. And thus the meeting increased in power, numbers, and results each night.

After preaching in the church one week, Pastor W. K. Bouton invited us to his church to preach on a Thursday night. (After warning his people not to come near our meetings, he had come himself. The Lord had convinced him of the truth that there was something deeper yet for himself and his church.)

The night on which I spoke at his church I had to ask the Lord not to let me be afraid or overawed by the visiting ministers who sat behind me on the platform and to give me liberty and power preaching his Word. He never fails. He remembers our weakness, praise his name!

As I spoke, hearty amens and hallelujahs came from all over the church. I felt that I must preach the truth without compromise at least once in this church, as they might never ask me again. When finished, I took my seat, not presuming to give an altar call in someone else's church.

The minister rose and said, "How many of you people who believe what Sister McPherson has said to be the truth feel that you have not received the baptism of the Holy Spirit in the Bible way and would like to receive this experience? Lift your hands."

"Sister," said he, and I noticed that there were tears in his eyes, "I wish to extend to you an invitation to stay in my church as long as you desire and preach these wonderful truths. You were crowded out in the building you had been using. Our church is considerably larger. Will you, in the Master's name, accept the invitation?"

Even this larger church was packed from the pulpit to the door and far out in the street at the next meeting. The windows were opened, and the people stood looking in on boxes or ledges.

One night having heard me declare that Jesus Christ was the same yesterday, today, and forever, that he still lives to save and heal and baptize with his Holy Spirit, some of my audience took me at my word. Great was the astonishment when, lifting my eyes, I saw coming down the central aisle a strange and pathetic little figure—a young lady, leaning upon two crutches. She was bowed over and twisted with rheumatoid arthritis and supported on the left and on the right, in addition to her crutches, by two friends. Down she came from the back row. It seemed to me as though everyone was looking at her. A little gasp of pity ran over the assembly.

I had had no experience in praying for the sick. Indeed, very little, comparatively, had been said or done about this great doctrine at the time. Yet in my sermons I had constantly proclaimed Jesus Christ to be the same yesterday, today, and forever. I believed it too—believed that he was able to heal. I was even willing to pray for one that was sick. But how I did wish that I could begin with someone who looked a bit more mendable than this poor little thing with her gnarled and twisted fingers, swollen joints, chin pulled forward until it lay upon her breast, and limbs that were drawn. Her hands were so helpless that she could not lift them to comb her own hair or feed herself.

But there she came, and it seemed she would never get to the front. Step—step—step. Gentle hands eased the poor little body along. I remember in the dead silence that had fallen upon us all how one crutch squeaked and a board of the floor creaked.

The eyes of the people looked first at the young lady and then at me. And I, God help me, felt my face flushing more each moment. But I cried out in my heart, "Oh, Lord, you are able to heal her, though I admit she does seem to be a hopeless case!"

During the message large tears had rolled down her face, and when the altar call was given, the girl, Louise Messnick, expressed to her friends a desire to come to the altar and be converted. Meanwhile, I had made up my mind to have a word of prayer for her that the Lord would strengthen her and give her faith. I intended to slip down to the front seat and there quietly pray with her. I tried to tell myself that the kinder thing to do was to make it as inconspicuous as possible. Perhaps away in the back of my mind there was a thought that if she were not completely healed her affliction would not be so noticeable there. But I gasped a little as I saw that the young lady was now being borne to the altar by the strong arms of her attendants. Being unable to kneel, lo and behold, they were carrying her to the central minister's chair.

Earnestly she prayed. Wholeheartedly she gave her life to Jesus. Inquiry brought out the fact that she was the child of a non-Protestant family. Before many minutes had elapsed, she had been not only converted but blessedly baptized with the Holy Spirit.

Then I prayed for her healing. I told her to lift up her hands and praise the Lord. "Praise the Lord! Praise the Lord!" rang out her clear voice. And, to the joy of all, the gnarled joints began to straighten out! She lifted her hands up, up as high as her chin, her eyes, the top of her head. "Oh!" she exclaimed, "this is the first time I have been able to lift my hands to the top of my head in so, so long! Praise the Lord!"

Up, up went her hands until both hands and arms were practically free. Her chin, however, had been pressed against her chest for so long that it seemed as though it had almost grown there, her neck being practically rigid. Her head began to turn now, and then the chin commenced to lift. She gazed heavenward. In a moment she was on her feet! Clinging hand over hand to the chancel rail, she began to walk as the limbs straightened.

Whether it was because I had until this time never seen such a sight I know not, but to this day the healing of that young lady seems to me one of the most mighty miracles I have ever known. She went walking out of the church that night, climbed into the car, and stepped out again at her own home. When her mother saw her walking up the garden path, and when one of her companions handed the mother the girl's crutches, she threw up her hands and cried, "Thank God! Oh, thank God!" and then threw the crutches down into the cellar to be used no more.

From that time forward, Louise became one of the constant

attendants at the meeting. She declared it seemed to her as she sat out on the piazza or ran the sewing machine which she now delighted in doing that all the neighbors for blocks around passed her door to inquire whether these things were true.

A couple of years later, I had occasion to conduct a meeting in the same church. Tripping down the aisle came a plump, rosy little lady who fell upon me like a tornado. "Do you remember me?" she demanded.

Looking at the sparkling eyes and clear complexion and the trim little figure, I shook my head and said, "It's not—not—Louise—"

"The very same, praise the Lord! I have been sewing, cooking, doing housework, attending the meetings. Our whole family has been converted, and praise the Lord for his goodness to me!"

Before I left Corona, Long Island, for Jacksonville, Florida, where I had felt the leading of the Lord for tent meetings during the winter months, the minister, without previously consulting me, announced that an offering was to be taken for my services in the church. Money had never been discussed between us.

A table was placed by the altar, a Bible opened upon it, and the people invited to lay their offerings on it. How they came, choking the aisles, laying silver and paper money upon the open pages. Thus the Lord supplied all our needs. The fields were waiting for the gospel, and the splendid offering with which the Corona Baptist Church had rewarded my campaign made it possible to carry it all the way south to Florida for the winter of 1916–17.

Another aftermath of that Corona meeting was the Lord's provision to me of that long-desired typewriter! This enabled me within a few months to begin to edit the *Bridal Call*. The first issue appeared in June, 1917, published from Savannah, Georgia. It was at first a little four-page country newspaper. But after three months I made arrangements with the Christian Workers' Union at Montwait, Framingham, Massachusetts, to enlarge the *Bridal Call* and publish it as a monthly sixteen-page magazine, seven by ten inches in size, with a subscription price of twenty-five cents per year. The issues carried my sermons, news, pictures of the campaigns, poems, and other articles. Now I could keep in touch across the miles with many of the people to whom I ministered in different parts of the country.

During the two winters I preached in Florida (1916–17 and

1917–18), the tent was pitched not only in Jacksonville and Tampa but in St. Petersburg, Orlando, Palm Beach, Miami, and as far south as Key West. It was during my campaigns in Florida that my mother arrived to help in the work.

I remember vividly one particular meeting which was held in a large wooden tabernacle in Durant, Florida, twenty miles from Tampa, and produced a doubting Thomas who was properly squelched. This man took special exception to the thought that the prayer of faith still saves the sick.

One Sunday afternoon when the meeting was at its height, this brother waited until the audience was dismissed to eat lunch. Then he started an opposition meeting just the other side of the fence that enclosed the grounds, setting forth his theory that miracles were only for the Bible days and that all supernatural power had ceased with the writing of the last chapter of the Book.

Meanwhile, I was preparing for the night service. The lighting problem in Durant had been a difficult one to solve, as the tabernacle was too far from the civic center to be supplied with electricity. Having decided that the kerosene and gasoline lamps in use there were not bright enough, I had brought with me a calcium carbide lighting outfit. There evidently was a defect in the apparatus, for suddenly, while I was making some adjustments, *the thing blew up.* Searing flames enveloped me.

My first thought was that the great wooden tabernacle would be burned. Somehow I managed to stay right where I was until I had turned off the tap and the flame was extinguished. There were only a few people in the tabernacle at the moment, and I remember how astonished they were. One man dropped to his hands and knees and crept under the seats clear to the door. He looked so funny that in spite of my pain I burst into laughter.

My face for an instant after the explosion felt joy cold, but in a moment it was flaming hot. What a peculiar sight I was! My face was black, and my eyebrows and eyelashes were gone, as well as my hair that was exposed. Fortunately I had on a tight-fitting hat. The pain was so violent that I did the most foolish thing possible. I ran and buried my face in a pan of cold water. As long as I could keep it in the water, excluding the air, the pain was alleviated, but the moment it was taken out, my suffering was intense. Some of the ladies came with soda and applied it to the blisters. Up and down, up and down, I walked under the trees, and all this time the crowds were gathering in the tabernacle.

Someone had succeeded in repairing the lighting system. I could see the automobile headlights coming up the road, hear the cars drawing up, doors opening and slamming, see the people going in, see the wagons lumbering up and unloading their quotas.

One thought above all others predominated: "What, oh what, will that brother say who told the people that the Lord no longer answers prayer on behalf of the afflicted?" Oh! O-o-o-oh! My poor face! Oh! O-o-o-oh! O-o-o-oh! The meeting—the meeting! Ten minutes to meeting time . . . five minutes to meeting time.

Meeting time, and still I walked up and down, scarcely able to endure the agony. Five minutes after meeting time. Ten minutes after meeting time. I had a never-late-to-service record. Some evangelists like to have the song leader start the service and carry it on for half an hour and then walk in fresh at the last moment for the message, but somehow I have never been able to do that. I have always loved to be in the service from the earliest moment to catch the spirit of it, to decide upon the tenor of my message.

Sure enough, my worst fears were realized. The man in question got to his feet, bold sort of a fellow as he was, and began to make a speech, assuring the people that there would be no meeting tonight, as the lady who preached salvation and divine healing was ill, having burned her face. The gist of what he said reached my ears, and I was shaken with righteous indignation. Rushing to the pan of water, I washed off the soda, at least all except one spot on the end of my nose which I missed and found later. With my stiffly starched collar bespattered with water, my eyebrows and eyelashes gone, and my hair singed, it must have been a rather wild figure that presented itself at the tabernacle door. But praying to God for strength and telling him I would go in the name of the Lord, I entered and mounted the platform.

I gave out the first hymn, my lips so stiff with the burn that I could scarcely articulate. At the end of my first verse I lifted up one of my hands and in naked and desperate faith exclaimed: "I praise the Lord that he heals me and takes all the pain away!"

A great shout went up from the camp. My intense suffering was relieved instantly, and right before the eyes of the audience the angry red burn faded from my face, the little white blisters that were forming disappeared, and at the end of the service the flesh had resumed its natural appearance. This turned the tide of the battle decidedly in favor of the present-day acceptance of the power of God, and the doubter was put to shame and silence.

Spring was at hand, the northern states were calling, the southern campaign was brought to a triumphant close, and I piloted the gospel car northward with my family. While my children slept in the back seat, I drove us toward Philadelphia and the scene of our nationwide camp meeting beginning in July, 1917.

Arriving in the city of brotherly love, we were welcomed by friends who aided me in the selection of a glorious camp site situated on a hill overlooking the river and sheltered by high, shady trees. Here too I found the tent of my dreams neatly stored in a warehouse. As we climbed the stairs to inspect its broadtop of ten-ounce U.S. army duck, double fill and double twist, double stitched with splendid ropes, block and tackle, iron stakes and jointed, lofty poles, my heart sang for joy. Valued at twenty-five hundred dollars, this spacious meeting house had been designed for a splendid evangelist who had done great things for God. But when the baptism of the Spirit had been preached, he had refused the light, taken a stand against the Holy Ghost, and was now set aside and ill for months.

The tent which God meant for our work remained brand new in its bag with instructions that it be sold for religious purposes only. We offered fifteen hundred dollars and were refused. "You cannot expect a reduction of a thousand dollars!" indignantly declared the salesman in the dark shadows of the great storehouse.

"After prayer," I replied, "that is all God wishes me to pay."

"I know nothing of prayer, but I do know the value of tents," he snapped, walking away and looking out of the window. There he saw, far below, my gospel car with the motto printed on it in letters of gold: "JUDGMENT DAY IS COMING! GET RIGHT WITH GOD!"

"H-m-m-m!" came his decision—and the tent was mine. Soon it was up and packed with benches, electric lights strung inside and out, a rented piano on the plank platform, and almost countless little sleeping tents piled upon the ground in bags ready for the erection of a tent city.

Banners were painted and swung across main thoroughfares. Musicians volunteered and polished up their technique for an orchestra. Hymn books were loaned. Handbills distributed, posters placed in every advantageous spot, the meeting was on!

Saints came from New York, Baltimore, Washington. Hundreds upon hundreds of godly men and women standing upon their feet, hands lifted toward heaven, eyes closed, and upturned faces streaming with tears as they sang the new song of heavenly anthems prompted by the Holy Spirit, provided never-to-be-forgotten sights and sounds. They prayed as I had never heard people pray before. Each one, forgetting his neighbor, forgetting all else but the God who answers prayer, cried out with all his might for a great revival.

Trouble arose upon the second night, however. It developed that the site of our campground had been used by the young men of a neighboring Catholic college for a football field. These young men resented our presence very much and patrolled the grounds day and night, keeping watch on everything and everybody, declaring that we had invaded their own hill, although I had rented it in a regular manner.

While an enormous crowd filled the tent, these young men by the hundreds formed a fringe on the outside. Every time there would be a manifestation of the Spirit, they would burst forth in peals of laughter, ridiculing and mocking. Finally their scoffing and jeering became so loud that it drowned out the voices of any who started to sing solos, lead in prayer, or speak.

The devil had carefully laid his plan. It so happened at this time that a riot took place in the center of the city which had called every available policeman, so there were none to keep order. Back and forth, to and fro, the mob surged on every hand. Detectives told me later that there had been a prearranged program to wipe out every tent on the ground that night, the young men having even gone to the length of concealing cans of kerosene and gasoline behind hammocks of grass that they might later ignite the entire highly inflammable canvas.

Speaking being impossible, the song leader simply directed the audience in the singing of such old songs as "Rock of Ages Cleft for Me," "Nearer My God to Thee," "It Is Well with My Soul," and "Jesus, Oh How Sweet the Name." "Oh, Lord," I groaned, leaning back in my chair upon the platform, "what shall I do?"

"Begin praising me out loud," answered the Spirit down deep in my heart, "for the joy of the Lord is your strength."

"But, Lord, how can I praise thee when I do not feel like it . . . when I feel like running away?"

"Do you praise me because you feel like it or because I am worthy?" questioned the Inner Voice.

"Because you are worthy," I answered. "Bless the Lord! Hallelujah! Glory to Jesus!" I began timidly, in a soft voice.

Instantly it was as though strong winds of thanksgiving lifted me above the danger and peril of the moment. My voice became stronger until at last I was truly shouting with my eyes still tightly closed, "Amen! Glory, glory, glory! Praise the Lord, oh, my soul, and all that is within me praise his holy name!"

The congregation caught the Spirit and likewise lifted their voices. As I praised the Lord, I seemed to see a lot of demons with outspread, batlike wings, each of which was interlocked with that of his neighbor, surrounding the tabernacle. But every time I cried "Praise the Lord!" I noted that the demonic forces took a step backward until finally back, back, back, they disappeared amid the trees. But now that I had once begun, it was difficult to stop, so I continued shouting, "Glory to Jesus! Hallelujah! Praise the Lord!"

Suddenly I noticed that from the place where the powers of darkness had been lost to view a great square of white-robed angels were advancing with outspread wings, each of which likewise was interlocked with that of his neighbor. Bless the Lord! With each "Praise the Lord," the angels took a step forward. On, on, on they came until they entirely surrounded the outer edges of my canvas cathedral.

Startled, I opened my eyes and looked about me. The young men who had been our tormentors were still there, but now they stood as quiet as mice, eyes rounded and staring as they looked upon me wondering-like. Then I arose and preached to one of the most attentive audiences it had ever been my privilege to address. When the altar call was given, the benches were thronged. The same young men, many of whom gave their hearts to Christ, came again and again, bringing the sick and afflicted for prayer. God marvelously answered.

War! Influenza! Tens of Thousands Die! Shortage of Coffins Delays Burials! Thus ran the headlines of the daily press; the epidemic had struck the East with full force. There I was with a long itinerary of meetings scheduled throughout Massachusetts, Connecticut, and New York!

Quarantine bans came down on public schools, theaters, and churches everywhere. Our banners fluttered listlessly over sorrowing thousands. The revival announcement pennants flapped limply in the humid autumn air. Yet miraculously in every city as I came to it, the bans were lifted only to settle again after the campaign was over.

I preached day and night. Worcester, Massachusetts, Hartford and Long Hill, Connecticut, were plague ridden, yet God graciously saved and baptized hundreds. These meetings were followed by a successful convention in New York City. Here, marvelous and outstanding instances of healing were observed, and Pentecost poured out.

On the way from New York to New Rochelle, I piloted my little family and automobile through a heavy, murky fog. My daughter complained of a chill, and I bundled her up in the lap robe. The very air seemed pregnant with disease and death. There was nothing to do but go on to our appointed eight-day revival. We took quarters in a tiny, sunless upstairs apartment consisting of two bedrooms and a kitchenette.

The epidemic was raging. Newspaper screamlines and photographs revealed that scores of dead lay in blankets upon morgue floors for days, as there were not enough coffins for their interment. Gravediggers were shown in a state of exhaustion as new recruits took their places and began digging feverishly into newly turned earth.

In this morbid, unpromising atmosphere, the New Rochelle revival opened. A wonderful spirit prevailed. Unprecedented crowds thronged the auditorium. Eager men and women overflowed every available seat, stood in aisles, and sat upon the floor of the platform. Every anteroom was packed, and throngs clamored at the doors. Steady processions of hearses and ambulances passed our portals even as I spoke. All of this produced a serious consideration of eternity which brought ever-increasing streams of men and women to the altar. The power fell, and scores whom we did not stop to tabulate were baptized with the Spirit.

On Saturday night I was stricken with the ravaging disease. Somehow I got through the service. On Sunday, though I spoke at all three services, I was taken with violent chills and fever. By Monday morning I was filled with such racking pain that it was with difficulty that I sat up in bed and struggled to do up my hair for the early service. Every moment was agonizing. The trip downstairs seemed endless. I staggered weakly across the street and was obliged to take a firm grip upon the pulpit in order to steady myself and keep from falling. Perspiration dripped from every pore, and I shook as with an ague. Yet—I reasoned— every one of these persons present in the eager crowd was a man or a woman whose soul faced immediate eternal decisions. I must—I must—go on! I must not fail them . . . this was my task.

Upon my return to the dingy little apartment, I groped blindly for the stair railing and slowly pulled myself up the squalid steps. I was met at the top landing with the news that my little daughter's condition had developed into influenza and double pneumonia. Fear gave wings to my feet, and I wove my dizzy way into her room. She lay unconscious . . . very weak and very small, beneath the coverlets. Groping along the walls for support, I felt my way to my own room and fell to my knees beside my bed. "Oh, Jesus," I sobbed, "everyone can stand just so much. You took Robert; d-don't take R-Roberta!"

Suddenly my own shivering and shaking ceased. I saw a vision of my Lord standing close . . . just before me. Slowly my eyes traversed the distance from his nail-pierced feet to his glowing eyes. Then, for one of the few times in my life, I heard his glorious, soul-thrilling voice speak to my heart, "Fear not. Your little one shall live and not die. Moreover, I will give you a home in California where your children shall go to school. Yea, the sparrow hath found an house and the swallow a nest for herself where she may lay her young."

Then the vision faded. With uncertain steps and tear-blurred eyes I made my way back to the dreary, unheated, front bedroom. Saints had prayed for Roberta, and she was immediately better . . . even conscious. Kneeling beside the bed, I murmured, "Darling, you are going to live and not die, and we are going to have a little home in California where you are going to go to school."

"Mama," she answered weakly, "could I have a canary bird too?"

"Yes, darling," I promised rashly.

At that moment, my son, Rolf, came into the room. "Mama," he said, "may I have a rose garden too?"

"Yes! Yes!" I cried, for my faith was strong at that moment, "Yes, wee man . . . a big, big rose garden in California."

In a short time we were both well but weak. I sold the car and bought a new one, strapped our belongings and camp equipment upon the running boards of the shining Oldsmobile Eight and turned the radiator cap toward the great unknown West.

California, Here We Come!

Late fall of 1918 . . . uncharted, unpaved motor roads . . . a brand-new seven-passenger Oldsmobile . . . my mother, my stenographer, and my two babies . . . four thousand miles ticking off on the speedometer . . . rain, snow, hail, blizzards, slippery red clay, and adobe mud.

But on clear stretches or on bumpy roads, my magazine, the *Bridal Call,* must be edited and mailed for the press. I would dictate mile after mile to the grumbling stenographer who sat at my side. Then by a campfire near the roadside she would type on my Corona.

An energetic, insomnia-ridden devil perched upon my shoulder and whispered, "Why are you leaving the East where you have worked for years and have made countless friends? What foolhardy, pioneer jaunt is this? You'll never make it! And even if you do, what then?"

All this, and only one driver in the party—myself. These were the facts, ingredients, and perils that made up my first trip to the "Land of the Setting Sun" and the incidental building of the mighty Angelus Temple which hundreds of thousands have since enjoyed. Looking back upon those weeks, I am filled with wonder that I ever accomplished the feat.

With Tulsa, Oklahoma, as our midway goal, we set forth. A Tulsa minister had written urging that I conduct an evangelistic campaign in his city. Much was our consternation when, having preached and left tracts in Gettysburg, Pittsburgh, and Clay-bille, Pennsylvania, Columbus, Ohio, Indianapolis, Indiana, Springfield and Barry, Illinois, Macon and Braymer, Missouri, Olathe and Iola, Kansas, and Ologah, Oklahoma, I received a telegram from Tulsa reading, "Postpone coming. All churches closed because of high death rate caused by influenza epidemic. It is not safe for you to be abroad in the land."

Staggered by the blow which reflected upon my interpretation of the Lord's leadings, I went to him in prayer. "Oh, Lord," I cried, "you know all about our dwindling finances, my westward call, my dependent little family, our utter reliance upon thee. Speak, Lord. Reassure me of thy call."

Quick as a flash the answer came, "Fear not. Lose not a single day. Go at once. The moment you arrive, the ban will be lifted and the church doors shall open." So on and on I guided the gos-pel car.

We reached the outskirts of Tulsa on a fine Sunday morning. The sun shone, the hour was early, and the first sound that greeted our ears was that of church bells. They rang in a chim-ing triumphant medley. Pulling the car to the curb, I hailed the first police officer and inquired, "What is the meaning of all those bells, chimes, and whistles?"

"The influenza ban has just been lifted, lady, and Tulsa is celebrating the reopening of the churches."

Dirty, weary, and wan, we received a hearty welcome from the pastor who had invited us. A bath, a good breakfast, and a season of prayer proved both refreshing and invigorating. A glo-rious revival followed.

In the midst of it, my mother was stricken with a mortal ill-ness of the throat and lungs. Persistent and insistent prayer to God spared her life, and together we shared that ear-splitting, en-thralling, joyous day when whistles were tied down for hours, bells rang incessantly, parading men and women danced, sang, laughed, and cried together, and the Armistice was declared.

World War I was over. The epidemic had lifted. God was in his heaven, all was well, and we were headed again toward sunny California.

Through thrilling lands of oil wells, coconut, and datepalms, orange, lemon, grapefruit, and walnut groves we wended our weary but triumphant way to Los Angeles, the "City of the Angels." Los Angeles differed little from scores of other cities we passed through. The streets were not paved with gold, neither were the boulevards lined with angels, but I had the feeling that here I would meet my destiny. Here was journey's end.

Among the subscribers to my magazine was one family that resided in the city. Turning our car down the wide stretches of Washington Boulevard, we approached the residence of Brother and Sister Blake. We paused before the widest gate I had ever seen and sounded our motor horn. As the great gate swung open and a smiling face greeted us enthusiastically, God spoke to my heart, "I will open the heart of California to you as wide as this gate." And bless the Lord, he did!

We had only two days to get the ache out of our arms before we opened our revival campaign in Los Angeles, after our long transcontinental gospel-auto trip with a car whose speedometer now registered over four thousand miles. Our campaign opened in Victoria Hall, a large upstairs auditorium having a seating capacity of about one thousand. This hall, we were told, had been almost empty. The dear pastor had been preaching in his shirt-sleeves to about a dozen people. But from the first meeting, crowds grew steadily. In a few days the people were not able to get into the hall. Prayer room, rostrum, stairway, and corridors overflowed, and many were turned away.

Here, in this "City of Angels," where the Pentecostal power had so wonderfully fallen fifteen years before on Azusa Street, we learned that several doctrinal differences had gotten the eyes of many off the Lord and that there was a dearth in the land. Hungry hearts were praying earnestly, however, and the Lord answered their prayer in a wonderful way. Those who had lost their first love caught the flame and reconsecrated their lives to his service. One night the Lord gave me for a text, "Shout, for the Lord hath given you the city!" Little did we know at this time just how wonderfully God had given us the city, first as our home, later in wonderful revivals, and now as a base for evangelistic work at home and abroad.

The windows of heaven were open, hundreds were saved, scores were healed, and large numbers received the baptism of the Holy Spirit. People complained that they could not get into the building, so the Philharmonic Auditorium, occupied by Temple Baptist Church and seating some thirty-five hundred, was engaged for the larger meetings. The rent was one hundred dollars for each three hours. This rental the Lord supplied through the plate offering at each service without any special appeal.

This revival was not man-made or woman-made but truly came down from the Heavenly Father. At times the whole audience would be melted into tears as the stillness and hush of the Holy Spirit descended upon the place. At other times it seemed as though the gales from heaven swept the place, and heavenly singing would be indescribable. Wonderful messages in the Spirit poured forth, and the glory of the Lord rested like a mantle upon the place.

All this time the Lord had continued to assure me that he would provide for me a little home for the children. He spoke to other people throughout the city on the same lines, insomuch that they were calling me up on the telephone with the word that God had been showing them that the children should have a home and a place to go to school.

On Sunday night, when the auditorium was packed to the doors with people, a young lady sprang to her feet, saying, "The Lord shows me that I am to give a lot to Mrs. McPherson. I have four lots of land and do not need them all. I am not called to preach the gospel, while she is, and by giving the land that the little ones may have a home and she may be free to come and go in the Lord's work, I will share in her reward."

A brother sprang to his feet, saying, "Yes, I will help lay the foundation." Others offered, "I will do the lathing," "I will do the plastering," "I will furnish the dining room." On it went until even the little canary bird and some rose bushes were promised. Now the canary and the rose bushes touched my heart and caused me to shout more than all else. The Heavenly Father had not forgotten.

When all was arranged, a day of dedication and earth-turning was set. After singing and prayer the saints formed a long line and marched round the lot single file, asking the Lord for the needed means with which to erect the little home.

Away back yonder, when out of the will of God, how I had struggled to get a little rented flat furnished, and what misery I had gone through! But now God himself was planning a home which would be our own, a home given and built by the saints, where every hammer drove nails of love into the building and into our hearts.

Just three months from the date the lot was donated, the "little gray home in the West" was finished and mother, myself, and the babies in it. Each blow of the hammer, each smoothing of the trowel was done by Spirit-filled brethren who shouted and sang as they worked, while consecrated sisters cooked for them and sang in the garage, which was erected first. What a little haven of rest it proved to be, that little home, a gift from the Father of love. But I was not to tarry there long. The gospel call summoned to meetings in other parts of the United States.

Five weeks in Denver—three in 1921 and two the following year! Glorious weeks of divine visitation! Blessings beyond the powers of description! How can I tell the thrilling story? Upon arriving in the "Mile High City," I beamed as I beheld banners stretched across several streets and posters almost everywhere advertising the meetings.

Because a labor convention had previously engaged the Municipal Auditorium, it was necessary to hold the first week of the revival in cooperating churches. On Sunday, June 19, people began arriving as early as 7 A.M. for the 10:45 A.M. opening service in the Second Congregational Church. For the afternoon meeting we moved to the largest Protestant auditorium in Denver, Dean A. C. Peck's People's Congregational Tabernacle, which also was crowded to overflowing.

So overwhelming was the response to the afternoon altar call, so thronged with suppliants was the small area between the front pews and the platform, that I longed to sacrifice seating capacity for altar space. But did I dare request removing the front pews? However, when Dean Peck asked after the meeting, "Sister, can you suggest any way to make more room at the altar?" I mustered the boldness to reply, "Only by taking up the front rows of pews!"

"But they are all fastened securely to the floor," came a half-hearted objection. "And besides, this is Sunday!"

"Never mind that! Souls are at stake," I exclaimed. So out came the pews.

That evening we had a larger space, but still not nearly large enough to accommodate the hosts who thronged forward to receive Jesus as Savior.

Attendances Monday, even in the afternoon, seemed larger— if that were possible—than those which packed the tabernacle on

Sunday. After the first divine healing service Wednesday night, when the lame walked and ran, throwing away their canes and crutches, the newspapers headlined the miracles, "The Deaf Hear! The Blind See! The Lame Walk!" Thereafter police had to be called to handle the crowds, since greater throngs assembled on the streets outside the church than were able to enter the building. "Oh, if we only had the Municipal Auditorium for this first week as well as for the coming weeks," I sighed.

That great auditorium is built in two parts, the theater end with its two rows of galleries and boxes, and the convention hall and dance floor end. A great stage and asbestos curtain separate the two sections and can, when occasion demands, be removed to make the building into one huge auditorium seating twelve thousand people and affording standing room for three thousand more. The management of the auditorium was confident that the theater end would suffice for the campaign. But when on Sunday morning thousands were turned away for the first meeting there, the management decided to allow people to assemble also in the convention hall section for the evening service, even though they could only hear and could not see the proceedings. The next morning a crew of men went to work to unite the two ends of the auditorium. Then the real crowds began to come. The entire building proved too small and many thousands had to be turned away.

The police chief was compelled to assign every available officer to manage the multitudes. And the numbers swelled with each ensuing service. Toward the end of the campaign, the police sergeant in charge of the crowds exclaimed to newspaperman Alva A. Swain, "I don't know how she does it, but this woman has captured Denver. We turn thousands away from every meeting and jam between fifteen and sixteen thousand persons into the building at every meeting. Last Wednesday night we turned eight thousand away. They are coming here in carloads from almost every town in the state. It isn't all cripples who are coming by any means. [an allusion to a charge by critics] She has a good, old-fashioned religious blessing. She has certainly captured this town, and no man, not even a president, could fill this auditorium two and three times a day for three weeks like she has done."

Not only was this a mighty revival in the healing of sin-sick souls but also in the healing of disease-ridden bodies. I wondered whether there had ever been, since the days of the Master, such an assemblage of sick, blind, and lame gathered together in one place. As the campaign continued, requests for prayer cards multiplied. At the last two services where these were distributed, some twenty thousand were registered!

Special sections were arranged for the sick and invalids who were able to walk and sit up. Other sections accommodated the bed-ridden and those in wheel chairs. Constantly it was necessary for me to emphasize that I am not a healer—even though the press on occasions referred to me as such—that I am but an office girl introducing sufferers to the Great Physician.

There was a lady high in social circles, but she did not strike me as being very spiritual. She was just as polished as she could be, but I cannot remember ever seeing a tear in her eyes or hearing her call out to God for souls in the meeting. But when I prayed, her ears, which had been deaf for years, were opened. She took off her acouphone (an old-fashioned type of hearing aid) and radiated excitement and joy. She could hear the talking and the singing. She was very effusive in her manner. She wrung her hands and said, "You will never know what you have done for me, Sister."

"I haven't done anything for you. Jesus did the work," I told her.

"Yes, but you prayed, and I am healed," she insisted.

"But I couldn't heal anybody. It was Jesus who healed you," I told her over and over again.

She left the auditorium hearing, but her healing lasted less than a week. And there was a reason. There usually is a reason when a healing does not last.

"Darling, has anything happened to you?" I asked her, noticing the difference in her manner about a week later. Her eyes no longer sparkled and glowed. It was as if she were shadowed by a dark cloud.

"I beg your pardon," she replied as she leaned over close to me.

"Don't you have your hearing?" I asked in a loud voice.

"I did for a while, but it didn't stay very long," she confessed. "I can't hear very well any more. But it still isn't as bad as it was before you prayed. But something has happened. Isn't it a shame that it didn't last?"

"My dear," I said, "other people have kept their healing."

"Yes, I see they have, but I've lost mine," she sobbed.

"What have you been doing?" I inquired.

"Oh, just the usual things," she answered. "Entertaining and being entertained. I've given several big parties. I've been to the theater. I attended a big card party. You know, just the usual run of social obligations."

This lady was doing the usual things, but she had *lost* her healing! "Look here, darling," I said, "you've done a very foolish thing in asking the Lord to heal you under those conditions. Do you realize you are bringing your body, which is to be a temple for the Holy Ghost, to the Lord and asking him to lay his dear, nail-pierced hands on your body and heal you? Why? So you could hear people talking about the next card they were going to play and listen to the stories they tell around the bridge table? Or did you ask him to heal you so that you might attend the theater and see the shows? Do you think you were asking for your healing for his glory—for his services?"

"I never thought about it that way," the lady declared.

When this little lady understood, we prayed for her again. The Lord opened her ears. And when I returned to Denver a year later, I found her a devoted worker in the Master's service. Needless to say, her hearing had lasted.

The 1921 campaign had lasted three weeks. I could spare only two in the following year, but the five weeks of those first two revivals in the Mile High City, together with happy experiences on several subsequent visits over almost two decades, have enshrined Denver as a most treasured and honored picture on my memory's wall!

To recount in detail the glories of the second Denver revival would sound very much like a repetition of the events already described. Jesus Christ did not change between the two campaigns. What he did in 1921 he did in 1922—as he will do in any generation when men respond to his Word with faith.

Oakland, California, and Australia

My last revival in America before the dedication of Angelus Temple was a great tent meeting in the East Bay city of Oakland, California. It was in this Oakland revival that the concept of the gospel as "Foursquare" dawned in my heart. I had not been completely content with the designations *Pentecostal* or *Full Gospel*, though I had used both on the masthead of the *Bridal Call* magazine. Because of the strong stand I espoused that in the public services of my campaigns all things be done decently and in order, with only those manifestations and demonstrations which exalt the Lord Jesus Christ, the rumor commenced circulating that "Mrs. McPherson is not Pentecostal." One Pentecostal magazine quoted criticism of my methods under the title, "Is Mrs. McPherson Pentecostal?" For some time I had used the phrase *the middle of the road* to describe my position. On one side of the road stands the cold, frozen, worldly church. On the other side loomed at that time the frenzied fanaticism boasting manifestations which brought discredit to the precious Holy Spirit. I stand in the middle, however, for a sane, wholesome power of the Holy Spirit which brings honor and souls to the Lord Jesus Christ. I have maintained this position without catering or compromising to the favor of either extreme. I seek to give no offense to either side but to keep life and doctrine straight to the Word. I take the hand of the one who is burning with fire and zeal and put it into the hand of those who are cold and dead, thereby lifting both through the Word and the Spirit to the sane, sweet, powerful, humble, balanced, soul-wining position.

In pursuing this course, it is understandable that I would be misunderstood. On the one hand, friends and former associates have hurled their favorite epithet for those who do not see eye to eye with themselves in all things, charging, "You're *not* Pentecostal." And on the other side, friends hit another whack and say, "You *are* Pentecostal." And so it has gone—whack, "You *are,*" whack, "You are *not.*" Between the two thrusts, it's rather easy to maintain the middle of the way.

"Well, are you Pentecostal, Mrs. McPherson?" many were asking. That depends altogether on what you mean by the term. Pentecost really means fifty, and at that time I was only thirty-one! This term, so far as we know, was not used by the early church. However, if by the word you mean that I stand for, believe, preach, and rejoice in the power of the Holy Spirit, the answer is that I assuredly do. Never have I compromised on this Full Gospel message. It grows sweeter and more blessed. I am not ashamed to be called Pentecostal. But for me the phrase *Foursquare Gospel* better described the ministry of Jesus Christ which I thrill to proclaim. Let me tell you how I commenced using this expression.

It was, as I said, during this revival in Oakland in July, 1922. The great tent was packed, with multitudes standing around its borders, unable to find a seat beneath the bigtop. The Spirit of God was manifest in a wonderful degree. The great audience listened with rapt attention to my message on "The Vision of Ezekiel."

My soul was awed, and my heart athrill, for the blazing story of that heavenly vision seemed to fill and permeate not only the tabernacle but the whole earth. In the clouds of heaven which folded and unfolded in fiery glory, Ezekiel had beheld the Being whose glory no mortal can describe. As he gazed upon the marvelous revelation of the Omnipotent One, he perceived four faces, those of a man, a lion, an ox, and an eagle.

In the face of the lion, we behold that of the mighty baptizer with the Holy Ghost and fire. The face of the ox typifies the great burden-bearer, who himself took our infirmities and carried our sicknesses, who in his boundless love and divine provision has met our every need. In the face of the eagle, we see reflected soul-enrapturing visions of the coming King, whose pinions soon will cleave the shining heavens, whose voice will vibrate through the universe in thrilling cadences of resurrection power as he comes to catch his waiting bride away. And in the face of the man we behold the Savior, the man of sorrows, acquainted with grief, dying upon the tree for our sins. Here is a perfect gospel, a complete gospel, for body, for soul, for spirit, and for eternity, a gospel facing squarely in every direction.

The whole tent was enveloped as I developed this exposition of God's Word. It was as though every soul there was aquiver with the harmony of celestial music. In my soul was born a melody that seemed to strike and be sustained upon four full quivering strings, as I thought upon the vision of the prophet Ezekiel. I stood still for a moment and listened, gripping the pulpit, almost shaking with wonder and joy. Then there burst from the white heat of my heart the words, "Why—why, it's the Foursquare Gospel. The Foursquare Gospel!" Instantly the Spirit bore witness. Waves, billows, oceans of praises rocked the audience, which was borne aloft on the rushing winds of Holy Ghost revival.

Since that day when the Lord gave me that illumination, the term *Foursquare Gospel* has been carried around the world, as vividly and fittingly distinguishing the message he had commissioned me to preach of Jesus the Savior, Jesus the Baptizer with the Holy Spirit, Jesus the Healer, and Jesus the Coming King.

A final shriek of the whistle! The scampering of a multitude of feet across the deck and down the gangplank! Laughter, songs, good wishes, smiles, flowers, and God-bless-yous from the thousand friends the press reported had come to see us off for Australia five days after the Oakland meetings closed.

The wild impulse for a moment to leap ashore or to cry, "Stop! Stop the ship! Take us back to shore. This is our country. Here are our friends. Here lies our work—our Temple nearing completion—our earthly all. We cannot leave it to go to the other side of the world on this boat!" But a second steadying thought made me realize that I was going on the Master's business to hungry hearts in Australia, to people who had waited many months. I must go now, if at all, for I would not be able to get away after Angelus Temple opened. Indeed, it would be years before I could conduct revivals, so heavy would be the press of ministry at the Temple.

Soon the S.S. *Manganui* nosed her way to open sea past the Golden Gate. The American shore faded to an indistinct shade and then vanished from sight. It took almost a month to get to Australia.

I had lived at too fast a pace to relax at first. Other passengers spent whole days in aimless wanderings, idle conversation, or playing cards, but my mind was constantly occupied with work to the point that I could not sleep at night. There was planning to do concerning details of the Temple's interior. I must draw designs for the dedicatory stone. The final editing of the September and October issues of the *Bridal Call* required my attention so that the copy could be mailed to the printer from the first port of call. Then lead articles for the November, December, and January numbers had to be written, besides a multitude of letters.

Slowly the days and nights passed, and finally we received notice that the ship would dock at Wellington on Friday morning and sail for Australia Saturday evening. However, the praying believers of Wellington had determined otherwise.

Without my knowledge, preparations were being made there for meetings. The Town Hall was engaged and advertisements posted which drew hundreds of hungry souls from the towns and cities of New Zealand for meetings announced for Friday night, Saturday, and Sunday. When word reached these planners that the boat would sail Saturday night, they refused to accept disappointment. "We must have the meeting," leaders resolved. "But what can we do?" some questioned in consternation.

"We can go to the ship office and ask that they hold the boat in the harbor," came the suggestion.

"I'll try," agreed another. "Perhaps the officials do not know that it is God's will for the boat to wait till Monday. I will tell them."

You can imagine the reception that brother's proposal prompted from the steamship company. "Hold the boat? The idea! Why, one thousand pounds could not hold it! Hold the boat over Sunday? Indeed! The idea is impossible!" snorted the official.

"Well, if you cannot, God can," was the parting statement of the petitioner. Soon a prayer meeting was in progress. Saints pleaded, "Dear Lord, hold the boat. Hold it till Monday. You might let the firemen go on strike, Lord, or send a storm if all else fails. Yes, Lord, send a wind, not enough to hurt the boat but enough to delay the arrival a few hours, to cause delay in unloading the cargo so they will have to stay till Monday."

Call it coincidence if you will, but the elements began to threaten. The barometer dropped. And though the sky looked clear, a wireless from New Zealand warned our ship to prepare

for storm. The crew lashed canvas over the open decks, put up
wind breaks, and readied the vessel. Then the storm came, rain
and wind and towering waves—a glorious sea depicting the
power of God—the first rough sea we had encountered, because
friends in America had been praying for calm weather. Indeed,
almost every experienced sailor on board had remarked that they
could never remember so calm a passage. But now, knowing
nothing about the praying people in Wellington, I wondered
what to tell the people in America when they asked whether we
had a storm.

When we made the harbor, it was not Friday morning but
Friday night. Notices were posted stating that the ship could not
sail till Monday afternoon. Two working days were needed to
handle the cargo, and no work of this kind was allowed on Sundays in New Zealand. How the believers in Wellington rejoiced,
for God had held the boat, and it had not cost one thousand
pounds either!

In services held in the Methodist church and in the Town Hall
scores of penitents knelt at the mercy seat to crown our Savior
as theirs. The songs, testimonies, conversions, hunger, hallelujahs,
amens, rejoicings, and tears seemed the same as those of God's
children in America and Canada. I could hardly suppress the
desire to stay longer or to come again to minister to these precious people.

A party of these New Zealanders sailed with us when the ship
resumed its voyage, headed for Sydney, Australia. The sea was
like a placid lake all the way. When we turned into the magnificent harbor of Sydney, a crowd of bright-faced Christians
were waiting on the pier to meet us, hoisting a large and brightly
painted banner reading

WELCOME
MRS. McPHERSON AND PARTY TO
AUSTRALIA
AND GOD BLESS YOU.

What a welcome they extended, shaking our hands, kissing us,
wiping tears from their eyes, shouting the victory. Australians
have a reputation for being cold and conservative in their de-
meanor, and some may be, but the people with whom we would
have dealing seemed as warm as our American audiences.

The day in Sydney was busy as I inspected prospective buildings and discussed plans for the revival which would conclude

the Australian itinerary. Then all aboard the Melbourne express for the overnight journey to the scene of my first Australian *mission*—to use the term most common "down under."

I doubt that any evangelist ever challenged a city under greater handicaps than those which from the first threatened disaster to this Melbourne revival. The company which had been promoting the meetings not only was small in numbers—that never had hindered us long—but also was ostracized and feared by most ministers and churchmen in the city, and for good reason. The leader had been attacking the Methodist church in print, saying, "I was a fool to join that denomination. In doing so I took the first step toward carnality." Upon examining some of the publications of this leader, I found views diametrically opposed to the teaching of the Word of God and the historic church on basic fundamentals. Sunday school classes had been abandoned by this company because this leader had abandoned belief in the infallibility of the Bible. Conditional immortality was espoused, with its ideas of soul sleep and total annihilation of the wicked dead. Unscriptural psychic demonstrations with overtones of spiritism were mistakenly represented as the blessed dealings of the baptism of the Holy Ghost (oh, Pentecost, what crimes have been perpetrated in thy name!). The whole cause of the Holy Spirit and divine healing had come into disrepute as a result of these excesses and errors. And when ministers and churches held aloof from this company's promotion of my coming meetings, the group printed and circulated handbills declaring that "no power on earth or in hell can hinder the revival."

The result was exactly as you would expect in such circumstances. Instead of bands, chairs, and ministerial cooperation and confidence, I faced a stone wall of resistance which had to be broken down, a mountain of prejudice which must be removed, a shattered confidence which must be restored, and a quagmire of doubt about my own doctrinal views which had to be cleared away before I could build with the help of God a solid foundation of sound faith and trust for the superstructure of the campaign to be built upon. But how should I proceed?

The only thing to do was to open the Good Book and with unswerving faith, even with a heavy-burdened heart, preach the simple Word of God. And God sent a mighty tidal wave of revival which in three weeks removed prejudice, swept over the city, and filled the platform with clergymen from practically every orthodox, evangelical denomination. Indeed, the very ministers who had written and preached warnings against the revival worked by my side with tear-brimmed eyes, helping welcome the hundreds of sinners home. The meeting ended in sweeping victory with pastors, Salvation Army bands, church choirs, and Christian workers wringing each other's hands, reading a new love in each other's shining eyes, promising to keep the revival fires burning, and all urging a return visit. How God swept back the curtains of clouds and utterly consumed the darkness from before his face!

There were many precious instances of divine healing in answer to prayer, but the Lord gave me a very definite check about emphasizing this ministry because healing had been unduly exploited prior to our revival. The great general need in Melbourne was for evangelism and teaching regarding the baptism of the Holy Spirit. Comparatively few physically afflicted people requested prayers for deliverance. But I myself fell victim to a badly ulcerated throat. The continual rain and cold 'drafts proved quite a test to me, especially since the buildings were not heated. I was chilled till sometimes I wondered whether I would ever be warm again! While others in the services could bundle up in warm wraps, I had to stand without a coat for hours. I took chills which lasted for forty-eight hours. Then a high fever soared. But I arose from bed in the name of the Lord and went out and on with the work. And as I went, I was healed. Praise the Lord!

As the Melbourne meeting progressed I was faced with the fact that the course of construction of Angelus Temple demanded my presence as soon as possible. In order to catch an earlier ship home, we had to revise the schedule for the missions in other Australian cities and commence the Adelaide meeting one week earlier than planned. This left only three days for advertising the revised dates. Melbourne ministers prepared a glowing testimonial which they forwarded to the Christian leaders in Adelaide.

The services commenced in the Exhibition Building with just a few hundred in attendance, but the crowds grew steadily until they filled the great auditorium to overflowing. Sinners came to Christ in every service, and Christians were stirred to wait upon the Lord for the enduement of power from on high.

The same story was repeated in the mission at Sydney. The auditorium was well filled at the first afternoon meeting and overcrowded at night with many having to stand throughout the service. The first altar call brought an instantaneous response. Men and women rose all over the building, coming down from the balcony and streaming forward on the main floor.

As this mission neared its closing, expressions of regret that it could not be prolonged were expressed on every hand. One well-to-do brother who had a reputation for his generosity in helping the work of God offered to pay the full fare of my party to and from America if in a few months after the opening of Angelus Temple we could return for just three weeks in Sydney! Another prominent businessman escorted us to Sydney's most expensive auditoriums, so that we would have a working knowledge of them in case we could return!

Few evangelists ever left a field with more testimonies to their ministries than I received from leading ministers of the cities where I held missions in Australia. Methodist, Congregational, Church of Christ, Presbyterian, Salvation Army, Baptist, Pentecostal, and other clergymen signed glowing and enthusiastic endorsements of the revivals.

But it was imperative for me to hasten home to Los Angeles.

A House unto the Lord

"Why, Lord, did you give us a home in far-off Los Angeles?" was a question often on my mind in the months after moving into "the little house that God built." Between the time construction commenced on this home and the end of the year 1922, I made no less than nine transcontinental evangelistic journeys. After a meeting in Philadelphia, Washington, or Baltimore, there was always the long train trip across the country to my children in our western home. "Dear Lord Jesus," I asked periodically, "wouldn't it have been better if you had placed our little home somewhere in the East or in the Middle West where it would have been more accessible?"

I had no idea at the time what a tremendous project awaited in the purpose of God. Eventually God gently but unquestionably began to show me that he had led me to Los Angeles, to "build a house unto the Lord." His message encouraged, "Shout, for the Lord hath given you the city."

When this burden first came from heaven, I tried to shake it off, supposing that the idea might be of self. But the call persisted. Then I shrank from such an ambitious task. Who ever heard of a woman without earthly backing or any organization behind her undertaking the raising of funds and the erection of such a building?

But louder and clearer came the call of God, "Build a house unto the Lord." Little did I imagine that this structure would be a mighty and glorious temple. Surely it would be a wooden tabernacle, an inexpensive, temporary, and very ordinary affair! If I had ever dreamed that the plan of God encompassed a building the likes of Angelus Temple, the audacity and seeming impossibility of so gigantic an undertaking would have alarmed me so as to muzzle my very mention of it. How little we knew of the plans of God which would be unfolded in the immediate future.

Certainly Los Angeles was ripe for revival. This great metropolis appeared to afford perhaps the greatest opportunity for God of any city in America. Thousands of tourists were coming from every state of the Union, many coming to reside. Statistics at the time indicated that two thousand a day were arriving. Their other needs had been provided for in the city—homes, amusements, highways, and parks. But, alas, there were few adequately large buildings where they might hear the Word of God in its blessed Pentecostal fullness. While there were several precious missions and churches which preached the full gospel, they were but a drop in the bucket compared with the need.

Each time I returned to Los Angeles there was added to the call of the Lord the urging of hundreds of letters and contacts emphasizing the need for a revival tabernacle. One day in the summer of 1920 the call rang so urgently in my heart that I climbed into the automobile and with my mother set out in search of land. Reaching the corner of Figueroa and Third Street, where we usually turned into the heart of the city, I was strangely impressed to drive on another block and then turn toward Glendale Boulevard. I had never been in this section of Los Angeles before.

In just a few minutes we reached Echo Park. "Oh, this is heaven!" I cried, "the most beautiful spot for a house of the Lord I have ever seen. It's right in the city, yet so restful." There flashed before my mind scenes in other great cities where I had preached. When the buildings had to be emptied between meetings, the people had stood in hot sun or rain hour after hour waiting for the auditorium doors to reopen. "Here they would have parks, trees, grass, and benches, picnic tables, rest rooms—everything they could desire to be comfortable between meetings!" I exclaimed to mother.

Just beyond the park we spied a circular piece of property. "What a wonderful site that would be for the tabernacle!" I exclaimed. Like a flash from heaven I visualized the general plan for the structure. There leaped within my heart the assurance, "This is the place!"

A real estate office loomed nearby. When we mentioned the property we had in mind, the agent declared, "But, ladies, that particular piece of land is not for sale. It's about the only vacant property in this district that is not on the market. A wealthy lady who has many real estate holdings owns it, but she refuses to sell any of her land. Other people have tried to get this property and have offered high prices, but she has always answered, 'No, I am not interested in selling.' "

"Well, praise the Lord," I replied. "I can see clearly that this is to be our piece of land. The Lord must have been saving it for us all the time."

The real estate man shook his head and looked at us doubtfully as we departed, probably thinking there was something missing about us somewhere. But I knew we had found the place. I commenced contemplating some of the advantages the tabernacle would afford. There would be no need to interrupt a revival, giving up a Monday night for a boxing tournament, Thursday for a grand ball, Saturday for some prima donna, as we had been compelled to do in many rented auditoriums. The tabernacle could be engineered so that I could make myself heard without the difficulty I had encountered in some of the large edifices.

A day or two later we were impressed to return and look again at the land. We found a sign advertising the property for sale and urging, "Snap this corner!" I took a lead pencil and sketched upon the signboard a diagram of the "house unto the Lord." We found our way to the property owner's home. The elderly lady told us she owned too much land. "I suddenly decided I am land poor," she explained. "This is the first piece of property I will sell." She offered us a splendid price.

It was time, however, to leave Los Angeles again to fulfill four months of evangelistic appointments. Through all those travels and meetings God kept the vision of the tabernacle before me. I put the fleece out to be absolutely certain that if this were God's place and time and purpose the property would remain available until our return. This looked improbable, as vacant lots in that section of the city were rapidly changing hands. However, upon our return, we found the door still open, so we purchased the land.

The first announcement of the proposed structure appeared in the January 1921 *Bridal Call* headlined, "Echo Park Revival Tabernacle to Be Erected in Los Angeles." It would be eighteen months before the name was changed to Angelus Temple and two years until the dedication. The transformation from a tabernacle to the temple was influenced by the tremendous crowds which thronged my campaign in the interval. Our original intention was to construct an edifice seating between twenty-five and thirty-five hundred. We soon learned that the city would not permit a building with a capacity so large to be constructed out of wood.

Consultation with Mr. Brook Hawkins of the Winter Construction Company resulted in tentative plans being drawn for a class C structure. I explained that we would build by faith as the Lord provided the money. We would not go into debt. "How much money have you to start with?" came the contractor's very natural question.

"About five thousand dollars," I replied.

"That should be enough to dig a good hole for a foundation," he commented.

"Well, you excavate and get your steam shovels to work," I instructed. "By the time you dig the hole, I expect to have money for the foundation." The people in my St. Louis meeting contributed sixteen thousand dollars, which I proudly brought home saying, "Now you put in the foundation, and by the time that is done, we will have enough money for the walls." The loyal friends of Denver and other cities where meetings were held rallied to the challenge. Money poured in by mail from *Bridal Call* subscribers. And all over the country friends became chairholders, subscribing twenty-five dollars to underwrite the cost of seating each worshiper.

Within a few months, however, a major decision had to be faced. "The crowds you are drawing to your meetings almost scare us," wrote the contractor, Brook Hawkins. "It would seem advisable to lay our plans so that in the future the building can be added onto to take care of the crowds you have here." After much prayer and considerable consultation, we deemed it best to enlarge the tabernacle at the outset, adding another twenty-one feet to the height of the structure to allow room for the second balcony, which was not included in the initial plans. This required changing from a class C building to class A construction and increased the seating capacity to over five thousand. The changes were engineered so as to use the foundations and footings which had already been installed, but additional foundations and footings were required to support the extra balcony.

This enlargement of plans and upgrading of construction naturally increased the cost of the structure substantially. Some of my friends grew skeptical, warning, "Sister McPherson, you are foolish to build so big and solid a building when Jesus is coming soon."

"But I want to leave my work so solid behind me," I replied, "that it will stand and stand. Maybe it will stand through the millennium when Jesus returns with his church, and someone will help tell the story in it of Jesus and his great eternal love. I want to build so solidly as if Jesus were not coming for a hundred years, though we are ready for his coming any day."

By the end of 1921 the words *Echo Park Revival Tabernacle* no longer stood for a fond but distant dream, a glorious but misty vision. The building was fast becoming a blessed and concrete reality, a solid base for the evangelistic work the Master had placed in my hands. How eager and anxious I was after another strenuous series of eastern campaigns and the transcontinental trip through snow and sleet to reach Los Angeles, where I lost no time speeding to the tabernacle site. Echo Park loomed ahead, but it was not the park or the lake that gripped my attention. I was straining for the first glimpse of the tabernacle.

Yes, there it was—that large circular property just at the entrance to the park. How beautiful for situation! How ideal its location! "Just think!" I exclaimed. "It hasn't been a year since the first announcement of the proposed tabernacle was made, and now the walls are going up!"

Of course, I could not remain in Los Angeles to watch the construction. Numerous campaigns kept me busy—campaigns which also prompted generous donations toward the expense of building. In Fresno, California, Mr. Hawkins visited the meetings, standing on his feet from early morning until almost midnight studying the surging crowds. Not a detail in our problems of seating and caring for the people, opening the way for hundreds to flock to the altar and getting them back to their seats, caring for the sick, providing prayer rooms, workers' assembly rooms, and choir rooms escaped his alert gaze. As he jotted down items in his notebook, people heard him say, "Now we must do this, we must change that, we must add such and such to the building."

Mr. Hawkins had brought with him the latest pictures of the tabernacle, showing how rapidly it was progressing. How I treasured these photos and others which came by mail. Night after night when I returned to my room from the meetings, weary to the brink of exhaustion, I found new encouragement and a source of fresh inspiration by holding those pictures in my hand and studying over every detail until my eyes closed in sleep.

For a while we expected that the tabernacle could be completed in the fall of 1922. However, the multiplication of details requiring planning and consultation postponed the opening until the New Year. Meanwhile, the contractor marveled at the progress of the work. "We are now at work in the huge dome," he wrote about June 1, 1922. "Everything is going along smoothly and entirely satisfactorily in every respect. We have not had one man injured on the job, that is to say, so that we had to have medical attention for him. This is almost an unheard of condition on a building as large as this one." Mr. Hawkins also often commented how he had never erected a structure where the men worked more contentedly or where the money stretched as far and lasted as long as it did in this edifice. Certainly the Lord was with us wonderfully in this respect.

At the end of my Oakland revival—my last city-wide campaign in America before the opening of the new building—Brook Hawkins addressed a meeting to report on construction. He told the audience, "I have been erecting large buildings for a number of years and am completing one now at Sixth and Hill Streets in Los Angeles to seat nearly four thousand persons that will cost two and one-half million dollars when completed. Other buildings of a similar nature seating not nearly four thousand persons have cost in the past anywhere from $800,000 to $1,500,000 and will only seat in the neighborhood of fifteen or sixteen hundred persons. Therefore when one considers that the temple will seat over five thousand people and when it is eventually all completed, including seats, organ, necessary decorations, furniture, carpets for the aisles, lighting, everything to make the building presentable, I am quite convinced that the total cost will not exceed $250,000." This was especially gratifying, since within a few years the value of the building was estimated as exceeding one million dollars!

The audience in Oakland listened with rapt attention as Mr. Hawkins outlined the amount of materials which had already gone into the structure: "There are over two hundred tons of steel, over twenty thousand bags of cement each weighing one hundred pounds, over 800,000 feet of lumber, and we have been able to use this lumber over and over again. There are many, many tons of rock and sand which go into the mixing of the concrete, for I want you to know that the entire building is of class A construction and is entirely fireproof. No wood is permitted in any part of the building except the doors and window frames, and perhaps here and there a wooden partition of a temporary nature."

Did you notice that in mentioning the seating capacity, Mr. Hawkins referred to the building as the temple? About the middle of 1922 the tentative name "Echo Park Revival Tabernacle" was dropped in favor of the enduring name "Angelus Temple." Certainly the term *tabernacle* was not adequate to describe the building as restructured to class A specifications.

I had two thoughts in mind in naming the building Angelus Temple: first, the Angelus, the ringing of bells, ringing from the belfry calling people to come to church. But my principal thought was the second—the Angel's Temple. Anyone visiting the church will notice that bells and angels predominate in the decorations within. There is a frieze work with bells on the front of each balcony. And angels are painted at the top of the walls, standing wing to wing, representative of a little glimpse beyond the veil that I was privileged to have in the autumn camp meeting of 1917 in the city of Philadelphia.

Because the Foursquare Gospel means Foursquare Good News, I did not want anything sad in the decoration of Angelus Temple. When it came time to choose the central motto to appear over the platform, someone suggested, "Woe, all have sinned and come short of the glory of God." But we all know that, and anyway, that would not be good news. What is the heart of the good news? The good news focuses on this point, "Jesus Christ the same yesterday, and today, and forever." That verse would become the scriptural motto of the Church of the Foursquare Gospel. I wanted Angelus Temple itself to be an illustrated sermon so that if anyone came into the Temple who was deaf, he could see the story of Jesus and the way of salvation! And many have!

The decoration of the dome engaged my attention. Some wanted to make it a night scene with stars shining. That might have been very beautiful but more likely would have proved gloomy. I said, "No, I want it to represent the day that it might speak to us of the Scripture, 'Work while it is yet day, for the night cometh when no man can work.' " Moreover, it was painted as the azure blue of the sky with white fleecy clouds to remind us that Jesus is coming in the clouds of glory so that I and others might look up at it while preaching and wonder, "Jesus, are you coming during this service? Will I be ready to meet you with souls if you come right now?"

But to me even all this was not enough. I wanted to tell the whole story of the good news in such a way that if anybody should come when no one was here to preach he would be able to look around and see the gospel. Stained-glass windows would contribute to this effect! On the boat trip to Australia I planned the windows, and the execution of those plans mailed back to America was one of the major factors necessitating my early return from down under. The windows could not be installed by the time of the dedication of the Temple, but in a few months all were put in place.

After designing the windows, I realized that some might wonder, "How is Jesus coming?" So we took forty feet, interrupting the organ grill, for a mural painting showing Jesus Christ accompanied by the hosts of heaven with their long, slender trumpets. Jesus appears in the center with outstretched hands, one reaching upward, signifying his promise to take his church to that land where there is no sin or sorrow, and the other hand is extended as if to say, "Bless you, my children. I am with you every minute of the day and night."

Speaking of the organ grill—in our original planning we wanted a pipe organ but did not see our way clear to contract for this instrument of considerable expense while raising funds to pay for construction of the building. Nevertheless, we had the architect include a space for an organ chamber if the Lord did provide the instrument. By the Easter after the dedication of Angelus Temple the great Kimball organ was pealing forth glorious melodies. I especially asked the designers of the instrument to include among its many stops chimes and harp.

The Temple was constantly on my mind on the return voyage from Australia. Numerous finishing touches required attention. A systematic explanation of the Foursquare Gospel was needed, outlining my teachings in general under the headings of Jesus the Savior, the Baptizer with the Holy Spirit, the Healer, and the Coming King. I also worked on the first of the Foursquare Gospel Battle Songs—this one to be used for the dedicatory service at the Temple. The chorus, containing a summary of the message, has become well known around the world:

> Preach the Foursquare Gospel,
> The Foursquare Gospel,
> Clear let the Foursquare message ring:
> Jesus only Savior,
> Baptizer and Healer,
> Jesus the Coming King.

Weeks before the official opening, Christian workers commenced flocking to the Temple for preliminary activities. The choir began rehearsing. An information bureau opened at the main entrance on Park Avenue on December 15, where musicians, ushers, and other helpers might register for service. A two weeks' convention was scheduled for the opening of Angelus Temple, with ministers from all over the country—spirit-filled Methodists, Baptists, Congregationalists, United Brethren, and others who had participated in our evangelistic campaigns—sharing the pulpit, with me. The year 1922 was fast fading into history. The New Year would soon dawn, and with it the dedication of Angelus Temple.

13

Angelus Temple —the First Years

From the day the doors opened on January 1, 1923, a mighty spiritual revival surged into Angelus Temple with ever-increasing power and fervor. Eight thousand converts knelt at the altars in the first six months, and fifteen hundred believers were immersed in the baptistry. Hundreds were healed and baptized with the Holy Spirit. One thousand young people covenanted together to serve as the Angelus Temple Foursquare Crusaders. And as the weeks and months passed, new outreaches commenced.

In February, the Prayer Tower opened, where prayer has not ceased as men gather in two-hour shifts during the night and women pray during the day, bringing before God thousands of requests which come by mail, telephone, and telegraph from all over the world. In the same month we instituted the Bible training school which would in time become LIFE Bible College—the Lighthouse of International Foursquare Evangelism. To house this school, a building had been erected on the corner of Lemoyne Street and Park Avenue, but from the very first day of classes it proved much too small, and sessions were consequently held in the 500 room of Angelus Temple. Eventually the five and one-half story college building was constructed adjacent to the church, and the original small structure was remodeled into a parsonage where I lived until 1936.

In March, on Easter Sunday, came the unveiling of Angelus Temple's glorious organ, one of the last installations in putting the finishing touch on the building. That organ—of all inanimate things, I love it the most. It seems to contain somewhere within its mighty pipes the epitome of all life. Oftentimes when the church is empty save for an isolated soul praying here and there, I slip inside and drop into a seat under the shadow of one of the pillars. And there, listening to its multi-throated melodies, the organ brings me peace.

Then came the challenge of radio! There were only two stations in Los Angeles in 1923. When I sat before my receiving set, over it came floating to my ears songs, music, recitations, as clearly and distinctly as though instruments were playing and voices singing right in the room. And yet they were being broadcast miles away. My soul was thrilled with the possibilities this media offered for the spread of the gospel. We secured time on a radio station and began broadcasting a few services. But the thought persisted that if Angelus Temple had her own radio station we could broadcast almost all of the meetings!

Representatives from Western Electric and the Times-Mirror stations assured me that such a broadcasting station could be installed in the Temple for between twenty and twenty-five thousand dollars. I learned that there were at that early age of radio already over two hundred thousand receiving sets within a radius of one hundred miles of Los Angeles. What an opportunity to spread the gospel!

I presented the challenge to the congregation and to the *Bridal Call* family. Would they respond with offerings over and above the operating expenses of the church? Months before, I had rejected the suggestion of a brother on the Temple's board that each member of the church should be assessed ten dollars a month. I replied that I would sooner resign as pastor and build another church than tax or solicit contributions from anyone individually. "Everything in this church," I declared, "is, by God's grace, going to be by the freewill donations of people who give voluntarily."

People said that it couldn't be done that way—that so gigantic an undertaking required guaranteed income. But God provided for the Temple. It was dedicated without debt. God provided for the operating expenses. And God provided through the love gifts of his people for the radio station. In February, 1924, KFSG— Kall Four Square Gospel—went on the air, broadcasting the glorious song, "Give the winds a mighty voice, Jesus saves!"

For three years I stayed close by Angelus Temple, preaching and teaching many times a week, conducting a daily "Sunshine

Hour" broadcast, writing, editing, publishing, and praying for the sick, besides carrying out a multitude of administrative duties. The revival swept on and out. Branch churches sprang up in adjacent cities and towns. I had thought myself busy in the old days, what with driving the car, putting up the tent, and then holding the services, but those days were effortless compared with the early years at the Temple. Then there was outside work to be done. Various civic and fraternal bodies and charitable organizations invited me to address them, and I welcomed the opportunity to take them the message of Jesus and his love. The city firemen wanted a raise in pay and called upon us for help. A branch church wanted me to help select furniture. There was absolutely no end to the things I found it essential to do.

In addition, the people who attended the Temple, both young and old people, must be kept as busy as I was. Then they would be as happy as I was, happy with the happiness of achievement in each doing what he could to help the Word a bit farther along. And keeping them busy was a big job for me by itself.

The Lord did send our way a number of marvelous ministers who helped shoulder the speaking load from time to time. The Crusaders especially enjoyed a Friday evening with Homer Rodeheaver, the famous baritone who had delighted countless thousands in the Billy Sunday campaigns. Mr. Rodeheaver was passing through Los Angeles en route to Japan, India, and Australia with evangelist W. E. Biederwolf. Dr. Biederwolf climaxed the evening with a wonderful gospel message. Another guest who blessed the Temple was William Jennings Bryan, who had been three times the nominee of the Democratic Party for the office of president of the United States and who had served with distinction as secretary of state in President Woodrow Wilson's cabinet. Mr. Bryan was devoting his later years to the upholding of the fundamental faith. How thrilled we were to have him preach in the Temple!

Meanwhile, the study body of the Bible school was growing by leaps and bounds. Something had to be done and done quickly to accommodate these future pastors, evangelists, missionaries, and Christian workers. On New Year's Day, 1925—the same day that the Angelus Temple float won the grand prize at the Pasadena Tournament of Roses Parade—a parade of trucks loaded to capacity with sacks of cement traveled to the vacant lot east of Angelus Temple, the site of the proposed Bible school building.

Childhood

*Robert and Aimee Semple
Chicago, 1910*

Far left: *Grave of Robert Semple in China.* **Center:** *Present-day Semple Memorial School, Hong Kong.*

Above left: *Aimee Semple upon return from China.* **Above center:** *Aimee Semp* *McPherson, Harold McPherson, Rolf McPherson, and Grandfather.* **Above rig** *Aimee Semple McPherson and Harold McPherson.*

Above: *Aimee Semple McPherson and Rolf K. McPherson camping out.* **Above right:** *Aimee Semple McPherson and Harold McPherson in St. Petersburg, Florida.* **Center right:** *The campaign car.* **Lower right:** *Nationwide camp meeting at Philadelphia, 1918.*

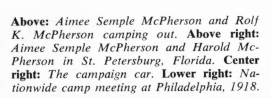

Above left: *Aimee Semple McPherson preparing the* Bridal Call *magazine.* **Above right:** *Cross-country travel, ferry trip, 1918.* **Left:** *Cross country to San Jose, California.*

e: The "House that God Built," gray home in Los Angeles. : The Bungalow Church pre- for Angelus Temple.

Denver, Colorado, stretcher day, 1921.

Above: *Camp meeting in Los Angeles.* **Left:** *San Jose, 1919.*

Above left: *San Diego, Dreamland Arena, 1921.* **Above right:** *Flying over San Dieg*

San Diego, Balboa Park

Dallas, Texas

Olympic Theater
Melbourne, Australia

Forum Auditorium
Wichita, Kansas, 1922

Memorial Hall
Dayton, Ohio

Above: *Angelus Temple groundbreaking.* **Right:** *Angelus Temple under construction; Rolf K. Mc-Pherson as a child.*

Center: *Angelus Temple under construction.* **Left:** *Angelus Temple on dedication day, January 1, 1923.*

Aimee Semple McPherson standing at radio mike, Angelus Temple, 1920s.

Above: *Aimee Semple McPherson at pulpit and radio, Angelus Temple, 1920s.* **Right:** *Angelus Temple interior during late 1930s.*

Angelus Temple exterior during night service, late 1930s.

Angelus Temple exterior during day service, late 1930s.

Angelus Temple baptismal service.

Angelus Temple dedication and Aimee Semple McPherson.

Present-day exterior, Angelus Temple.

Above: *Present-day interior, Angelus Temple.* **Left:** *Aimee Semple McPherson on revival tour, early 1930s.*

Above left: *LIFE Bible College.* **Above right:** *LIFE Bible College, fourth floor class, late 1940s.* **Lower right:** *LIFE Bible College and the parsonage.*

Climbing atop the largest truck, I spoke for a few minutes to the assembled throngs, explaining my plans and hopes for this great building. We "sold" the sacks of cement for a dollar each so that everyone could have part in the foundation of the structure. The donors received as souvenirs of the joyous occasion a small golden bag labeled "cement." A year later the school building, though not completely finished, stood five and one-half stories tall, eclipsing Angelus Temple in height.

During the construction period, I was often disturbed by the noise accompanying the building of the school. This would begin early in the morning, sometimes disturbing my rest after late night services. Since the parsonage was just a few feet south of the structure, the noise also interfered with my writing and preparation of sermons and lessons. For that reason, I often would drive after the evening meetings to some hotel, usually the Ambassador, but occasionally to the Alexandria and Rosslyn, where I would register for the night and spend part of the next day working on messages. At the Ambassador I always requested room 330 because it was at the end of a corridor and directly across the hall from a room occupied by one of the Temple members. Thus, I was not really at any time alone, and our doors were often left open so that we could visit back and forth.

Little did I realize at the time what sinister innuendoes would be manufactured out of my resorting to hotels for rest and quiet. It never entered my mind that the enemy would counterattack in wrath because of the former bootleggers, gamblers, dope addicts, and white-slave victims who gave themselves to God at Angelus Temple and then told their secrets—secrets of poison liquor supply and rum-running activities, the addresses of speak-easies and gambling dens, names of dope traffickers, and horrible facts of white-slave interests—to listening radio audiences. Hoodlums who had been ignored by the authorities suddenly lost their "protection" because action had to be taken as a result of such telling public revelations.

But the storm was not ready to break—not quite yet. The sinister growl still lurked underground. Not until I returned from the Holy Land would the tempest unleash its ferocious fury.

I was to have a vacation! For three years mother and I had been busy in Angelus Temple. God had given us hundreds of thousands of friends in this area to which he had directed us. All the offerings of the past years had been plowed back into the work of the Lord. We had not invested in real estate or lovely homes or oil wells as some evangelists had done. I know of no reason why an evangelist should not spend his money that way if he wants to, for it is given as a freewill offering of the people, and if they do not want him to spend it in that manner, they should tie a string to it when they give it. But we did not want to amass personal wealth. We wanted to turn it all back into the work of God. And, of course, we invested our energies as well as the offerings. How tirelessly we worked! But now associates were warning that continued exertion at the same pace would endanger my health. So it was proposed that I take a vacation—what would be the first real vacation since I entered the evangelistic ministry at Mt. Forest, Ontario, years before.

I wanted to take mother with me, but it was felt we should not both leave at the same time. Mother would hold the fort in Los Angeles and care for the many thousands of details which no stranger could know or understand, while I was to have this lovely trip. My heart was singing to think that I would get a real rest, and yet it was with a rather tremulous heart that I approached the time. Could I leave the work? It was going on so well with one accord. The people were so loyal and wholehearted. There was a man in the Bible who sowed seed, and while he slept, the enemy came and sowed tares in his field. I had always hesitated to go away for long lest the devil come and sow tares. There never had been any to speak of in Angelus Temple. It seemed we were so much of one accord, and everybody was such a booster for the Lord, for the church, and for souls. But the Lord was laying it on my heart that now was the time to take a rest.

So at last, after three years of constant service day and night in Angelus Temple, the great event was to happen. The tickets were purchased. Roberta would accompany me at least as far as Ireland. Then I would proceed to France and then on to the Holy Land.

The people gave us a wonderful send-off at the railroad station in Los Angeles. Thousands gathered to say "good-by, God bless you and bring you safely home." There were cameras everywhere —a big flat car all full of photographers. "What will people say," I wondered anxiously, "when they see me in the moving pictures after all I have said about them?"

When the train arrived in New York, I congratulated myself that I was able to slip into the city unnoticed. Now, I thought, I could really begin to rest. Everybody on the train knew who I was, and I was asked to pray for the sick and to tell them about Jesus. How happy I was to do it, only I was supposed to be resting.

The next morning we sailed. When I entered the stateroom, I found people had packed it full of flowers, fruits, and baskets of good things. "Sister," one lady accosted me, "do you remember me? I was converted in your meetings in Brooklyn." "I was healed in your meeting in New Jersey," another testified.

At last came the announcement, "All ashore who're going ashore." Later, with a big, deep-throated groan, the ship was off. We watched New York fade in the distance, and then we were bounding away across the billows toward distant Europe.

Roberta and I paid a visit to Robert Semple's parents on the beautiful Emerald Island of Ireland. Our plans were for my daughter to remain with her grandparents while I proceeded to the Holy Land.

One of the highlights of my visit to London was the tour through the cloistered aisles of Westminster Abbey. I saw the graves of martyrs marked on the floor of that beautiful edifice. I saw the doors where they had entered with the processions and I could almost hear the words, "Open the doors and bear him in." Great monuments might crumble into dust, but this was living stone.

To several invitations to preach while I was in England I replied uniformly, "I am resting, not preaching." The ministers seemed more sympathetic than disappointed, for some had visited Angelus Temple and knew the heavy work load I had carried. They agreed I deserved a rest. But some of those precious British Pentecostal believers commenced to pray that somehow the Lord would direct me to preach in their midst if it were his blessed will.

Meanwhile, I took off for France. The airplane trip was wonderfully smooth, and the scenery breathtaking. How my heart yearned over Paris. I went to the Eiffel Tower and climbed up, up, up to the top. As I looked over the city, I thought of Jesus looking over Jerusalem and weeping. I longed to see a real Holy Ghost revival in Paris but, though I looked carefully, I could not find one. The churches I did visit were so filled with tourists wanting to look at the treasures in them that it seemed to rob them of all spirituality.

I proceeded south in France toward the Riviera, where I would sail for the Holy Land. But one night in the historic town of Nice the Lord seemed to impress upon me that I should go back to London. There began a battle between faith and reason. Not until the third night, when the Lord directed me clearly and distinctly, "My child, I want you to return to London and preach," did I yield to his leadings. The next morning I telephoned the secretary of the Elim churches in London that I was coming to preach for four days. The airplane trip back to England proved exceedingly rough. A gale wind blew, and the plane arrived one hour late.

Ministers and newspaper reporters welcomed me to London. The press wanted an audience, which I granted. The interviewers, however, seemed disappointed because I preferred to talk about Jesus more than about myself. One reporter complained that he got only a very few particulars because I kept "going off talking about spiritual subjects." But I had come back to England to preach Jesus.

The Tabernacle was packed, and we had to have overflow meetings. The people came from far and near to listen to the message from God's Word. So glorious were the meetings that the ministers commenced urging me to remain and conduct an extensive campaign. A public hall seating eight thousand persons was available. Several times while my decision was pending, I prayed, "Lord, I want to be in thy sweet will, but you know how I want to walk where you have walked and pray where you have prayed, and see the places I have been speaking about all these years, that I might be able to better describe them. But thy will be done, dear Lord." I was willing to forego the trip on to the Holy Land, but God seemed to guide me to continue onward. I did agree to come back to London on my return journey and preach in the Royal Albert Hall before leaving for home.

Meanwhile, Roberta had decided that she wanted to accompany me on the journey, so she bade good-by to her father's people in Ireland. We hastened on our way back across the English Channel and down through France to Marseilles, where we boarded a ship which took us to Port Said in Egypt. We crossed the Suez Canal in a small ferry. Natives dressed in quaint costumes attracted our attention. The women wore veils, some

completely covering their faces, and others with only eyes showing above the edge of the veil.

"Oh, I wish I could see!" I thought as I pressed my face to the
window in an effort to see the passing country. Here at last was
the land the Bible spoke of. Would it be anything like that which
I had pictured? Would I be disappointed? Perhaps I had done
wrong to come, for all my life since childhood I had been building up of the fabric of which dreams are made a lovely Holy
Land. I had seen it as it was in Jesus' day in my mind's eye.
Would it be changed and different? Would the people be modern?

Looking out as we neared the Holy City, it seemed that my
worst fears would be realized, for I was looking upon modern
scenes. There were beautiful homes of brick and stucco that
would do credit to California. Then there were stores and plate-
glass windows, telephone and telegraph poles, and nice looking
restaurants. And there were newsboys crying, "The New York
paper!"

I just crumpled up then. Oh, I was going to be sorry that I
came. I know many people who want to see the Holy Land but
fear that very same thing—that they will be disappointed.

Just then a man passed the door of my compartment. He had
helped us with our luggage the day before, and he was a man
who was well acquainted with that part of the country. "Sister,"
he comforted, "you are still outside the walls. You are looking at
the modern city of Jerusalem. The Jews are coming back, and
these are their settlements. There is a Russian section, a Polish
section, a German section. However, you will find that Old
Jerusalem will be unchanged."

That was some comfort, but I was not going to build my hopes
too high until I had seen for myself. At last we came to the station. The train did not go all the way to the old city. We would
have to continue there by automobile.

"Oh, there are the walls!" I exclaimed some time later.

"Yes," replied my guide. "The walls are solid, for they have
been restored."

My heart began to beat fast. How I rejoiced at seeing the walls!

At last we came to the Damascus Gate. That was as far as
you could go by automobile. You could not drive a car through
old Jerusalem because of the narrow streets and the many steps
up and down all along the way. All the loads there are carried
by donkeys, camels, or by men.

Hundreds of people crowded old Jerusalem wearing native costumes much like the ones of Bible days. They carried burdens and sold their merchandise. I wondered if Jesus looked on scenes like this when he walked Jerusalem's streets so long ago.

I could not stay in my hotel. I wanted to travel every moment. So sometimes I started out without a guide. Thus I came to the wailing wall where Jews weep and mourn over their lost temple and nation. It was the most awful sound I ever heard. "Oh, God, give us back our temple! Give us back our land! Drive out the Moslem and give us back our land! Send the Messiah! Oh, God, send the Messiah and save thy people!"

I longed to put my arms around them all and tell them that the Messiah had really come, that Jesus is he and that we have a temple not made with hands where we may worship Christ today. Sometimes there were few, sometimes many, but they never turned to pay any attention to the tourists. It seemed almost sacrilegious to stand there and watch them, but they paid no attention.

We visited other areas besides Jerusalem—Nazareth, Jericho, Hebron, Joppa, Galilee. The days passed so quickly they seemed like a dream. I wish I could go back and stay in the Holy Land a year and go everywhere. But the time to leave had come. We would make a quick trip through Egypt because I wanted to see where old Pharaoh oppressed the children of Israel before Moses led them forth in the Exodus.

We came to Cairo and to the great pyramids. I was thrilled as I saw those huge piles built by the genius and strength of men so long ago. From Egypt we embarked for Italy, where we visited Venice, Rome, Naples, and Pompeii before traveling onward to London to preach in the Royal Albert Hall. The British press gave us headlines across all the papers and wrote up the story of the meetings wonderfully. My treatment at the hands of the newspapers in England in 1926 was quite different from what I would face on my next visit to London.

The hall seating twelve thousand people was packed to capacity from the arena to the dome. I spoke on the Second Coming of the Lord at the closing meeting on Easter Monday. From London we went to Belfast, Ireland, where I had the privilege of telling the story of Jesus in the coliseum. The lord mayor of the city invited us to have our pictures taken with him. He showed us about the city hall and sat on the platform, attending as many services as possible, thanking God for the revival.

But now we must return to Los Angeles and resume the work. What a glorious welcome awaited us upon arrival there! I had no inkling of the storm which would break about me in less than a month, threatening my life, my reputation, and my ministry.

Kidnapped!

How suddenly it all happened! One moment sunlit skies, singing, preaching, considering bright plans for immediate extension of the Master's work. Then the next moment came horror, wild fear, rough hands, the roar of a car, and I lay prone upon the floor of that car!

It took me absolutely unaware, that sudden abduction by unknown plotters. If anyone in all the world had even been completely happy and busy with a life utterly full, it had been I. Then suddenly the trap sprung! I really should not have been surprised, for there had come warnings which I had ignored, dismissing them as pranks or cranks.

Such a church as Angelus Temple, of course, would naturally have its enemies. My desk drawer bulged with lists of addresses where laws against bootlegging and narcotics were constantly and flagrantly violated in that "world" which is ruled completely and unquestionably by the powers of Satan. That underworld is no myth to one who has knelt beside penitents at the altar and heard them sob out stories of crushed hearts and broken lives which might have been ruined forever had these victims not encountered the Jesus I preach.

Time and time again converted gamblers, dope addicts, boot-leggers, and white-slavery victims rose from knees to send thrilling testimonies out over radio station KFSG as well as to the Temple audience. In recounting their experiences, they had named people and places where they obtained narcotics and liquor or where they had gambled away homes and fortunes.

Friends warned me, "Sister, you'll get into a lot of trouble fighting sin so boldly. The underworld and its 'higher-ups' won't stand for these exposes!" And frequently the postman delivered envelopes containing letters and notes threatening that kidnapping and death would ensue if we did not "lay off."

"Kidnap? Impossible!" I imagined, even after one Los Angeles newspaper a year before the ordeal published a headline article claiming that reports had uncovered a plot to abduct me! The idea was unthinkable. Such things just don't happen to an evangelist! We had dealt telling blows at the underworld, to be sure, but the thought of anybody striking back with a blow at the church didn't impress me as worthy of serious consideration.

But then it happened. I had been home from the Holy Land just three weeks. What wonderfully busy weeks they had been. "I won't need another vacation for a long time to come," I had announced. "I am going to work steadily—as hard as I can."

I began planning, projecting conventions, engaging speakers. The Bible school building construction had been completed during my absence, but decisions had to be made concerning its decorating and furnishing. Painters, artists, and decorators consulted me about details of the finishing touches. My preaching schedule called for sermons Wednesday afternoons and evenings, Thursday, Friday, and Saturday evenings, and Sunday mornings, afternoons, and evenings. In addition, I was teaching in the Bible school where seven hundred young men and women were studying for the ministry as pastors, evangelists, and missionaries. The seniors would soon graduate, as the spring term was nearing its end. My examination papers were out. It was a very busy time.

Sunday, May 16, 1926, found the Temple crowded to capacity at all three services. I had to give my sermon that night, "The Scarlet Thread," to three audiences, emptying the Temple after the first two sessions and then seeing it fill quickly again.

Ordinarily I did not speak at the Temple on Mondays or Tuesdays. However, because people were requesting so insistently that I give a journey-log of my trip to the Holy Land, I agreed to present this on Monday night, illustrated with slides.

The streets around the Temple were packed with people by 5:00 P.M. The doors were opened, and the auditorium breathlessly jammed by 6:00. By 6:30 the streets outside were again crowded with people who refused to go home. I gave my journey-log to the first audience, speaking until 9:30, then dismissed those thousands and repeated the same story to a second congregation. But even the Temple could not accommodate the throngs who came, so I announced I would repeat the travelog on the following night. But by the time that service should have started, the Southland supposed I had drowned.

Tuesday, May 18, 1926. In the morning I went downtown to do some shopping. My daughter, Roberta, needed a new dress for school, and I wanted a new dress too. To the best of my recollection, it was about ten o'clock when I drove away from the parsonage. I parked in front of Bullock's Department Store. After purchasing a dress for Roberta, I looked for an outfit for myself. I found a black and white dress which I liked very much but decided I wanted Emma Schaffer, my secretary, to come down and look at it. "Would you hold this dress for me?" I asked the saleslady, and she put it aside.

I am going into these details because some months later witnesses would appear who thought they saw me at the Clark Hotel at exactly the time I was at Bullock's. Fortunately, the Bullock's saleslady, Mrs. May Dunton, remembered the time of the transaction and gave affadavits to that effect. I also stopped in a small shop near Bullock's whose proprietor, Mrs. Hamilton, remembered my coming. Then I drove home. Harriet Jordan, the dean of our Bible school, came to the parsonage to consult me, and she declared I had returned before 11:00 A.M.

Because I had given up my two rest nights for speaking, mother said to me, "Darling, your cheeks look pale. You get ready and go to the beach this afternoon and get a little outing."

"Fine," I said. "Will you come along?" Mother sometimes accompanied me on such outings. Her swimsuit was already in the car, left there from an excursion on the previous Friday.

"No, darling," she declined. "I have to get the advertising ready and the church bulletins on the press."

I asked Roberta to go with me, but she had to go to school.

Then I invited my secretary, "Miss Schaffer, will you go?"

"Yes, I'll be glad to," Emma answered.

Wearing a white and yellow sport outfit, I left the parsonage with Miss Schaffer. We greeted a number of people on the sidewalk outside and mentioned our destination.

I carried my bathing suit and cap, also my Bible, concordance, and some papers, intending to work on some sermons in the quiet of the beach.

It took longer than usual to drive to Ocean Park, for I got lost going out Pico Boulevard, which was quite torn up at that time. I got off the right road in trying to get back onto Pico from the detour. Once at the beach, I parked at the Ocean View Hotel at the corner of Ocean Front and Rose Avenue.

I was joyous with the thought of getting into the water. But I was also hungry. Emma and I walked down to a little eating place, where I ordered a waffle. Miss Schaffer got some popcorn. Then I rented an umbrella tent and dropped down on the sand. My secretary sat beside me. I spread out my Bible and notebook and worked for a few minutes before going for a swim. The billows rolled in, and I swam out into them, hand over hand. I love to swim, but it seemed I should be working on my messages. Besides, the water was rather cold.

Back at my tent on the beach, I finished the outline for one of the next Sunday's sermons and was about to begin work on another message when I began to think about the travelog I would repeat that evening. Because this presentation would be especially slanted for children, I decided I wanted some changes made in the music. And I wanted two new slides prepared for the program. I spoke to Miss Schaffer, who did not swim. "You are dressed, dear. Would you be so kind as to go and phone the musical director about the music and order the slides? My eyes are tired, so I guess I'll have another swim while you are gone. That won't leave you alone so much here." I told her just the route I expected to swim.

"All right," she said. "Don't go too far now."

"Oh, I won't," I answered. "I'll be all right." I had no idea how far I'd go before I would see any familiar face again.

I walked out the little boardwalk, swam out almost even with the pier, then went over toward the pier before starting back toward the shore. I noticed some lifeguards out there practicing and I stood about knee-deep in the water watching them drill.

How happy I was, singing a snatch of a song to myself. I had no fear of anything.

While standing there, I heard my name called. I don't recall whether the party said "Sister McPherson" or "Mrs. McPherson." I frowned a bit, thinking "I can't even go to the beach without being recognized." I looked in the direction of the summons and noticed a man and a woman apparently waiting for me. The woman was crying, and the man seemed greatly agitated. They came toward me as I emerged from the surf, both talking at once, almost incoherently. "Our baby is dying, Sister," they exclaimed. "The doctor has given it up. We have come all the way from Altadena with the child. Oh, please come to our car and pray for the baby."

"How did you know I was here?" I asked almost automatically, not at all suspicious of the interruption. Many times while I had been out riding horseback or driving my car another auto would draw up alongside, and I would be whisked away to some hospital or to the scene of an accident to give the victims what comfort I could in the name of Christ.

"We called at the Temple, and your mother told us you were here," came the explanation. "She said that if we could find you, she was sure you would pray for our child. You will come, won't you?"

I didn't suppose for a moment that they hadn't called the Temple. When I need to be reproved, most often it is because I have been too trusting. I assume people are telling me the truth and do not question their sincerity, just as I did that fateful day.

"Well, I can't go, not just now," I declared. Those words were hardly out of my mouth, however, before the thought flashed, "These people will think you care more about a swim than about a dying baby. Shame on you! Don't think about swimming now, but go pray for the child." "Wait till I go up and get dressed," I said.

"But the baby is dying, Sister," the woman pleaded. "Every minute means so much. Even if the baby does die, we would feel better to have had you pray for it."

How that touched me! "Well," I proposed, "I'll run back to the tent and get my robe." The tent was pitched about one city block away from where we were conversing at the shore.

"Won't this do?" the woman asked. On her arm she had a dark coat made of a sort of cravenette material. As she asked the question, she slipped the coat over my shoulders. The garment covered me, so I decided it would be all right to wear. I still had my bathing cap on and walked in my bare feet.

"I knew you would do it," the woman exclaimed happily as we moved across the sands toward the boardwalk. Upon reaching the walk, the lady ran ahead, saying she was nervous about being away from the baby.

The man directed me up Navy Street, where I spied a car with the rear door open. Another man sat at the wheel, and the motor was running, but I paid no attention to these strange circumstances at the time. My interest was in the woman sitting in the back seat holding a bundle which she clasped tightly to her breast. Naturally, I supposed this to be the dying baby.

"Just step in," the man said as we reached the auto.

I was glad to do that, for I couldn't reach the baby from the running board of the car. Many times I had stepped into ambulances or automobiles which drove up in front of our house, so the invitation to enter the vehicle did not strike me as strange or suspicious. However, as I stepped inside, the man gave me a little shove, a push from behind. Down I went onto the floor of the car. I didn't cry out or make any fuss because I was too surprised and startled. I couldn't imagine what was happening.

Immediately the bundle of robes the woman had been cradling as a baby came down upon me. Something wet and sticky was pressed roughly to my mouth. A firm hand held the back of my head. I struggled weakly for a moment, then lapsed into unconsciousness. The last sound I remember was the motor accelerating as the driver sped off.

Some weeks later I would be told by an attorney who claimed to be in contact with my kidnappers that they said they had used a sort of rubber mask to administer the anaesthetic—a procedure by which, they said, you are all but gone with just one gasp. Several hours afterwards, the lawyer advised, the abductors gave me a quarter of a grain of morphine. Whether this attorney had actually heard from the kidnappers, whether he was the victim of a hoax, or himself the perpetrator of a hoax will probably remain a mystery, for he was killed in an automobile accident before we could confirm or refute his claims. But my abduction was no hoax. It was tragically real. My face was red and very sore for some time afterwards as a result of the administration of the anaesthetic.

How long I was unconscious I have no way of knowing. Whether after the effects of the drugging wore off I drifted off into fitful sleep is also uncertain. However, long before I came to, my disappearance was explained as drowning. The Temple organized a beach patrol to comb the coast for my body. This belief apparently complicated the plottings of my abductors, for their ransom note was greeted as a hoax aimed at extortion.

Of course, the beach patrol turned up no body. I was very much alive but quite the worse for wear. When I awakened, I was sick at my stomach and in bed, vomiting. A lady was holding a basin and bending over me. "Where am I?" I wondered. I looked about the room, taking note of the surroundings. There was wallpaper on the walls, so I knew I wasn't home, for my room has no wallpaper. I noted the foot of the bed; it was enameled. We haven't any enameled bed.

"I must have been in an automobile accident," was the first thought to enter my mind as I blearily surveyed the room. "I've been in a wreck and have come to a hospital." I lay there, looking and blinking. "Where am I?" I asked the woman beside the bed. "What has happened?"

She didn't answer me at first, so I asked again. Then the woman called, "All right, Steve, come in." Two men entered. By now I remembered the couple at the beach and their driver. These were the same people!

The heavyset man called Steve stood by the bed. The other man kept more in the background, though both looked down upon me. I no longer was wearing my bathing suit but had on a white cotton nightgown. I looked up at these men and asked them what was going on. I cannot remember their exact words at first, for my mind was still somewhat befogged. The gist of their conversation was that they had planned this snatch for a long time, and this was the first opportunity they had had to get me.

I asked them why they had taken me, and they told me I would be held for ransom and that they were going to "get that damned Temple." I definitely remember that they used the expression *get*. I grew very much excited and sat up in bed, pleading with them. "I must get back to the Temple!" I exclaimed, still wondering whether this was a ghastly joke. I was still quite nauseated. And how my head did ache! The trio broke out in laughter.

"Moth⦁ˑ must be worried to death," I continued. "Besides, I cannot be spared from the Bible school. I have examination

papers out." This especially worried me. But my captors just
sneered and said, "That's all right. You will have to forget that.
If you are a good girl, maybe you'll get to go home soon." My
further pleadings proved to no avail. Finally, one of the men
with an impatient gesture growled, "Be quiet."

The first time I was alone in the room I gave way to an impulse to scream for help. I climbed out of bed and staggered
to the window. This was boarded up almost to the top, but there
were a few cracks through which I hoped my cry might be heard.
I called, but my weak voice sounded almost as if it were mocking
me. The woman burst into the room, put a hand on my shoulder,
jerked me away from the window, and shook me angrily. Then
she thrust me back on the bed, commanding, "Stop that!"

As soon as she withdrew again, I went back to the window.
Almost beside myself, I cried out again. I did not care what they
would do to me if only somebody could be made to hear. This
time all three of my captors rushed in, grabbed me before I had
been able to scream more than once or twice, and gagged me with
a handkerchief bound tightly over my mouth. But they left the
gag in place only a few minutes. When they removed it, they
warned that if I made any further outcry they would put the
gag back and leave it there.

My abductors did not tell me at first how much money they
were asking for my ransom, nor did I think to ask them. I did
request that they send word to my family that I was alive, and
they answered, "You bet we will."

The days wore on. How desperately I missed my Bible! It was
the longest period of my lifetime that I had no access to the Word
of God. I tried to witness to my captors. After my return, the
district attorney asked me if I tried to convert the woman kidnapper, and I replied, "I tried to convert them all." But to his
question, "Did you have any success?" I had to confess, "No, I
am afraid I didn't, Mr. Keyes."

I lost all track of time. I would pace up and down the floor
pleading, "How long will this continue? I must get home." The
man called Steve—the pretended father who met me at the
water's edge—seemed to be away a great part of the time, but he
would show up at the house between trips. The other man was
there most of the time, though I saw very little of him. The
woman, who told me I might call her Rose, slept on a cot at the
foot of my bed. I can see it all now—the memory still haunts me.

Here was my bed. In a corner was a curtain behind which clothes were hung. Over there was a door leading into a small bathroom with basin, tub, and toilet. There was indeed such a bathroom in this first place of my captivity. After my deliverance, some writers would misrepresent my testimony and make fun of the idea that such conveniences could have been found in the desert shack to which I was transferred a few days before my escape. I never said there was a bathroom in that desert shack. On every occasion when I related my story I emphasized the differences in accommodations between the first house where I was held for a little over a month and the primitive cabin where I was confined for two or three days. It was the house, not the shack, that had the bathroom.

I remember vividly other details of that first place of captivity. There was an old-fashioned table and dresser. The wall had blue-striped paper with pink flowers climbing up and a narrow border. The ceiling appeared to be plastered. My impression was that it was a two-storied house, for I was quite sure I heard footsteps overhead. But I cannot be absolutely positive. I was never allowed in any parts of the house other than the room with my bed and the bathroom. Rose brought my food to me. She did very little cooking, whether or not it was because she was lazy I don't know. Most of what I ate was canned foods, but we did sometimes have boiled potatoes, which for me made a nice variety to the meals.

One day when Steve returned from one of his trips, I heard him storming out in the other room. I heard him ask angrily, "Don't they think we know a damned dick when we see one, even if he is beribboned?"—or something like that. At the time I did not know what ignited that outburst, but I later learned of the first ransom letter delivered to the Temple. Dated May 24 and mailed from San Francisco, it was signed by the revengers and demanded five hundred thousand dollars for my release. Mother said that this letter, when she received it, made no impression on her mind because at the time she was convinced that I had "gone into the water and had not come out of the water" and that my "spirit was with God." So she turned the handwritten note over to the authorities. Somehow this revengers letter vanished from the locked secret files of the Los Angeles Police Department. Two months later a newspaper printed what purported to be a photographic copy of this letter, but mother said, "I believe it is not a picture of the original letter, because the letter I received and turned over to the authorities was difficult to read, almost undecipherable, while the one in the papers is quite easily read."

At any rate, mother said the first ransom demand gave special directions regarding how to make contact in the Palace Hotel lobby in San Francisco the following Saturday. The messengers with the money were to wear the kind of ribbons we use for Angelus Temple workers' badges. Mother was strictly enjoined to send no dicks. Since she believed I was dead, she sent no one. But the police sent two men, wearing Temple ribbons and carrying a bundle to represent the ransom money. No one approached these detectives. If my captors were indeed the authors of the revengers letter, Steve was not fooled by the men at the hotel. He knew a dick, as he said angrily, when he saw one, "even if he is beribboned."

When I learned the amount of ransom these kidnappers were demanding, I was almost wild. "Why, our people cannot pay that!" I insisted. "That's almost as much as our plant is worth. Nobody on earth could raise that!"

"Oh, they will raise it all right," they declared. "You've got that many people who would give a thousand dollars each to get you back."

"You'll never get it," I persisted.

"We will get it," they boasted confidently. But from their conversation I gathered that they were having considerable difficulty making my mother believe that I was alive. She insisted I had drowned, and they were trying to break this opinion down. I never told anybody this before except my attorneys because I was afraid people might think I was telling a wild tale, but my captors said that they had people at the Temple representing themselves as detectives and reporters—that these men were on the inside and knew everything that was going on.

From time to time I tried to question Rose to draw out some details which might be helpful to the authorities after my release. But she was noncommittal. "That's enough, dearie," she would reply. "We don't go into that, dearie." It was always dearie, usually uttered in a very gushy way. She did tell me she was a nurse, and she struck me as such, but as the kind of nurse who would work in a psychopathic department to take care of some obstreperous person.

I must say that for the most part there were no insults nor

affronts from Steve or the other man. Whether Rose was the wife of one of them I never determined. Sometimes I feel that those folks were almost kinder to me than some of the people I had dealings with after I made my escape and got away.

Apparently the next step to my captors to extort the ransom was the contact made by two men with R. A. McKinley, a blind lawyer with an office in Long Beach. On the Monday morning after the Saturday when the rendezvous at the Palace Hotel in San Francisco as directed in the revengers letter failed to materialize, Attorney McKinley told officers of the Long Beach Police Department that two men who gave their names as Miller and Wilson entered his office and claimed they had kidnapped me at the beach and were holding me prisoner until their object was achieved. They wanted the blind lawyer to act as a go-between with my mother in an effort to collect twenty-five thousand dollars ransom. "We chose you because you are blind and thus can't identify us," they said. I presume they put the figure down lower than the revengers demand because they had been unable to convince my mother that I was alive.

The next day Mr. McKinley told his story to Los Angeles County District Attorney Asa Keyes and Police Captain Herman Cline. These authorities were skeptical, but the lawyer suggested that my mother be contacted and asked to submit several questions which only I could answer. The answers supposedly would prove whether Wilson and Miller really had me in captivity. Mother cannot recall whether it was Mr. Keyes or Captain Cline who phoned, but it was one or the other. This latest story sounded so melodramatic, so surfeited with villainy, that she was incredulous. Still my body had not been washed ashore, and she felt she should not overlook the possibility, however improbable the events seemed. So four questions were prepared for the blind lawyer, which he passed on to Miller and Wilson when they accosted him later, this time on the street. I understand also that on another visit these men beat this blind lawyer in his own office.

Rose drew me out so cleverly that at first I did not realize I was being questioned. The day Steve returned from one of his trips she remarked, "It is certainly hot. A hammock would feel good today." Then casually, "Do you like hammocks? Did you ever have one?"

"Yes, we had a wire hammock," I replied, "out in the country. When I was a little girl."

"Did you have it on the piazza?" she asked.

"No, we had it out under the apple trees."

"Did you ever sleep on it?" Rose continued. I answered, "Yes."
In a little while the conversation changed. "Do you like dogs?"
Rose wondered.

"Yes, I am very fond of them."

"Did you ever have a dog?"

I told her about little Gyppy at my childhood home. Without
realizing it, I had answered correctly mother's first two questions.
Just then I noticed Steve standing in the doorway with a peculiarly pleased yet furtive look. He apparently had been eaves-
dropping in the other room. Something about his face made me
suspicious. "Why are you asking me these questions?" I said.
"What's the idea?"

"Oh, nothing," Rose shrugged. But I knew better. Finally they
told me that they were soon going to let me go. "The old lady
will be coming through with the money pretty soon," Steve declared. He meant my mother. "If you'll just go ahead and answer
the rest of these questions, she'll be convinced you are alive."
They then showed me a portion of a newspaper, with the story of
how mother had been approached through the blind lawyer and
had provided the questions I was to answer.

"I won't answer any more questions," I said resolutely. "I'm
not going to let them raise the money."

"You will if you know what is for your own good! You will
answer those questions and answer them quick!" Steve used pro-
fanity to enforce his command.

"I won't do it!" I insisted.

"Oh, you won't, won't you?" he sneered. With a quick motion
he grabbed my wrist and stabbed his cigar down hard against
my fingers.

I just winced and said, "Go ahead." He stopped and seemed to
be a bit ashamed. The burns weren't serious, hardly enough to
mention, but the scars were there for a long time. When I appeared before the grand jury in July, one of the jurors asked
about the marks, which were still visible.

Not long after this I believe my captors began another initiative
to get the money. I heard them talking over their predicament.
They seemed worried about how they could collect the money
and avoid being caught. I heard the clatter of a typewriter. It
sounded to me as if it was being operated by an amateur. I would

not learn about the second ransom note until after my escape. Rose clipped off a lock of my hair. Later she cut another. I gathered from the snatches of conversation I heard that these were further attempts to convince my people I was alive. Steve came in and looked at one of my fingers, which bears a peculiar mark where it had been cut with a corn sickle in my childhood. "If the locks of hair don't convince her people," he told Rose, "we can send that finger next." I don't know whether he was serious in that threat, but I suppose he was capable of carrying it out.

Soon after this came the night they moved me. I had retired. I don't know for how long I slept, whether several hours or just a short time, but Rose awakened me. "Get up," she ordered. "We are going to move. Get into your clothes." They said they were taking me for a short time to a place where nobody could find me. I had a feeling that I would soon be going home—that they were moving me to a safe place while they put over their final coup. So I was willing to go.

They blindfolded me and led me out to the car. The woman had taken the narrow mattress off her couch and placed it in the bottom of the car. They made me lie on that. They tied my hands and feet—not uncomfortably but loosely. Once we were under way, my blindfold was removed. There was no baggage in the car except a lunch basket. Rose and the driver were the only others in the car. I didn't know where Steve had gone. Whether this was the same car in which I was abducted I cannot say for sure, but I suspect it was different.

I have no idea what time of night we left. I judge that we traveled several hours before dawn, but I fell asleep. We traveled all the next day. A couple of stops were made for comfort, but that was out in the country, and no landmarks were evident. It was desert. During the day I thought, "Thank God! We must be going home." Somehow I imagined we were in Imperial Valley or near Palms. I supposed I was getting nearer home but hoped they weren't getting the ransom.

Once during the trip they put a gag over my mouth, but it wasn't on long. Most of our driving must have been in open country because I did not hear the rumble of traffic. If there were towns, the driver apparently circled around them. The roads were mostly smooth.

Night had fallen when we reached the destination. The car

stopped. They blindfolded me lightly again and took me into a cabin. Then they told me about a newspaper report that my mother had collapsed. That was the last stroke. I had stood everything else, but when I heard that news, it seemed that something snapped. I began to cry out and moan. I became sick and hysterical and could not eat anything.

To the best of my recollection, Steve was at the shack when we arrived. Apparently he had brought with him the brown khaki soldier cots, the camp chair, and a few utensils. I did not pay too much attention to the room, but it was my impression that the walls were dark. I believe the floor was wooden. However, when I returned to the desert after my escape, in an effort to locate the shack of my captivity, one of the buildings we inspected had an earth floor so treated and smoothed and hardened by some preparation that it deceived me. When I came out of the shack, the authorities asked me, "What kind of a floor did it have?" and I answered, "A wooden floor." They took me back inside and showed me I was mistaken, but before that I believed it was wood.

The men were very little in evidence at the shack, keeping in the second room or leaving the cabin on business, since I overheard them talking about going to the city. I remained perfectly miserable. The weather was much warmer here than at the first house. "It is so hot," I complained to Rose. "It is so hot. I can't stand this heat."

"It's not as hot as in Honduras," she commented. Then she remarked, "Now, dearie, if your mother behaves, you will be out of here perhaps by Friday."

But I did not have to wait until Friday. An opportunity to escape occurred on Tuesday. Rose and I were alone in the shack. The men had driven away in one of the cars. Rose brought in a small tin basin, and I washed. I did not seem able to walk. I just kept saying, "Mother, poor mother," like a child, remembering the news that she had collapsed. I couldn't help thinking how much she must be suffering.

Rose announced that she was going away to get some provisions. Her words as nearly as I can recall were, "I am going out for a little while for supplies. I will be right back. But I am going to have to tie you."

"Oh, please don't tie me," I begged. "I can hardly stand. You know I will just fall."

But she said she must tie me securely. "You will be all right.
It won't hurt a bit. Lay on your side, dearie."

"Won't you tie my hands in front rather than behind my
back?" I pleaded. "It makes it so uncomfortable." But she insisted that I turn over. After binding my hands, she tied my feet.
The material she used was a stitched strapping similar to bed
ticking. It didn't cut into my wrists. She did not gag me. I suppose
she thought it wasn't necessary that far away from civilization.

Rose left the room. I heard the car start and drive away. I lay
on my cot with my heart racing. It was the first time since my
abduction that I had been left alone. "Praise the Lord!" I thought.
"Here is an opportunity to get away." I realized that if I could
get my feet loose, I would have a chance. But I felt so weak.
Would I be able to walk? I began to pray.

I commenced to pull my feet and wiggle them loose, but the
bands didn't budge. I began trying to loosen my hands but soon
realized it would be impossible to free them that way. Then I
looked at the five-gallon tin can across the room. It was a can
such as we used to have for maple syrup, with a top that had
evidently been roughly cut off. I wondered if I could perhaps get
to that can and cut the straps. I rolled off the bed and across
the floor to the can. It was against the wall. By leaning back, I
managed to saw the strap binding my wrists back and forth
upon the sharp edge until my hands were loose. I did not cut my
wrists.

A reporter named Collins of the *Herald* newspaper in Los
Angeles would later challenge, "Mrs. McPherson, I don't believe
your story, because no one could cut their hands loose in that
way without cutting their wrists." The authorities and others
voiced similar skepticism. So we tried it one night at home.
Mother tied me as I lay on the couch with a can across the room.
It took me thirty seconds to roll off that couch up to the can and
cut my hands loose. I did not cut my wrists at all. On four different times I tried this and each time was successful in cutting my
hands loose without lacerating my wrists in the least, as several
witnesses can testify.

After freeing my hands, I went to work unloosing my feet.
This was easy. Weak and trembling, I struggled to my feet, praying for God to give me help. Though scarcely able to stand at
first, strength began coming to me in a God-given flood. I made

my way to the little window and climbed out. It wasn't much
of a drop to the ground.

I would often be asked afterwards, "Why didn't you go out
the door?" But I didn't stop to think of the door. It was closed,
while the window was open, and the window was not high.

After reaching the ground, I didn't stop to look at anything
—not even back at the shack. My one thought was to get away
before Rose or the men returned. I expected every minute to hear
the sound of the automobile coming back to the cabin. I commenced to run across the desert terrain as fast as my trembling
legs would carry me. The day was cooler than usual for that
region, though still warm. The sun was not terribly hot, even
though it was probably about noon when I made my escape.
Desert dwellers would later confirm that the day was cooler than
any for some time either before or after.

As I went, I prayed as I had never prayed in my life that God
would enable me to make the journey to safety. I didn't stop to
observe my surroundings. My thoughts were chaotic. I don't
know that I really could define them. I ran until I got tired and
then slowed to a walk. I ran and walked and walked and ran.

As I went I had no hat—nothing to protect my head and face
from the sun—so I made a sunbonnet out of my dress, gathering
it up around my head. This gave complete protection from sun-
burn, as the garment was made of a heavy, closely woven fabric.
It afforded as good a break from the sun as any umbrella could.
I turned it over my head and held it around my arms, which of
course made me go slower. But I continued on and on.

Fortunately, I do not perspire easily. Someone weeks afterward quipped that if I had sweat more then, I would not have
been sweating so much later—during the ordeal when every effort
was exerted, albeit futilely—to break down my story.

There were times when I was especially tired. I would sit down
for a while before resuming the trek. I wondered, "Am I going
around in a circle?" My lips felt parched, and my tongue was
dry, but I was not suffering acutely—physically. I was fortunate
that during most of the day my travels led through a somewhat
elevated region several degrees cooler than the flat desert. Though
I had had all the water I wanted to drink that morning, naturally
I became thirsty in the afternoon. I wanted a drink of water, but
I can't say I was dying for it.

The hike was such a nightmare that I can hardly recall all the incidents. The terrain, however, was not especially rugged or rocky. Certainly there were cactus and catburs that would stick you, but these I managed to avoid. The country was not one which would cut up a person's shoes by any means. Deputy District Attorney Ryan himself said that he could walk two days on it without his commissary shoes being marked. I did occasionally, however, stumble on stones as I journeyed.

Just how far I walked in all, I do not know. Some who followed what they believed were my footprints estimated I hiked twenty miles. It seemed to me more like a hundred miles, though of course it wasn't. My hips got very sore in walking. Every time I put my foot down, the joints seemed to hurt. I would lie down and get up, walk or run for a while, then lie down again. Why weren't my clothes more soiled when I reached safety? That was a question with which I would be hounded for months. I thought at the time that my clothes were filthy, but the sand in that desert was like snow in the respect that you can brush it right off. It didn't stain as would dirt or soil.

I assumed I was traveling north, as the sun was to my left. I am just guessing now about the time, but I think it was around 3:30 in the afternoon when an eminence I later learned was called Niggerhead Mountain loomed in the distance. I resolved to try to reach it and climb up to survey the country. Fortunately, by walking toward a definite goal, I was now safeguarded against wandering in circles.

Before I reached this hill, it grew quite dark. The moon was up, and stars were shining. It was a beautiful night, but I who love the heavens was in no mood to enjoy their glory then. I remembered with increasing dread many stories of people who had died in the desert, hopelessly lost, perishing for food and water. "Oh, God, thou who didst lead the children of Israel across the wilderness and didst guide them in all their journeys," I prayed, "thou hast never failed me before and thou wilt not fail me now. Guide my weary footsteps to safety, for I am lost and sore distressed."

Hardly had I uttered that earnest plea for help when, having mounted a small elevation at the foot of Niggerhead Mountain, I saw a glow in the sky. There was a cluster of lights too low and too bright to be stars. It must be—it was a city! How far away it seemed, yet there it lay! Thank God! I would learn afterward that the glow in the sky was the smelter fires of Douglas, Arizona, and the dancing white lights were those of the adjoining village of Agua Prieta, Mexico.

How many miles was it to those lights? Could I make it? As I continued onward, I came upon a good road. At first I thought, "I will sleep on this road tonight, and if a car comes to pick me up, all right. If not, I will go on in the morning." I was so very tired.

I got off the road and tried to compose myself for slumber, but soon a slight rustle in nearby bushes brought to my mind the thought of the creatures that live in the desert. I feared a gila monster might come. So I got up and started hiking again. The road made the walking so much easier!

I proceeded until I came to a small building on my left. I found out later it was a sentry hut. I walked around this house shouting, "Help! Is anybody here?" There was no answer. I saw no sign of life so I went back to the road and continued on. I would go on as far as I could and then sit down at the side of the road. At times I walked with my eyes closed, eyelids refusing to stay open.

Eventually I heard dogs barking in the distance. I saw the great dark form of a building loom ahead and a fence which later proved to be the line fence between the United States and Mexico. The building was about three hundred feet to the right of the road. I renewed my cries, "Hello! Help!" To me my voice sounded like a little whistle in that vast wilderness. But the dogs increased their barking and snarling as I stumbled toward the building, continuing my calls, "Help! Won't you please help me?"

A man emerged from the structure, swearing at the dogs and telling them to be quiet. His voice sounded gruff, with a foreign accent. When he approached, I realized he had nothing on but his underwear. He was unshaven and looked frightening. Some people have asked why I did not stop there. If they could have seen the man that night, they would know why.

"What you want?" he challenged me.

"I want the police," I said.

"What you done?" he asked suspiciously.

"I haven't done anything," I answered. "But I want the police." Because he didn't seem to understand English too well, I decided not to tell him the details of my ordeal. But I did say that I had been kidnapped.

"Who took you?" he asked.

"Some people," I answered. "Have you a telephone? I want to call the police."

"No, we no have phone," he said.

"Have you an automobile?" I pressed.

He said, "No."

"Have you a horse?" I asked.

"No."

"Will you go with me to the town?"

"No, I work all day," he said. "You better come in and stay until morning."

"Have you a wife?" I asked.

"No."

"Are there any women here?"

"No."

"What is this building?"

"A slaughterhouse."

"I will go on now," I told him. "How far is it to the first house where there will be a lady?"

Instead of answering, he kept asking me questions. "Who are you? What you want? Who kidnapped you? What you done?"

I said, "Please tell me how far it is to a house where I can get the police or where there is a lady."

Finally he grumbled something about it being a mile. I cut across a gully back to the road and made my way toward the town. I had to lie down frequently. Twice I came to houses. Each seemed to have a dozen dogs. The big ones growled, and the little ones yipped, so I didn't stop at those little houses because now I could see bigger ones ahead. I thought I might find a policeman. The lights of Agua Prieta were going out—lights I later learned marked dance halls and drinking resorts.

Soon I came to a house bigger than the rest. It had a hedge growing around it and looked as if the people living there would be respectable and responsible. I stumbled to the gate. A dog barked as I began to call. My knees were wobbling like jelly. I felt I could go no farther in search of a policeman. "Won't you please help me?" was the only thing I could think to say.

"Who are you?" a man's voice called out. "What do you want?"

"I want the police. Have you a telephone?"

"No," came the reply, "but there is a telephone across the street, one block."

"One block—just—one—more—block—now," I was saying

to myself dully. I had entered the gate and climbed up three steps to the porch. I turned and descended those steps and started for the telephone. I reached the gate at the end of the walk and there I fell, with my head down and my body on the upper part of it. They tell me I lay there something over an hour. Mr. and Mrs. Gonzales—the people who lived there—at first thought I was dead. They lighted matches in my face, but my eyes would not dilate. They supposed I was dead and that they dare not move me until the coroner came. When they discovered I was alive, they covered me with blankets.

When I regained consciousness, I begged, "Water! Water, please!" And they graciously provided it. How good it was! I called for a second glass. Why hadn't I asked for water at the slaughterhouse? For the same reasons I did not remain there. In my already upset frame of mind, the man's appearance prompted me to get along quickly. He was too eager for me to come in.

Mr. Gonzales raised my head while his wife chafed my hands. I still seemed shrouded in a mist of semiconsciousness. "Señorita, Señora, what is the matter?"

How good it was to look again at kindly faces. I thought of Rose back at the shack—of her hard, cruel look that even her gushing dearie could not hide. How different was the face of Mrs. Gonzales, now bending so anxiously over mine. How beautiful she looked to me. The next faces I saw were Mexican too, kindly and anxious. I learned I was in Agua Prieta, across the Mexican border below Douglas, Arizona. I told them I was Mrs. McPherson, but that didn't mean anything to them. "I have been kidnapped," I explained.

"How were you brought here?" they asked.

"In a car." When I said I was brought in a car it was used against me. But I did not mean I was brought to Agua Prieta in an automobile but brought into Mexico from Los Angeles in a car.

"Get me American police officers, and they will understand," I pleaded. Finally they got an American taxi driver, John Anderson. "I am Mrs. McPherson," I told him. He drove me to the police station in Douglas. The officer there wanted me to get out of the car, but I said I couldn't. I was utterly tired out and exhausted.

"Who are you?" came the question.

"I am Mrs. McPherson."

"I do not believe you. Many people have said they were Aimee Semple McPherson, and they were not."

"I don't care whether you believe me or not. I am Mrs. McPherson and I want to go home."

"You are sick," I was told. "You should go to the hospital. Would you rather go to the hotel or to the hospital?"

"The hospital is all right," I replied.

"Have you any money?"

"I haven't a cent."

Police Officer Patterson pondered for a moment and then said, "I will stand for it for you. If you are not the right woman, I will take a chance."

Nobody at first would believe that I really was the right person. The taxi driver took me to the Calumet and Arizona Hospital, followed by Officers George, Cook, and O. E. Patterson, who arranged for my admission. They took me in, dirty, with my hands covered with grime, my face and my shoes white with desert dust, as was also the rest of my apparel. A nurse put me to bed but did not offer to give me a bath. She picked out some of the cactus spines from my legs and rubbed something on my toe where a blister had broken, a blister caused by the fact that the pair of shoes that I had been wearing had been too large for me. I think they were Rose's shoes.

I had no rest for some time. People came in to look at me. "Are you Mrs. McPherson?" they would ask.

"Yes."

"I don't believe it," came back the verdict.

One man paced up and down a long while before he asked, "Would you mind letting me smell your breath?"

"No." I couldn't imagine what he meant by the request. I didn't realize that it wasn't altogether unusual for a dazed woman to turn up in Douglas in the wee hours of the morning after a night of carousal in the saloons across the border in Agua Prieta, Mexico. This man supposed I had been drinking and was only imagining I was Mrs. McPherson.

After noting my breath he said, "That is all right. Now I can testify you are not drunk. You may be an impostor but you are not drunk."

Eventually they called in Editor McCafferty of the Douglas *Dispatch*. He took one look at me and said, "That's Mrs. McPherson. I know because I covered her meetings in Denver."

Meanwhile, I had been pleading that my family in Los Angeles be notified. When the news first reached mother, she was naturally skeptical. A nurse burst into my room, asking what I could say to prove who I was. Quickly I searched my mind, then repeated little things about my girlhood that no one but my immediate family would remember. I told the nurse to say that the scar on my finger was from a cut suffered when a little girl and that the man who cut me in that accident was named Pinkston. I mentioned my pet pigeon, Jennie, and the cat named Whitetail.

But there had been so many rumors, so many sensational reports that I knew nothing about—so many times word had come, "She is here." "She is there!"

"Can you manage to come to the telephone yourself?" the authorities asked.

"Could I?" If that telephone had been a mile away, even a mile of desert road, I would have gone to it. They took me in a wheelchair to another room where there was a phone. The man who was talking to mother was giving a description of me. He then turned and said, "Mrs. Kennedy wants you to tell her the birthmarks on your children."

"Roberta has a strawberry on her hand," I replied, "and Rolf has a raspberry on his back."

That convinced mother. I was given the telephone. I could scarcely hold the receiver or control my voice in that first eager greeting. And back over the miles of wires came the voices I had never expected to hear again. In that Douglas hospital, clinging to the telephone with the nurses smiling around me, I breathed this prayer of joy, "Thank God! Oh, thank God!"

Joy was unbounded at my end of the line, but at the other end, so they told me afterward, it overflowed all banks and leaped all barriers of restraint. In the Temple and Bible school the congregation and students gave a shout. Services and classes were forgotten on the instant. Leaping to their feet, people danced down the aisles. The most dignified and imperturbable faculty members were seen to jump three feet into the air. Through crowded doors the throngs swept down the stairs, scorning elevators. They dashed out into the streets. Commandeering anything to make a noise—Temple drums, pans from hardware stores, whistles and bells from drug stores, horns and whatnots from any place—they formed a big, ever-growing impromptu parade of celebration.

The festival of joyous noise attracted the entire district, and people came rushing out of homes and stores to join the fete. "Sister will soon be home!" erupted from many lips. But I was not home yet. By the time I would arrive in Los Angeles, storm signals would be threatening the happiness of my homecoming.

It Really Happened

How marvelous that our God shrouds the future with an impenetrable cloud and drops a veil over all the tomorrows of our lives so that no one of us may know what a day or an hour will bring forth! Marvelous and infinitely kind—for if we knew all that the future held, we might not always have the stamina to march on. Had I been a seer with prophetic eye the night I stumbled through the desert, I might have placed some symbolic significance in the fact that the first sound I heard was the ferocious barking of dogs, the first substantial building I came to was a slaughterhouse, and the first person I met was a butcher! Had I known all that was to come, would I have had courage to go on?

In weaker moments, during the tribulations of those following hideous days, I felt that, had I known what was coming, I might have cried out that night in the desert, "Father in heaven, I can never drink this cup! Let it pass. Oh, let it pass from me!"

No sooner, however, would I stand again in the pulpit to preach, no sooner would I look out upon the sea of upturned faces of those who listened to the Word of God, than I would realize the unworthiness of such weakness. In that atmosphere of faith and love, I would be made to know that God, who will not suffer us to be tested above that which we are able to bear, would have given me the grace to say, "Thy will, oh my Father in heaven—thy will, not mine, be done." I should also have known that "truth crushed to the earth will rise again" and that right would vanquish wrong. I should also have known that on the tenth day of January, 1927, the telephone would ring, and that when I lifted the receiver to my ear I would hear the voice coming over the wire announcing that the case had been dismissed.

And now in Douglas, Arizona, at the Calumet and Arizona Hospital, I was in telephone contact with my mother at Angelus Temple in Los Angeles. Her joy—and mine—was inexpressible. She told me she would take the train down to Douglas and accompany me home. Then she sent word for me not to talk—not to tell my story. In the meantime, so many reporters had come, and these newsmen were clamoring for the story. I did not know any reason why I shouldn't tell it. I was willing to tell everybody and anybody that asked me.

The door to my hospital room burst open, and in trooped the reporters and photographers, armed with cameras and flashlight powder and bristling with questions. Scores of them representing papers all over the world—interviews, questions, snapping cameras, and booming flashlights until my head reeled. Several times I nearly fainted. What confusion! What a scene! The place was literally bombarded and attacked by industrious representatives of the press.

Quivering and weak though I was, I tried to answer all their questions. I frankly and truthfully told them everything they asked, even to the most minute detail. Squad by squad they came in turn to hear my account. Nothing would do but I must tell it all over again and again. Nurses protested that the newsmen were disturbing me, but still they came. As the door of my room would open, the resounding boom of a flashlight would blaze out, torturing me, in my extremely nervous state, like the searing burn of a red-hot iron. All day Wednesday, all Thursday morning the grilling continued.

But at last the greedy cameras seemed satisfied, and the last sensation-hungry reporter had hustled off to a telephone or to the telegraph office. Surely now I would be allowed to rest. But hark! With cutouts open and horns honking in the distance, louder and louder, closer and closer, descended a *new*, thundering herd from the depot. More reporters, more photographers, and the same wearying, monotonous question-mill started again, grinding out its tireless rounds of whys, wheres, whats, whens, whos, and hows. It seemed that this second onslaught would surely finish me. But somehow I survived, still answering as patiently and as courteously as I knew how.

At length the nurses succeeded in getting everyone out of the room and bade me rest, saying, "Your family will be here soon." My every nerve strained as I anticipated the reunion. A car drew up. There had been many cars, but instinctively I felt that this was *the* car. My arms opened. I tried to still the trembling of my lips. Mother and Roberta and Rolf were at the door. My darling family!

But crowding through the door with them came a tall, heavy-set police detective from Los Angeles and his smooth-faced, young son-in-law, an assistant in the district attorney's office. Disappointed at being deprived of a few minutes alone with mother and the children, I hastily dropped the curtain over the expression of emotion that one shows only to one's own.

My mother bent over the bed and whispered to me. Since that time I have been questioned by the authorities about what she said. Efforts were made to show some sinister implication in the conversation. But mother simply asked me the question any mother would ask her daughter under the circumstances—if I was all right. I told her I was.

The authorities never gave me a second alone with my family until they had extracted every bit of my story. The tall detective introduced himself as Captain Herman Cline and his son-in-law as Deputy District Attorney Joseph Ryan. These men told me that it was imperative that the pictures be posed all over again that they might appear with me. How I wished that they had not intruded at that time, in those first moments of reunion. I wanted to tell my family of my love and happiness at seeing them again. I wanted to be alone with them for a while after fleeing what might have been the jaws of death. But as the children rushed into my arms, each of the two men pulled up a chair and sat down, one on either side of the bed. I wondered vaguely at their lack of courtesy and understanding, but there they sat, joined a few minutes later by another stranger, a stenographer brought in at the request of the two men. My family was pushed aside, and the question-mill began all over again. For what seemed to me to be hours on hours they questioned me regarding each minute detail of my experience.

I gave them my story simply and truthfully. They pressed me to describe my kidnappers. Steve, I told them, appeared to be about forty years of age, about five feet nine or ten inches tall, weighing around two hundred pounds. His eyes were brown, and his complexion light.

"Was he getting gray?" my inquisitors asked.

"I did not notice that he was."

"Did you notice anything peculiar at all about his teeth?"

"No."

"Had he any marks or scars on his face?"

"No, I noticed no peculiarities about his features, although he had some lines in his face. And when he would be talking, he would draw his brows together."

"Were his eyebrows heavy or light?"

"Not bushy, but rather heavy."

"How about his dress?"

"He usually wore a brown suit. I think I saw him once in a gray suit. The hat he wore was a soft fedora."

The questioning changed to the second man—the one who drove the car in which I was abducted. "Do you think he was an American?" the officer asked.

"I assume so. I did not hear him talk much, but I didn't notice anything strange in his accent when he did talk."

"How old a man was he?"

"I should judge he was between thirty-five and forty."

"His height?"

"About six feet."

"What do you think he would weigh? Was he heavily built?"

"He had a flat chest. He was rather bony. It is hard to guess his weight—say about one hundred sixty pounds." To further questions I answered that he was dark and his beard was noticeable even when he was shaven. It would show black. He had lines around the corner of his mouth and an upper gold tooth.

"How near the front of his mouth?" they asked.

"Quite near the front. I am not exactly positive, but I think it was on the left side."

"What kind of clothing did he wear?"

"He was dressed mostly in black clothes, I think."

"Do you remember anything about his hat?"

"I do not remember a hat."

"Now this woman called Rose, do you think she was an American woman?"

"I think so."

"How tall was she?"

"A little taller than myself."

"How tall are you?"

"Five feet, five inches," I answered at the time. Later I was measured at five feet three and one-half inches.

"You think she was taller than you?"

"Yes, she was bigger than I—an inch and a half or two inches taller." I estimated her weight at one hundred eighty-five pounds. "She had plump arms and was rather heavy set and full chested."

"Was she light or dark?"

"Her hair was black, her eyes were dark brown, her face was rather olive but not dark."

"Did she wear long hair?"

"No, bobbed hair. A bushy bob."

"Was her hair straight or kind of kinky?"

"It was not straight. It was betwixt and between, and it would come out forward on her cheeks and was a little longer in the back."

"Did she or any of these people talk with a foreign accent at all?"

"No, not that I noticed."

"Did she have any marks or peculiarities at all?"

"Her lips were rather full, and I think her nose was a little wide. She did not have long eyelashes, but there were no blemishes noticeable."

"How did she dress?"

"She had a black dress on when she went out. Her hat was grayish with a green crown. I think it was a kind of a tweed mixture."

"Would you judge that the three of them were partners? Did they all seem like people that took each other on equal terms?"

"I would say that Steve was the leader and that this woman was a close second."

I felt that I had given Captain Cline and Mr. Ryan a complete description of my kidnappers. Certainly I answered their every question. Imagine my surprise when from time to time afterward one of the reasons advanced for doubting my story was that I had not been able to describe my abductors! Yet the newspapers had carried the questions and answers of the entire interview almost word for word! I say "almost" word for word because there were some slight errors which twisted the meaning. The officials from Los Angeles told me the stenographic report of the interview would be brought to me to read and sign, but I never saw the story to proofread it or sign it. The first I saw of it was when I read it in the press.

I left the hospital as soon as I was able and went with my family to the Gadsden Hotel to rest and regain a little of my strength.

The authorities asked me if I felt able to accompany them into the desert on a search for the shack. "I don't even know which direction it was," I answered. "I only know I came in by the road by that big mountain." However, I agreed to go, though I knew nothing about tracking. Where my footprints branched from the road there was hard shale. The footprints could no longer be followed. However, the officers told me before I left with them that trackers had found my footprints some thirteen miles away— that the trail led toward a certain ranch which they mentioned by name. "The shack must be in that section of the country," trackers assumed.

Because skepticism had already surfaced over the possibility that I could make the trek through the desert without water, I offered to go without water the day we were searching for the shack, even though that Friday was warmer than the Tuesday of my escape. Indeed, I said that I would be perfectly willing, if my word was doubted about water or about the condition of my clothing, to prove that my trek was possible by walking the same distance without water in the same desert. But a newspaperman riding in the car as we drove on the desert said, "No, Mrs. McPherson, don't be foolish. Here is a drink of water," and he held it up to me. I wondered why no one in authority seemed to want to let me walk into Agua Prieta again from the distant places where my footprints had been found. I repeated the same offer to the grand jury some weeks later, but there was no apparent interest in allowing me to confirm my desert trek. However, the hubbub continued in attacks on my story on these very issues of water and clothing.

As the posse returned through Agua Prieta to cross the line to Douglas, the presidente of the little Mexican village indicated his desire to speak to me. He said, through an interpreter, that he wished to talk with me privately. Leading the way into a cafe, the official went into a booth, asking an American interpreter to follow. The presidente glanced around furtively and started to talk. I asked why we had to talk alone. "There is nothing to be discussed that cannot be said in the presence of the police officers." But this official was quite insistent that what he had to say was for my ears alone. And no wonder! For what he said placed him in the vanguard of that column of opportunists who were to come saying whatever anybody wanted them to say for money.

"Mrs. McPherson, I have been offered five thousand dollars by some people to give a written statement that I do not believe your story of kidnapping and desert experience to be true. Now I need the money, but I have no particular desire to hurt you. If you could see your way clear to—oh, probably pay me as much as I have been offered, I am sure I would find it convenient to give a statement just the opposite to what they want—that is, that your story is true and that I am convinced of it."

A blackmailer! Here was a man coolly making a proposition that if he were not paid so many American dollars he would give a written statement to the effect that my experience had never taken place! Face to face for the first time (but not the last time by any means) with an unscrupulous person who wanted to exact a toll to keep from lying, I walked out of the cafe, hardly dignifying the swarthy plotter with an answer. This was the beginning of a series of offers from corrupt people who desired to take from me and my church everything of material value we possessed. My position seemed to be a signal for countless charlatans to gather in the hope of extorting material gain.

The presidente shortly thereafter denounced my story and of course ridiculed the idea that he had attempted to blackmail me. However, the interpreter during the interview furnished me with an affadavit corroborating that the official had solicited a bribe. Unfortunately, the interpreter had been convicted of crimes some ten years before, and the authorities refused to put credence in his affadavit.

When I returned to Douglas from the desert that Friday afternoon, I was appalled by a report of the rumors which were flying in doubt of my story. "My heart and soul are tied up in Angelus Temple," I told Captain Cline and Mr. Ryan and the reporters.

"There is nothing in the world that I wouldn't do to stop these untrue and soul-searing rumors. Before the God in whom I have every faith and utter belief, every word I have uttered about my kidnapping and escape is true. If I have been unable to answer any question propounded by a score of newspapermen, detectives, attorneys, friends, even my own family, I have told them I do not know or I don't remember. My story is true. I have permitted every reporter to ask any question, and when I knew the answer, I gave it." My ordeal was one which only a person who has actually passed through it could visualize. It was not the kind of escapade a person would concoct in his imagination. The Douglas, Arizona, chief of police, Percy Bowden, called attention that no one could possibly create such a startling sequence of events in his mind. If I had been inventing a story, it would have been a quite different one than the account I gave. I gave that account because it was true, and my story was never shaken or changed in any material point, as commentators would grudgingly admit after the long months of trial that followed.

The hour came to leave Douglas. We would return to Los Angeles on the Southern Pacific's Golden State Limited, leaving Friday evening about 9:15. A crowd of people gathered at the train, and I addressed them in what must have been a somewhat weak voice. How earnestly I wanted to express to all those wonderful Arizonans my gratitude for their courtesy, love, and care. In weeks to come, they would maintain their faith in my integrity and produce emphatic evidence corroborating the story of my desert trek.

The railroad officials had told me that a special car had been provided for my party, but when I got into the car, I found that the party consisted of my family plus a host of newspapermen and photographers who almost crowded us out. The newsmen were still asking questions and demanding interviews. I tried to be polite to everybody, but I was so tired—so utterly, unspeakably weary and weak. The white face and the black-circled eyes that looked back at me from my mirror caused a second glance to be sure that it was really I.

The same men who had sat at each side of my bed in the Douglas hospital and who would be ever in the background of the picture for weeks to come were also on the train. They would question me for awhile, go to the reporters who had the telegraph blanks in their hands, come back and talk to me, then again report to the newspapermen, to whom they were most obliging and anxious to help get stories.

This pair—Captain Cline and Deputy District Attorney Ryan—told me after we left Douglas that there were a couple of men up the line in Tucson who declared they had seen me there walking down the street alone a short time previously. Conveniently our train would pass through this town some time after midnight. I might retire now for a little while, they told me, "but please be ready to meet the two men."

"How absurd!" I exclaimed. "I am so tired! I want to do everything to assist the officials, but this is so unreasonable and so uncalled for. I was not in that town and I am so tired."

But the officials said it would be to my best interest to be up and dressed lest one of the reporters write up a story inferring that I feared to meet the men. My eyes opened wide at the threat which the suggestion seemed to contain. Despite my weariness, I felt I must meet these two men and settle this thing at once.

When I finally had a few minutes alone with my mother in our Pullman section, she said, "My dear, I have been with the reporters, and they are not going to believe your story."

"Why?"

"They just are not going to believe it," she said. "You are in for trouble. Why do you talk so much?"

"Why, mother, they asked me what happened, and I told them."

She seemed quite worried and thought we should refuse to talk about the ordeal. But I couldn't see why, even though I had been astonished by fantastic rumors concerning my whereabouts. One was that a Dr. Weeks claimed I had been at his place and that he had performed some operation on me, after which some people had driven me out into the desert. The nature of the alleged operation was impossible in my case, but the rumor that I underwent such surgery would simmer for some time before its absurdity was proven by medical records.

At any rate, before I had left Douglas, Dr. Weeks's secretary came and said she knew she could identify me as the woman he had treated. Percy Bowden, the police chief, asked me if I would be willing to meet this woman.

"I certainly would," I agreed.

Dr. Weeks's secretary was honest. She looked at me and said, " I have never seen this woman before."

Meanwhile, a Douglas pastor called on Dr. Weeks to track the rumor to its source. Dr. Weeks denied he said he saw me, adding, "All I saw was a car containing two women and a man driver about midnight on June 22, and I saw many cars that night. It is absolutely unfair to Mrs. McPherson or to me for the newspapers to make anything out of my story. I did not treat any woman as the papers say, and it is dirty for the papers to make such a statement." But the innuendo would persist.

Probably this is the best place to mention another rumor which attempted to establish that I was deposited in Mexico a short distance east of Agua Prieta by an automobile which drove out from that town, turned around at a fork in the road, and returned to the Mexican village. Officers Murchison and Patterson of the Douglas police department and desert tracker C. E. Cross found the tracks of an automobile which had indeed followed that route, but they could make no connection with those automobile tracks and my footprints, as Mr. Cross later testified emphatically under oath. I was not in that car. But innuendoes continued to connect me with it.

Would the rumors never cease? What would the witnesses say at midnight? Should I refuse to face them? Should I keep silent hereafter as mother advised?

When the train stopped in Tucson, two men climbed on board. The officers had led me to the middle of the car and had me sit where the light was strongest. The reporters crowded around me, sensing some dramatic story. The two witnesses approached. Mr. Ryan asked them, "Can you pick out the woman here whom you saw in Tucson?"

There was only one other woman in that railroad car besides my mother and daughter. She was a newspaper writer. I arose and said, "I am Mrs. McPherson." The first man took one look at me and then stated, "I am mistaken. I have never seen this lady before. I am sorry to have disturbed you, madam."

The second man gave me a brief glance, then blurted, "Sure! I have seen her before. She looks like the woman I saw walking on the street."

That was the signal for pads of paper to flash into sight, pencils to start careening madly over yellow telegraph blanks, carrying stories to the world. Some reporters did not even stop for the end of the conversation but dashed for the door of the car to file their wires.

I sat back stunned, waiting for Captain Cline and Mr. Ryan to cross-examine my identifier, but they did not make any effort. I had to do my own questioning.

Of course, that "identification" triggered a newspaper story. Here was a man who had an indistinct, fleeting glimpse of some woman with a hat low over her face and had identified her as a woman he had never seen before. This was my first experience with "identifications," many of which were to follow, some even more absurd than this. Against the unreasonable injustice of all of them I was just as defenseless and helpless as I was against this particular one. And, of course, all were flung to the world in newspaper headlines.

I went back to bed, but further sleep that night was out of the question. By the time the typewriters had settled down and the hubbub of voices was stilled, daylight was streaming through the windows, and hands were again knocking at my door. There were people to be spoken to from the train platform. In fact, throngs had congregated all along the line. Captain Cline would summon me at almost every station. "Come out and see the people." He wanted me to introduce him each time we stopped, and after he took a bow, he would whisper, "Introduce Mr. Ryan." I introduced them as two wonderful gentlemen who had come all the way to escort me home, and the people would cheer them heartily. I was still struggling against the suspicion that they were for some reason trying to undermine my story. From time to time in the days to come the press would quote them as stating their belief in my story, but shortly they would change their tunes. In fact, Mr. Ryan would eventually call me a fake and hypocrite in open court and state that he knew when he first set eyes on me in the hospital in Douglas that I was not telling the truth about my ordeal! If this was in fact his initial attitude, I wonder why he maintained any pretense of believing and investigating my account. And why did Mr. Cline repeatedly throughout the train trip to Los Angeles comment upon the absurdity of the idea that I had voluntarily disappeared? Was it all a façade? I was still giving them the benefit of the doubt as we sped over the rails toward Los Angeles.

When others at the depot saw merely the sea of faces upturned and what appeared to be acres of white uniforms, I, through a mist of tears, caught the spirit of loving friends, thousands of whom had been converted in our meetings, throngs with whom

I had prayed in hours of sickness and distress. The Sunday school children whom I had watched grow up from tiny tots; the members to most of whom I had administered the ordinance of baptism and communion. The branch churches from the country round about. The Silver band playing joyously.

Other people saw a beautiful car and a chair decorated with flowers; but I saw only the loving fingers that had fastened the blossoms there. The idea of my church officers carrying me over the heads of the crowd and lifting me into the car—me, who had carried *them* around, figuratively speaking, for so long!

Imagine, if you can, the joy of that reunion between pastor and people, the reuniting of the little undershepherd and the flock. With brimming eyes I made my way down to the Temple altars and fell upon my knees behind the pulpit where a thousand times I had stood and preached the gospel of Jesus Christ.

Oh, the peace, the comfort, the rest ever to be found in the sanctuary of the Most High! How often was I to find peace and comfort in that same sanctuary during the days of coming storm; days when the devil would strike his second blow and hurl across our sunny seas the darksome cloud of his evil fury; days when he would lash the waves of public opinion into a confused tempest of foam-flecked mad billows, with his whip of innuendo, diabolic plot, and intrigue, and start what he hoped would be a cataclysm that would sink us beneath the waves of oblivion.

As I knelt in prayer, I could hear the thousands of people pouring down the carpeted aisles, the soft, humming undercurrent of excitement subdued by a deep, reverent spirit of praise and worship which permeated the atmosphere. The great circular rows of shining mahogany seats, tier upon tier, were filling like magic. Fifty-three hundred people were seated there in a trice, and still they came, standing on the stairs, by the walls, in the aisles, fire rules seemingly forgotten for the moment.

The great stained-glass windows high in the Temple walls depicting scenes from the life of Christ shone with soft afternoon radiance. The slanting rays from the upper amber windows in the highest balcony were golden streams of liquid sunshine, falling athwart abalone-tinted walls of blue, gold, and rose. They touched the great mural painting of the Second Coming of our Lord with ten thousand of his hosts which spans the bronzed grill of the mighty organ, awakening each figure to life and causing the golden halo around the Master's head to shine as the sun, illuminating the cornice and tinging the clouds in the lofty dome which seemed to have caught and imprisoned forever the color of a California sky.

Esther Fricke, the organist, was in her place at the organ, her skilled fingers caressing the keys, rousing the chiming bells into rhapsodies and paeans of thanksgiving.

My heart swelled within me when I thought of all God's goodness, his love, his mercy, of how he had spared me to preach the gospel. Of the thousands who had been brought to his feet through the preaching of his Word. Of the strongholds of Satan laid low, of the broken lives that had been mended, and of the fallen that had been lifted from the miry clay and the sinking bogs of unbelief to the sunlit tablelands of his great salvation.

When I thought of the sick who had laid down their crutches, and the stretcher which had been borne out empty, blind eyes that had been made to see, deaf ears that had been made to hear, and of the halt and the lame that had been made whole in this place, when I thought of the hundreds of young students who had surrendered their lives to Christ and were now in training in this theological school that they too might go forth to kindle a glow of sacred love in myriad other lives, then my heart over-flowed with joy and thanksgiving.

Then, when I thought of his great mercy in sparing my life and bringing me safely home, I covered my face with my hands and bowed there at the altar, overcome with gratitude. Kneeling there, I observed that multitudes of others, like myself, had been involuntarily drawn to the sanctuary. In fact, since early morning the people had been gathering in the streets and pouring into the Temple to offer prayer and praise. Since shortly after dawn there had been hosts of them there who would laugh a while, pray a while, sing a while, and cry a while from sheer joy. But now every one seemed to have settled down into the spirit of real communion with the Lord.

Bowing my head, I thanked God for these wonderful people, this glorious Temple, thanked him for the steps that had led to its erection.

The voice of the organ beat and throbbed—a living thing that filled the Temple and stirred the soul with hope and heavenly exaltation. Of the storm of trouble and persecution which was to fall upon the heads of the worshipers, sweeping them incessantly with its fierce fury for months to come, there was no indication discernible here.

Beneath the sweet treble notes of the organ and the accompanying soft intonation of the deeper bass there was a muffled and undertoned mumble that was even now growing into a rumble and would soon burst into a roar of gathering thunder from the subterranean caverns beneath our feet. But we knew it not.

When the volume of the organ sank into a tremolo of deep feeling during the playing of the last verse, my happiness at being with my people was so great that no quiver of foreboding penetrated my conscious thought. I did not know that even then the enemy was setting up his heavy artillery, preparing his smoke screen through which he would fire away at the church. I did not know that even then the jaws of a great steel-like trap were being baited and set in readiness to snap.

Snap! Bang! Flash! Boom! Clouds of smoke rolling heavenward!

Startled eyes and heads of worshipers lifted and turned in wonder toward the line of attack. The sacred precincts of the church had been invaded. Strange faces and forms were moving in our midst.

There are strangers—and strangers. We were accustomed to new people coming constantly from the ends of the earth to Los Angeles and, of course, to Angelus Temple. But these were strange strangers. Their eyes looked, not with the hunger and thirst of people coming to the house of God solace bent, but with a curious, roving restlessness, with narrowing, unsmiling inquiry. Theirs were the eyes of a hound on the scent or a dog on the trail.

From that time, for months to come, the firing continued with scarcely an intermission. The stories which the press flashed around the world at first concerned my appearance in Mexico and Douglas, Arizona, and contained the account of my kidnapping; but from this point on they grew more and more sensational to satiate the appetite of sensation-loving America. The writers had been sent out for a good story, and a story they must fetch. My unfortunate experience was too good and too sensational, from their point of view, to let die immediately. A great newspaper seller. It must be kept alive.

The first story having been read and digested and repeated for several days, it was desirable to add to it a little new spice and thrill. What could be more spicy or more thrilling for a sated, blasé, and bored press, fed up with the usual choice bits of gossip, sensation, and scandal, than a suggestion, than an inference, and than at last all but a charge that an evangelist pastor of a great Temple and founder of a Bible school, had been there, or yonder, with this one, that one, or the other one during the time that she had been held captive?

I do not believe the newspapers meant to be malicious. But so insistently, like pattering rain upon a tin roof, did these impish, absurd stories fall that they became a torrent, and the fact that practically each one was disproved the next morning seemed to make no difference. It was news, and there was no apology for printing the first story, which had been exploded almost as soon as sent hurtling over the lines. The second and third followed and were the sensation of their brief day.

Though unbelievable and wildly inconsistent, so persistent were these stories—any kind of a story, so long as it fanned public interest by casting the light of aspersion upon my veracity—that some people who did not know me or know my life could not be blamed for believing this absurd, paper-selling propaganda. Yet, unspeakably hurt as I was, I had a peculiarly detached feeling. It seemed to me that they were speaking of someone else entirely. But I am getting ahead of my story.

As soon as we arrived home in Los Angeles, Captain Cline told me he wanted me to go to the beach and show him how the crime took place and the exact spot where it occurred. He wanted me to go that very day, but I was too weary. A day or two later he and Mr. Ryan brought a big car and a Los Angeles *Times* reporter to the parsonage (I don't think I saw the pair of them thereafter very often without a *Times* reporter). I joined the two officers, Mrs. Ryan, and the driver in the automobile. We started for the beach. On the way they asked me many questions from all angles, and I answered. At Ocean Park I showed them exactly where the tent was on the beach, told them how and where I swam out and back, and where the people met me. I took them with me across the sand, showed them where the woman left us to hurry ahead and where the man and I had walked on behind. I showed them where—to the best of my memory—the car was parked.

"It is impossible that the car was parked there," the officers told me. "You can see it is a no-parking zone." As if a no-parking sign would deter kidnappers!

I admitted the possibility that I might be mistaken, that the car may have been parked on the other side of the speedway, but I still believe I was right about the first location. And a short time later a witness came forward who claimed he had noticed a car parked there about the time I was kidnapped.

On the way home Captain Cline advised me to go to a doctor and have a thorough examination to substantiate my story. Later I did this. The foul rumor was persisting that I had disappeared to have an abortion. The medical examination and the records of my surgery on the east coast after the birth of my son adequately exploded that myth. But it did not altogether squelch the circulation of that rumor.

Captain Cline came constantly to our house. One day he appeared with another officer who was carrying a book with pictures of criminals in it. They asked me to peruse the volume and see if I recognized any of the photos as resembling my kidnappers. Photographers were on hand to take my picture looking through the book with the officers.

One day Captain Cline told me he thought it was time for me to have an attorney.

"What for?" I asked.

He mentioned doubts about my story and thunderings about a possible grand jury investigation. "If you get this certain attorney, he will keep you out of trouble," Captain Cline said. "It is Paul Skenk. It may cost you fifty thousand dollars, but it is the thing to do."

I really did not see any need to hire an attorney and did not contact him. That night, however, a telephone call came. "I was asked by Mr. C. to call," the voice said. "This is P. S. speaking. I want to talk to you about the case."

I rejected the overture, and from that time on, Captain Cline's outward attitude changed. I have an idea that if I had retained this attorney, there would have been no grand jury investigation, or it would have proceeded altogether differently.

One matter which kept controversy simmering was the "avengers" letter demanding a half-million dollars ransom for my release. This was a typewritten document in contrast to the handwritten "revengers" ransom note which reached the Temple shortly after my abduction and later disappeared from the Los Angeles Police Department's locked files. Mother did not open this second letter until Tuesday, June 18—the day of my escape. That morning, Miss Schaffer handed her the envelope. Apparently it had reached the Temple on the previous Saturday by special delivery. When mother opened the envelope, she found a lock of hair wrapped in two sheets of typewritten paper. The letter read, in part:

> We have your Aimee in our power. Here's a lock of her hair to prove it. If this isn't enough for you, we'll send along that finger of hers with the scar on it. That ought to convince you. We are going to send a second letter, which you will get Friday, with directions as to how you are to deliver to us $500,000 in currency. We mean business, and we know what we are doing. No use your trying to put a lot of dicks on our trail. Get wise and do as we say.

The letter also stated that many rumors of my being seen in various cities had been started by the kidnappers for the purpose of keeping hope alive in the hearts of Angelus Temple followers so that they would be in a more receptive mood for ransom offers. Upon my return, I learned that on one single day during my captivity I was reported to have been seen in sixteen different widely separated localities! The letter contained my answers to some of the questions mother had sent to Attorney McKinley and warned that the people who held me prisoner had "power to ruin Angelus Temple and lower Aimee's name."

Mother showed Roberta the lock of hair. My daughter believed it came from my head. Mother was more cautious, as she later explained. "I had been fooled too many times by people who claimed they had seen my daughter or had her captive, so I fought hard not to believe this lock was Aimee's, much as I wanted to believe. When I heard her voice on the telephone from Douglas the next day, and when she told me that they had cut her hair, I then knew that my first instincts were right."

This letter had been mailed on June 18 on a train somewhere between El Paso and Tucson. Apparently the kidnappers intended it to be read before the memorial service for me at the Temple on Sunday (for the church had given up hope that my body would be found). They probably believed that a fund-raising effort would be launched to secure the ransom. However, the delay of the letter in reaching mother hindered that procedure.

But the press and authorities pounced on that delay, hinting that mother had actually seen the ransom note but suppressed it until after the memorial service in order to raise a memorial fund. They also raised a hue and cry over the fact that the special delivery stamp had disappeared from the envelope. Mother insists that no such stamp was on the letter when it was handed to her. She stated, "There were two two-cent stamps on it. I had been disturbed with many letters containing all manner of messages—some purporting to have word from my daughter in the spirit world, others with information she was here, there, and everywhere. I noticed with distress the answers to the questions but figured they were questions anyone could have answered had they lived in our Canadian neighborhood." With reference to the memorial fund innuendo, mother issued formal denial that anything of the kind had been instituted. A carry-on fund had raised about $4,700 in cash and $29,500 in pledges, but this money was all for the finishing expenses of the Bible school building and had been subscribed almost entirely by the different departments of Angelus Temple. "Absolutely no money was asked for a monument," she emphasized.

What had happened to the special delivery stamp on the avengers ransom envelope? Mother surmised that if such a stamp was still affixed when the letter was delivered, someone in the Temple office handling mail might have removed it. Otherwise, the matter was as much a mystery to us as to the authorities, who launched an investigation.

I have often thought if nearly as much effort had been exerted to track down my kidnappers as was wasted on futile investigations of trivialities and on attempts to break down my story, the case could have been quickly solved. And mother was especially critical concerning the disappearance of the first ransom note, stating that "many crimes have been solved through less evidence than that one handwritten letter." Had it been available for investigation, she suggested, the kidnappers might have been traced. But when it was needed, it had vanished from the police department's locked secret files.

The grand jury subpoenaed a parade of witnesses. It became quickly evident that the district attorney and his staff were more interested in discrediting my story than in obtaining indictments of the kidnappers. Mother felt we should refuse to appear at the sessions, but I agreed with our dear friend, Superior Judge Carlos Hardy, that we should give our testimony.

On July 8 I appeared before the grand jury. About three months later, when my attorney, W. K. Gilbert, heard the transcript of my interrogation read in municipal court during the subsequent preliminary hearing, he exploded with disgust, telling the court, "I have been here at the bar twenty five years, and I have heard enough today to turn everybody's hair gray."

District Attorney Asa Keyes and Deputy Ryan questioned me concerning every aspect of my kidnapping, captivity, escape, and desert trek. Because so many questions reflected doubt that I could have made the journey without water, without soiling clothes and shoes more than they were, and without worse physical affliction, I repeated an offer I had made in the past. I told the grand jury, "I would be perfectly willing, if my word is doubted upon water or upon the condition of my clothing, to go and walk the same number of miles without water and in the same clothes to prove to the gentlemen that condition of my lips and tongue." I added, "I do not consider that a great length of time to go without water."

In response to questioning, I repeated my description of the kidnappers and mentioned a matter I had reported previously to the authorities after my escape. I had noticed two strangers standing out in front of the parsonage for several days before I was kidnapped. Almost every time I came in or went out, they were there, usually under a tree. I remarked about the men to at least a half dozen people, wondering who they were. Whether there was any connection between them and my abduction I do not know, but their vigil strikes me now as somewhat suspicious.

The authorities questioned me closely concerning several matters which—to me, at least—seemed to have no bearing on the case at hand, and they reflected credence of despicable rumors which were easy to refute. Their interrogation indicates the hostile spirit of the inquiry.

Mr. Keyes addressed me, "It has been stated to me on several occasions that, to use the expression we used to use, that you were run out of Denver at one time. Is there anything to that?"

"Oh, no!" I exclaimed. "The mayor was on the platform at almost every service when I was last in Denver, and I might refer you to the mayor and to the business firms there and to Judge

Ben Lindsey, who is nationally known. And when I left, they gathered washbaskets of roses and poured them in the room until I was ankle deep in roses."

Mr. Keyes then repeated a similar rumor—that I had been run out of some town in northern California, specifying, "I have forgotten whether it was Oakland or some other place."

"It is perfectly untrue," I replied.

"Fresno?" the district attorney pressed.

"No, I would bring, gladly, if such were permissible, pictures of all those cities and of our affairs."

For a while attention was focused on my hair. Mr. Keyes said, "I want to ask you a rather personal question. Is that hair that you have in sight all yours?"

"Yes."

"You don't wear a switch?" he asked, betraying skepticism.

"No."

The appearance of my hair would remain a subject of controversy well into the preliminary hearing months later, when, finally, at the suggestion of my attorney I put an end to doubt that it was all mine by taking it down and putting it up again in a matter of minutes. But what my hair had to do with the kidnapping, I fail to understand.

The rumor that "trouble" at the Temple prompted me to disappear was also explored by Mr. Ryan's questioning. He inquired whether at any time prior to the kidnapping I had any trouble with Miss Schaffer, my secretary. Of course, the answer was no.

"Did you ever state to Miss Schaffer that you were going to discharge her?" he pressed.

"No," I answered.

"And did she state back to you in reply that you didn't dare discharge her? That the information and knowledge that she had would blow up the Temple, if she should—"

The insinuation was so ridiculous that I interrupted, "Never! Miss Schaffer is like one of the family."

"Did you have any trouble with the ushers out there?" he continued, naming three in particular.

"I had a little misunderstanding with some of the ushers, yes," I replied. "Nothing of a serious nature—nothing more than comes up with any pastor."

"Let me ask you this question: Do you know of your own

knowledge whether Mrs. Kennedy struck one of the ushers during the discussion?" Mr. Keyes proceeded.

"I never heard of such a thing," I answered.

At one point in this line of questioning I was asked whether I thought these disgruntled ushers might have planned to perpetrate anything sinister. Of course, the idea was ridiculous. I added that we had had fewer misunderstandings in Angelus Temple than in any church I had ever been in.

The district attorney introduced the name of Kenneth G. Ormiston into the investigation. Because this name had been linked with mine before and would be again, although altogether without justification, I reproduce here in length the questions by Mr. Keyes and my answers as appearing in the transcript.

Question: You know a Mr. Ormiston, do you not, Mrs. McPherson?

Answer: I do.

Q. Who is he?

A. He is a man who used to operate our radio station KFSG.

Q. How long did he work there?

A. Practically ever since the radio was installed. That would be about two years and a half, I should say—two years.

Q. When did you last see him?

A. I last saw him one evening when he came to the Temple after my return from Europe. He was there one Sunday evening. I had finished preaching and saw him standing talking to Mr. Ballard at the organ, and just saluted him like that (indicating), said, "How do you do?" and passed on.

Q. Did you also know his wife?

A. I first became acquainted—can I tell you how I first met her? I first met Mrs. Ormiston under peculiar circumstances. Mr. Ormiston had disappeared from our radio department, leaving us with no operator. I came to go on the air, broadcasting my morning prayer service for the hospitals, and found that the radio was dead. So, of course, we began to inquire where Mr. Ormiston was and got Mr. Hawkins, who is a friend of his, and recommended he go and hunt him up. And he asked at home, so his wife came down telling us that they had had some quarrels, that they had quarreled frequently, and that he had left home, and she was going back to Australia and brought a letter from Mr. Ormiston explaining their difficulties. Soon after that, Mr. Ormiston returned looking very bedraggled and like he had been through a siege of sickness or something. We brought both of them into our house and she was quite determined to leave him but we had prayer with them, told them the serious step they were taking, and to by all means hold the home together. Finally they kissed and made up. That was how I first met Mrs. Ormiston.

Q. Well, did she ever intimate to you, Mrs. McPherson, that the reason she was having domestic difficulties was that she was claiming—whether true or false—that Mr. Ormiston was too friendly with you?

A. Oh, not at all. I had hardly spoken to Mr. Ormiston, hardly knew him at the time.

Q. Well, let's put it at a subsequent date, then?

A. Yes. At the end—one evening I wrote a letter to Mr. and Mrs. Ormiston stating how very careful I always had to live at the Temple, never having even walked up the rampart with anyone except a couple of ladies. My life is lived like an open glass house, and Mrs. Ormiston had invited me out to their house for dinner. Something I very rarely do is to go to any of the parishioners, but I had gone to this one little dinner which she had asked for so long. And after dinner, Mr. and Mrs. Ormiston and myself, at their suggestion, had gone over to see a new radio station which Mr. Ormiston had installed for Warner Brothers, and went on later for a dish of ice cream somewhere near there, and someone had seen me. I cannot move anywhere without someone recognizing me, and this had been commented upon, and I heard three different things. "Well," someone said, "Sister McPherson has Mr. Ormiston on the platform with her," and I had also heard Mr. Nichol's name—he is the man who plays the cornet—my mother asked him to lead the singing quite a little bit—and someone says, "I saw Mrs. McPherson and a man and girl out at this place," and I was worried about it because I have prided myself perhaps as every woman does on my name or character and defied anyone to put their finger on anything in my life that would be the least shadow of doubt—pardon me on that—so I wrote this letter, and explained how careful I must be. I know that then Mrs. Ormiston, instead of laughing at it as I would have, acted in a peculiar manner, and she said, "Well, you know my husband is kind of flighty"—that was her term. She said, "He smiled at a girl who put cream in his coffee the other night." She thought he was a little that way, but I just smiled it off and thought nothing more of the matter until later something was said. But I understand as to my being mentioned in any connection by Mrs. Ormiston, she denies that and says that must be a mistake, and I have that on very, very good authority. And we have a letter very recently from Mrs. Ormiston, a very friendly letter thanking me for all my interest and kindness.

In response to further questioning, I forthrightly denied every insinuation that I had seen Mr. Ormiston at any time in the hotels where I resorted for rest and study in the time before I left on my first vacation. There never was any relationship between me and Mr. Ormiston other than that of an employer and employee. This is the absolute truth. But how do you silence slanderous scandal once it is broadcast?

The last questions asked me by the district attorney pertained to reports that I planned to make a world tour. My mother was in agony when this doubt of me arose, and she said, "Darling, I think you will have to make a world tour." Mr. Keyes suggested —these are the exact words as they appear in the grand jury transcript—"Well, one of the reasons that you might have for pulling a stunt like this is for the purpose of getting worldwide advertising or publicity for the sake of helping you in your work." His bias clearly was showing.

To this idea, I replied, "That would not be necessary." I told how the Royal Albert Hall in London was packed three times a day to the doors when I was there. "People came from Sweden and Denmark," I pointed out. "And I have a most lovely invitation to come back. "

Near the end of my testimony Mr. Keyes recalled a request I had made earlier. "You say you want to make a statement to the jury?"

"Oh, may I?" I responded. "I have tried to confine myself just to the questions, but I have had it on my heart all day that I would like to speak a word. I didn't know whether I would have the privilege." I looked at the faces of the grand jury members, then commenced, "I realize that this story may sound strange to many of you—that it may be difficult for some of you to believe. It is difficult for me to believe sometimes. Sometimes it seems that it must be just a dream. I would to God that it were—that I could wake up and pinch myself and know that it was not true. I want to say that if character counts a little and if a person's past life counts a little, that I want you to look back. Our family has been a family of ministers on both sides. My mother gave me to God before I was born. My earliest training has been in Bible and religious work. As a little child, I lined the chairs up and preached to them as early as five years of age, and gave my testimony. I was converted at seventeen, married an evangelist, preached the gospel in my humble way at home, and then sailed for China, never expecting to come back to this land but willing to give my life for Jesus. They buried my precious husband there. I came back with my little baby in my arms, born a month after her father died. I took up the Lord's work again as soon as I was able to go on. I have had no great denominations back of me but have been inspired only by my love of God, my love of the work, and of his precious Word. But I began very humbly.

"Now, until this crushing thing that none of us can explain why even God would permit, although we cannot question like that—it would be wrong to do that—before that came I was on the pinnacle of success as far as my work for God was concerned. But I have not always been there. I began preaching to farmers, ranchers, under the trees to farmers in their blue overalls sitting on the grass and using the piazza as a mourner's bench. From there, with the sixty dollars that came in the collection, I bought a little tent, a poor little tent very full of holes, and from that I saved my money and bought a bigger one, and that has been the history.

"I have never put my money in oil wells or ranches or even clothes or luxuries. My great thought has been always—and this can be absolutely proven—for the service of the Lord and my dear people. I am not saying this in any unkindness, but I would rather never have been born than to have caused this blow to God's Word and to his work. I had rather I had never been born or have seen the light of day than that the name of Jesus Christ, whose name I love, should be crucified and people would say, 'See what her mother did,' but the blow to my work is the greatest thing.

"The turn in my career came at the International Camp given at Philadelphia. I could bring to you, I believe, hundreds of thousands of letters and telegrams over the route from friends in different cities, and during all these years no one has ever said that they saw me out with a man, nor never has my name been linked in any way with anyone like that. I don't believe that I have told lies or cheated or done anything that people could put their finger on.

"I traveled for two years with a tent. I drove my own stakes, patched the tent, and tied the guy ropes almost like a man. And then came the times when we began to get the bigger buildings and theaters and buildings costing sometimes as much as a hundred dollars a day in buildings where I have preached to as many as sixteen thousand in a day.

"Then came the building of Angelus Temple. I came here to a neighborhood that had no special buildings in it, got a piece of land and hired horses and scrapers and bossed the men myself and went out to build the foundation myself with my little capital. I told people my dream to preach the gospel as God had given it to me, and they came to me to help me, not here, but from other cities, through the *Bridal Call,* my magazine. I have been here for years. I have visited the jails. We have workers in the penitentiary. We have appeared at almost every bedside we could reach in the county hospital, and at the county farm we journey each week to gather the old folks and preach at the shops and factories to men at noon. We have never turned anyone away but give free food and clothes. And my life, I feel, has been lived in a spotlight.

"Naturally, I have preached a gospel which made some enmity. I have gone unmercifully after the dope ring, gambling, liquor, tobacco, dancing, and made the statement I would rather see my children dead than in a public dance hall. I have, perhaps, laid myself open to enmity in those lines about evils in the schools, et cetera, but in everything I have tried to live as a lady and as a Christian. And I just want one more thought—it is so kind of you to grant me this opportunity. It does mean so much. I will feel happier for having said it. The thought is that no one should doubt my story. Perhaps you are skeptical; I don't blame anyone, because it does sound absurd, but it did happen, ladies and gentlemen.

"Suppose one should doubt it. A trained investigator, it would seem to me, would need but look for a month to refute the story, so would I get by? As one said who was here at this moment, they couldn't think of any other reason than that I might be insane. I would not work with one hand for seventeen years and just as I saw my dearest dreams coming true, sweep it over. And not only that, but attempt to heal little babies in Christ who were too weak to stand. Motive? If I were sick—someone said, 'Maybe she went away to rest'—but it was not that! I had just passed an examination for life insurance a while ago, and they said I passed 100 percent. Amnesia? It could not be that. I am willing to have my mind examined or any test that could be put on that. And as for falling in love, I am in love with the work I do.

"There might be a baser motive. I almost blush to mention it in the jury room, but some might think it. They say the waters of the mind are like the waters of the sea that cast up strange things and that I might be in trouble of some sort, and had to go away and come back. I would like to say, although I apologize for having to mention such a thing, that I had a thorough examination upon coming home, although that was not necessary, as the history of my case for twelve years back would show that such a thing would be absolutely out of the question.

"Other motives, I can think of none. Had I gone away willingly, I would not have come back. Publicity? I don't need that. The Sunday before this happened to me my Temple was filled three times. Monday night it was filled. I can think of no other motive. And I pray—I don't need to ask that you will give me your most earnest consideration and that you will pray about it on your knees, because it concerns the church and concerns Christ, and the eyes of the world are on a religious leader and upon this case, and people may come and say, 'I saw Mrs. McPherson here,' 'I saw her in a dance hall there,' 'I saw her in a saloon there.' Just take a look at me; look at my children and my family. Of course, that is one thing; I am powerless; my hands are tied. I don't fear the most rigid investigation of my story, for my story is true. The only thing I fear is—I don't say a frame-up, but mistaken identities, people who might be up here or there who might think so-and-so, but I don't think anything like that will be found to be true, and I would like to have you call me and ask me. And I do thank you for allowing me these few words."

To my dying day I must proclaim my story of the kidnapping and escape is true. It did happen. It really did happen just as I told it. But it would be months after the grand jury hearing in July before official attempts to break down my story collapsed.

A Modern Babel Collapses!

The grand jury hearing continued for several days after I appeared on July 8. My mother and my son testified, as did a number of our Temple workers. Mr. McKinley, the blind lawyer from Long Beach who claimed my abductors contacted him to act as a go-between, also was called as a witness. But the interrogators from the district attorney's office continued their efforts to discredit my story rather than to obtain from the grand jury an indictment of my kidnappers.

Witnesses were called or quoted who claimed they saw me here, there, and almost everywhere during the period of my actual captivity. Deputy District Attorney Joseph Ryan announced to the grand jury that Dennis Collins, a night mechanic at a garage in Salinas, California, had positively identified me as the woman who accompanied Kenneth Ormiston to that garage on May 29. Mr. Ryan claimed the mechanic identified me from photographs.

However, Mr. Collins in Salinas denied he made any identification. He told Judge J. A. Bardin and Monterey County Sheriff W. A. Oyer that the woman he saw with the man believed to be Ormiston was of dark complexion and that she had dark eyes. The mechanic signed statements on the back of two photographs of me—a front view and a profile—declaring, "The photograph of this woman does not resemble the woman I saw with Ormiston the latter part of May, 1926, at the Highway Garage in Salinas, California." He said the woman looked younger than I.

On July 15 an automobile dealer from Tucson, C. A. Pape, repeated to the grand jury a claim he had made earlier, namely, that on June 20 he saw me and Harry D. Hallenbeck at a roadhouse in Agua Prieta called the International Cafe. Mr. Hallenbeck was the contractor who had erected our Bible school building, and he owned a ranch in Arizona. The innuendo was that I had spent the time of my absence there.

Fortunately, Mr. Hallenbeck was able to prove to the satisfaction of the district attorney's office that he was not near Agua Prieta at the time concerned, and people at his ranch scoffed at the idea that I was there. But isn't it ridiculous that anyone should say that they saw me coming out of a roadhouse? I sometimes felt it almost useless to deny rumors like this, for one has no positive way of disproving them. But the proprietor of the International Cafe, Mr. Ike Levy, furnished unexpected help by swearing in a notorized affadavit that I had not been in his establishment and that he had not seen me in Douglas or Agua Prieta. In addition, Mrs. V. R. Umphrey gave a statement to detective Nick Harris that she was probably the woman Mr. Pape saw. He was mistaken about Mr. Hallenbeck. And he was mistaken about me.

In view of the manner in which the district attorney's office conducted the hearing, it is no wonder that a majority of the grand jury voted that "there is insufficient evidence to date to warrant an indictment." I leave it to the reader to judge the accuracy of Mr. Ryan's statement which followed, "The evidence was presented to the grand jury absolutely from an unbiased viewpoint."

Just after the grand jury ended its investigation, my attorneys issued the following statement:

> The close of the official investigation into the abduction of Mrs. McPherson marks the end of the first phase of the search for her kidnappers. California, Arizona, and Mexico, have been searched, not for the criminals, but for evidence against the evangelist. And after the combing there is no such evidence. Mrs. McPherson's story, related time and again, to officials and others, remains as firm and unshaken as the first time it was told.

The attorneys concluded, "The official investigation not only bears her story out and proves it true but reveals her to the world as a truthful, upright woman who has withstood the attack in a religious, God-fearing manner. Today she stands vindicated and unafraid."

But the challenges to my story were not over. An anonymous tip sent the investigation off on another tangent. The scene shifted to Carmel, California. Apparently Mr. Ormiston had spent ten days there with some woman in a cottage rented from Mr. H. E. Benedict under the name of Mr. and Mrs. George McIntyre.

Joseph Ryan entrained for the north, carrying photographs of me, in an effort to prove I was that woman. He interviewed a number of people and reported back to District Attorney Keyes, "There is no doubt in my mind but that Mrs. McPherson and Ormiston were here from the morning of May 19 to the night of May 28."

Mr. Ryan's "evidence," however, was nowhere nearly as conclusive as he supposed. Mr. Benedict penned the following statement on the back of the photographs of me: "There isn't a thing about this photo that suggests to me Mrs. McIntyre who occupied my cottage in Carmel-by-the-Sea the latter part of May, 1926." He dated the statement August 17, 1926. Mr. Benedict also gave a statement to Judge J. A. Bardin that the biblical annotations or memoranda which were found in his cottage after the departure of the mystery couple were in the handwriting of Mrs. Benedict and that the Bible found there was also the property of his wife.

In spite of the weighty testimony of Mr. Benedict and others who swore they had not seen me, Mr. Ryan persisted in his efforts to connect me with Carmel. The press hinted at clashes between this deputy and his chief, Asa Keyes. The district attorney made conflicting statements in early August, announcing that the Carmel evidence "in no way was binding as has been indicated in unofficial reports." He called it "far from conclusive." He conceded that it had "collapsed." A new grand jury had resumed the investigation. Reports filtered out that material differences were evident between the statements of Mr. Keyes and Mr. Ryan before that body.

When Mr. Keyes remarked that the Carmel evidence "failed to stand up under closer scrutiny," he apparently was referring to the "fingerprint" evidence. Certain books and a spice can found in Mr. Benedict's cottage had been expected by the authorities to link me undeniably to the place. It was announced that a fingerprint expert would go through the books page by page. The press reported that Sergeant Barlow failed to obtain fingerprints from those volumes. The experts also reported that they could not identify the prints on the spice can either because they were "too blurred." This was not quite the truth. I learned later that prints were indeed identified on both the books and the can, but those fingerprints belonged to the newspaper reporters who had been in the cottage. The newspapers did not print this fact at

the time. Some of my friends, however, wondered whether the
books and can might have been planted there in the cottage by
someone whose fingerprints did appear on these items.

Another kind of "evidence" by which the authorities attempted
to prove I was the woman at Carmel was the "grocery slips"
which were found in the yard near the back door of the cottage
in late July by Mrs. Ryan, who had accompanied her husband
on the investigation. Imagine, grocery slips which were supposed
to have survived in the grass for more than two months! And
Carmel is a coastal city, with frequent fogs and dews! The authorities declared that undoubtedly these were in my handwriting.
Interestingly enough, several items on the list were commodities
I never use!

These grocery slips became involved in a mystery of their own
when in early August they disappeared in the grand jury hearing
room. One of the jurors was accused of disposing of them, which
she stoutly denied. The grand jury gave her a vote of confidence,
but the suspicion persisted against her. Investigation convinced
the authorities that this woman had no connection whatever with
me or the Temple.

I tried to pay as little attention as possible to the multitudinous
stories which titillated the public through the press after my return to Angelus Temple. The newspapers during these weeks continued to herald any and every new suggestion or wild surmise a
reporter would think up. It seemed to be a free-for-all. Papers
were selling like hot cakes, and the press had found one victim
who would not retaliate. When my friends urged me to fight back,
I recalled some very good advice a judge gave me after the bad
publicity commenced. "It's very hard to outstink a skunk," he
said, "so don't try."

Then one day a woman who introduced herself as Lorraine
Wiseman (she should have said Lorraine Wiseman-Sielaff) appeared at Angelus Temple and told Mrs. Blanche Rice at the
information desk, "I know the woman who was at Carmel. It was
my sister." Mrs. Rice said she was so excited she did not know
what to do. She ran upstairs and told mother, who asked that the
woman be brought to the parsonage. I came to the door, but
mother warned me away. "This is a very smart woman," she said.
"I haven't figured her out yet. I don't know whether she is a detective or a spy. I think she wants to say she identifies you. I want
you to keep out." So I did.

The woman talked nervously to mother. I did not see her on this occasion or at her next visit. Mother sent her to see Judge Carlos Hardy. Eventually I was present and heard her complete story.

We recognized that Mrs. Wiseman-Sielaff's story was rather unsupported, but she seemed so in earnest and was such a nice-appearing woman that I was certainly taken in by her. She professed that she was burdened with guilt at keeping silence—that she felt she would lose her soul and go to hell if she didn't tell.

This woman related that her sister had gone to Carmel with Mr. McIntyre, that she had been ill and was going to have an operation and had sent for her (Mrs. Wiseman-Sielaff) to nurse her. This sister, she said, had not been seen at any time, and those who had seen a woman at the Carmel cottage had seen her (Mrs. Wiseman-Sielaff) and not the sister. Lorraine Wiseman said she was sure that the witnesses there who had seen the woman at the cottage would recognize her. "I want to clear this thing up," she professed, proposing that she go before the grand jury and tell her whole story. However, she hoped to keep her sister's name out of it, because she said her sister was young, pretty, and unmarried and did not want this to ruin her chances in life.

I agreed that it was quite right that her sister should not be exposed in public.

Mother and I felt this story should have some substantiation before it was published in the press and so informed the newspapers, to whom Mrs. Wiseman-Sielaff gave statements.

My attorneys had not seen this woman up to this time. Mr. Veitch came in at one of our interviews and shook his finger at her and asked, "Are you after money?"

"Oh no!" she exclaimed. "No! I do not want any money. I have come on my own expense. I can show anybody where I drew seven hundred dollars out of the bank and am paying my own expenses. No one ought to ask for money in a case of this kind."

Mrs. Wiseman-Sielaff came out to our house almost incessantly. She would come around to the back door quickly, open the door, come in, and close it behind her. "I have a taxi out there," she sometimes said. "I don't think they followed me. They might kill me if anybody knew I was here to aid you."

I made light of her apparent fears and told her she was overly nervous and wrought up.

"I have had several death notes already," she insisted.

Mrs. Wiseman-Sielaff soon began to grow bolder. She would come more often and stay longer. She said she had a room at a hotel but wanted to be at our parsonage to talk about the case. We kept asking her what verification she had of her story, and she seemed to feel badly that we had any question in our minds. When she was there at dinnertime, we would say, "Sit down and have a bite to eat with us." We had always kept open house and open table. She ate with us. She commenced staying later and later. One night, as she seemed to linger and linger, mother whispered to me, "I wish she would go. She worries me." It was so late, and she seemed so fearful that someone was following her, that when midnight came, I invited her to stay overnight. "If you care to remain," I offered, "you may occupy my room."

I went up, changed the sheets, and put on fresh pillow slips. I slept in a hammock on the porch. The next morning she said she had slept well and felt wonderful because the great cloud over me was going to be lifted by her testimony.

One other night she remained too late to go home. It was hard for me to see people until after our meetings in the Temple. This service ended about ten o'clock. She still had not said much of significance until after midnight. This time she said she had been knocked down by an automobile while waiting for a streetcar in a safety zone. "I tell you," she insisted, "there is an effort on my life. One time I was struck and broke two ribs, and now this time. They have a blind attorney, and now they are trying to get me." I gave her my room once more and again slept on the hammock.

One reason we accepted Mrs. Wiseman-Sielaff was that she used the names of prominent men. She was going to Asa Keyes, was willing to go to Mr. Benedict and to go to Carmel. She seemed to be willing to submit to any test. I heard her telephone the foreman of the grand jury and Judge Keetch. She claimed that Judge Keetch had interviewed her in his home. She said she talked the case over with him there and later at a place where she claimed he asked her to meet him in his automobile. This woman declared that the judge did not want her to go before the grand jury but before a special committee which they would appoint and which would settle it then and there.

Imagine our surprise when the Los Angeles newspapers exposed Mrs. Wiseman-Sielaff as a hoax! Police arrested her as a passer of bad checks. The press revealed that she had once been committed to a state asylum, and that, in order to obtain fifty dollars for "funeral expenses," she had falsely advertised in a newspaper that her only son had died. Her husband had divorced her for "ungovernable lying."

We received a demand for money to put up bail for this woman. When we did not come through, she gave the newspapers a terrible story to the effect that mother and I had hired her to "confess" she was at Carmel.

Upon the testimony of this woman a "prosecution" against us was built. Mother and I were charged with obstruction of justice and conspiracy to fake evidence. Of course, this "admitted 'star' " witness later, according to the press, changed her story several times, finally making another confession, this time to the effect that we had not hired her but that she had come at the instigation of an accomplice to extract money from us. But I am getting a bit ahead of the story.

You can imagine my agony at seeing my name blazoned forth in the daily press in so sordid a manner. Worse than that was the poignant anxiety as to what effect the persecution would have upon others. The thousands of little children, our Bible students with hearts free of care and full of faith and love and blossoms of promise, could I be submerged without them sinking too?

Surely it was imperative that right must triumph and these sinister attacks fail, lest defeat drag the banner of the cross in ignominy. The truth must win out. My precious people must be spared. What happened to me did not so much matter. My concern was the church.

No matter how bewildered and tired and bruised I felt from the battle, I must needs bathe face and eyes with cold water, don a fresh uniform, gather up my Bible and the armful of roses which friends invariably provided, and make my way down the long rampart to the pulpit in Angelus Temple.

It was a blessed lifesaver too—this service of the King—which demanded my best each day. No sooner would I reach the platform than jaded nerves would be stilled, the harrowing jangle of what seemed to be a world gone mad would be hushed, and the stinging pain would cease. And after each meeting I would mount the stairs to my parsonage room with every ruffled feather smoothed, feeling as though I had been bathed in healing oil and that the alabaster box of Christian love had been poured over my drooping head. Then I could go out and face the duties of the coming day with courage high.

But there were some nights when my couch was a rack of anguish. As long as I could bear the physical inactivity, I would lie still, trying to take some much needed rest, wide, sleepless eyes staring up into the blackness of night until it reeled with circles and wheels of light. Then I would get up and walk the long upstairs corridor, up and down, to and fro in ceaseless pacing, hands pressed first over my eyes, then over my mouth to keep back the little cries and moans I feared would awaken the household. At times I would look out upon the Temple, the silvered radio spires bathed in moonlight, and up at the school building that towered above the parsonage. Somehow the mere gazing at the solidity of those walls of steel-girdered masonry comforted my heart, for they seemed to be symbolic of the strength of the Rock of Ages upon which this work was founded.

Often, before my hot eyes closed in slumber, I would hear the fresh voices of hundreds of young students as they came trooping through the gates for the morning classes where they were training for the Foursquare ministry. At length exhaustion would claim its own, and I would fall into a stupor for an hour or two until the duties of the day again came clamoring at the door demanding attention.

I have often been asked how, while this great travail was upon me, I was able to withstand it physically or mentally. Other women, other men, people told me, would have gone to pieces. Yet the fact remains that, through it all, I performed my pastoral duties just as before. Even during the court proceedings, while sitting under such enormous stress, I was permitted by God's grace to conduct the services each night, preach to vast congregations, visit and pray for the sick, baptize hundreds of candidates, minister to the various children's and adult Bible classes, console the bereaved, and do all those things which are imperative when one is entrusted with the keeping of a flock.

Because the malicious tongues of scandal became so blatant and the cleft of opinion had reached such a crescendo, I had called for a showdown. Over the radio and through the press I asked everyone who was muttering around in the dark to come forward and say what they had to say in the light of day.

I called for a showdown, and—I got it! And as my high-school son would say at the time—"and how!" The names of those who said they had seen me here, there, and yonder, or who had volunteered to the newspapers other wild and absurd tales were listed and supoenaed—much to the discomfiture of a number who found it one thing to make wild statements and quite another to repeat and prove them under oath.

We welcomed the day when the matter would be taken to the preliminary hearing before a judge of the municipal court. We hoped that there or later before a jury in superior court—if the case would really be brought to trial—the hand of the real instigators of the persecution we were undergoing would manifest itself and the trail be struck which would lead to the unraveling of the whole.

Etched in my memory is the night before the opening of that hearing. The glaring headlined expectancy of newspaper scandalmongers! My endeavors to arrange our busy days that we might be free to absent ourselves from some of the pressing duties of so great a church! The preaching of the evening sermon to the assembled thousands who surged in the streets and filled every nook and cranny of the great edifice! The giving of the last altar call before the big guns were actually loosed—the thronging forward of penitents to kneel and pray! The sea of hands that reached out to mine, the brave smiles, the words of cheer and confidence—such as might have been given to a Christian before entering the lion pits of Rome's old Colosseum! The constant ringing of the telephone, with newspapermen asking, "How do you feel now?" "Have you any fresh statements?" "Are you preparing to leave town?" and a hundred and one questions that seemed very foolish and mystifying and childish and endless—oh, so endless.

Suddenly, very tired, I threw myself down upon the bed for some much needed rest, muffling the phone bell and turning off the lights. Eventually I slept, but at dawn I awoke with a start. What was it? Oh, yes, this was the day I was going to court!

Rap, rap, rap! A man is hammering! What? Who? All eyes are fixed upon a door. A young man enters. Scraping chairs. "Stand up!" The young man, Judge Blake—looking scarcely out of his teens—nodded to those in the front seats which had been reserved for the favored to whom, according to the press, the judge had personally issued tickets. These spectators drew a long, quivering breath of anticipation as their beaded eyelashes fluttered at the handsome jurist. They were set and ready for the action.

Up with the curtain! On with the show! The droning of voices reading some stereotyped phrases. The winning smile from the bench as its occupant turned to be photographed. The firing of flashbulbs, unrebuked in those early days of the hearing. The calling of some unfamiliar name. The clicking of a telegraph instrument, temporarily fastened to a window ledge to carry the news to all the United Press papers of the land.

The opening of a door at the right! A door that was soon to become the door from the chamber of horrors—the witness anteroom. The slap-slapping of a man's shoes on hard floors. The first witness had arrived. He gave his name as Ralph W. Hersey.

What is this that the witness is saying? He had been at Carmel-by-the-Sea where it had been reported I had been seen. ". . . As we were driving around the corner—descending a hill—I observed on the corner a woman walking. She was Mrs. McPherson."

I was frozen, chilled, horrified, and astonished. Lead pencils were scribbling. Telegraphs clicking, cameras flashing. It was unthinkable! I felt that I must leap to my feet and cry out, "Stop! That is untrue!" or do some other unallowable thing. My attorney turned and instructed me to sit still, explaining that the cameramen were just waiting with lenses trained on me. The voices of questioner and witness went on.

Question: Describe in your own way the circumstances under which you saw her.

Answer: The first time was May 25, 1926, about five o'-clock in the afternoon. I was driving down Ocean View Avenue, descending a hill, and as I turned a corner I observed a woman walking, dressed in a white suit and a dark, soft, small, tight-fitting hat.

Q. Did you look at her?

A. I did.

Q. Can you say now who the lady was?

A. I can. Mrs. McPherson.

Q. Did you know Mrs. McPherson at the time?

A. I did not.

Q. Where did you go after you saw the lady?

A. To the home of my friend nearby, Mr. Compton.

Q. What did you say to him and what did he say to you?

A. I said, "Hello, Paul, I think I just saw Mrs. Liston, who purchased your house when we were here last time." He asked, "Where did you see her?" and I said, "Up in the corner."

Q. Mrs. who?

A. Liston—(spelling) L-i-s-t-o-n.

Q. That was not the woman you thought was Mrs. McPherson, was it?

A. Absolutely.

The witness proceeded to relate that his friend Mr. Compton dismissed as impossible the idea Mr. Hersey had seen Mrs. Liston because Mrs. Liston was out of town. Thereupon the discussion of the incident had ceased at Compton's house. The questioning continued:

Q. When was the first time that you changed your mind about it being Mrs. Liston and concluded that it was Mrs. McPherson? When did you change your mind?

A. Oh, those dates were separated probably only—two months and a half apart.

The witness mentioned later that Mr. Moore of the Santa Barbara *Morning Press* called upon him at the Santa Barbara club at the end of that period, "and we discussed the matter."

Q. Mr. Moore was a newspaperman and looking for news, wasn't he?

A. He was, I suppose.

Q. What suggestion did Mr. Moore make to you that would suddenly cause you to give birth to the idea that the woman you saw two months and a half before, and thought it was Mrs. Liston, was Mrs. McPherson?"

The district attorney offered an objection that the question was argumentative and not proper cross-examination. My attorney, Mr. Gilbert, replied, "In defense of my client I have a right to find out a few things about the working of this man's mind who can travel past a woman fifteen miles an hour, around a corner, down hill, with the sun in his eyes, and make up his mind two and one half months later that the woman, dressed in a low, tight hat, is a certain woman he thought at that time was another woman."

The attorneys for the defense and prosecution wrangled for some time. Eventually Judge Blake sustained the objection.

Mr. Gilbert pressed the witness concerning the steps by which he reached his opinion that the woman he had seen in Carmel was me. Mr. Hersey replied that he came down to Angelus Temple on August 8.

Question: Whereabouts did you sit?

Answer: I didn't sit.

Q. Where did you stand, then?

A. I stood in the doorway, facing the platform.

Q. How far from the platform where Mrs. McPherson was preaching?

A. About one hundred fifty feet.

Q. How was she dressed?

A. In white. Blue cape.

Q. And her hair was done up?

A. On the top of her head.

Q. Over a hundred feet away, she had no hat on, you saw that lady preaching a sermon and you made up your mind that it was the same lady you had seen months before as you drove past her and glanced at her head, covered with a tight, low hat?

A. Yes.

Q. Let's get your reason for the court.

A. Elimination.

Q. All right, give us your process of elimination.

A. The woman I saw had on a hat.

Q. A hat?

A. It was unusually large.

Q. Picture hat?

A. No, sir, it was a small hat, tight-fitting hat.

Q. And did you see the hair of the woman on the street corner?

A. No, sir.

Q. And after going into the Temple you saw a woman preaching who had auburn hair and you saw a woman on the street whose color of hair you did not know and you start your eliminator to work and when you got her hat off you found that she had auburn hair. Keep on, if your modesty will permit it, with your elimination.

A. I found very unusual eyes.

Q. And you were more than a hundred feet away at the Temple when you were there?

A. Yes.

Q. Do you know the color?

A. No, but unusual.

Q. What was there unusual about the eyes? You don't know, the color, don't even know the color now?

A. No, don't know the color now.

Q. All right. What was there unusual about the eyes?

A. Large, open, brilliant.

Mr. Hersey added that he had never seen eyes quite like that before. My attorney concluded his cross-examination sometime later with this challenge: "I will ask, if your honor please, that sometime during the examination, to have this witness with the court and counsel find out the door where he claims to have stood and seen Mrs. McPherson and ask someone to stand where she was for the purpose of showing that it was a physical impossibility for him to have seen the shape of the eyes, little less their color, peculiar or otherwise. That is all."

Then five more witnesses paraded to the stand—witnesses who had had my pictures shoved beneath their eyes continually in newspapers and in the hands of investigators—witnesses who had thrust into otherwise quiet lives an exciting incident which would naturally absorb their thoughts and make an indelible imprint on their minds. Four of these claimed to have seen me, according to their own testimony, not to exceed from ten to thirty seconds, and the other one not to exceed over a minute and a half. These were people who never had seen me in person until that day in court.

These witnesses' descriptions of the woman at the Carmel cottage gave her hair all the shades and colors of a rainbow. One said she had blonde hair. One said it was black. Another insisted it was red, and yet another said it was brown. They gave her age all the way from twenty to forty. One said he was "drawed" by her eyes. Others said she wore dark goggles and was never seen without them. An examination of the testimony of these people ought to convince anyone that the testimony of each fell by its own weight. So I was expecting a favorable press that night. I went home with a glow of anticipation to wait for the next editions. I did not have long to wait!

"Extree! Extree! Read all about it for three cents! Aimee identified! Yes, identified. Read all about it."

Springing to my feet, I trembled in righteous indignation as the raucous cries of the boys shattered the sacred precincts of the church, indignation at the cries and the message they carried. This could not be so. Identified! What were they talking about?

Quickly calling one of the large dailies, a bored voice answered, "City Editor."

"Please, oh, what is this the boys are calling?" I pleaded. "They're shouting something about my being identified. What can they mean? Please stop them."

"Now don't get excited," almost yawned the bored voice.

"Those birds said they recognized you. It makes a good headline. We got your side in the story."

Well, anyway, they had "my side" in the paper, even though you'd never guess it by listening to the newsboy or reading the headlines. So I bought a paper and looked for "my side."

Yes, it was there, like this: A column about one man's "identification" of me and this at the bottom of the story: "Mr. Hersey said at first he thought the woman was someone else but soon corrected this error."

What a silly little goose I was then to actually expect a newspaper to "play up" anything reflecting credit on me. Later, when responsible witnesses from Carmel testified that I positively was not the woman they saw there, the papers usually relegated the account to an inconspicuous column. I had to learn the bitter lesson that, as a reporter told me, it wasn't news if it was good. Not once or twice, but day after day my heart bled as I read how some reporter had taken a heated remark of some lawyer in anger or the statement of some discredited witness to build it up into a headline and a "lead" to their stories until the average reader's picture of the day in court was as far from true as night from day. From this time on, for years and years, those who were dependent upon the press for their information about me and my work could not help but get a distorted and perverted picture. Fortunately, I had my publications, the *Bridal Call Foursquare* and *Foursquare Crusader,* which we launched during this ordeal, and radio station KFSG. Through these we endeavored to get the truth across to the public.

The second day of the preliminary hearing brought help from the prosecution's own witnesses. Two men who had been brought down from Carmel to identify me disappointed the district attorney.

However, my attorney, Mr. Gilbert, had not finished his cross-examination of the last witness to appear on the first day of the hearing. Mr. Ernest Renkert, who delivered wood to the cottage, had claimed he saw me in the yard. He admitted that he had seen a picture of me in the *San Francisco Bulletin* just after my disappearance. This was a few days before he allegedly "saw" me. He admitted he had read of the twenty-five thousand dollars reward which had been posted for my recovery. Mr. Gilbert pressed, "After you knew that this twenty-five thousand dollars reward had been offered, why didn't you go to some officer and tell them about having seen this lady in the yard where the wood was delivered?"

The witness answered lamely, "Because I thought it was newspaper talk."

My attorney also asked Mr. Renkert about the color of hair the woman he saw had. The reply came, "Blonde or auburn or whatever you call it, brunette, they are all alike to me." Another mistaken identification had betrayed its flimsy foundation.

But the next witness was a man who would settle all doubts, once for all, according to newspaper publicity anticipating his appearance. From the fuss and furor in the press and in the prosecution's camp, it was apparent that the officials had arranged for this identification to crown their efforts and overshadow the weak and short "long-distance identifications" of the previous witnesses.

The stage was set. The telegraph instrument had stopped ticking. The reporters and spectators were waiting for the intense moment when this witness was expected to say, "Gentlemen, that's the woman!"

The right-hand door opened again. The man who entered looked like one whose word would carry great weight. Deputy District Attorney Murray stood up to conduct the questioning. His voice radiated the victorious tones of a brave warrior who had drawn a bead on his prey and is about to pull the trigger—in this case me, a woman—big game. William H. McMichael gave his name and occupation—stonemason. He testified he had worked on the boundary line on the south side of the Benedict property over a period of three months, including every day except two between May 18 and May 29, the time the mystery woman was at the house.

Question: Directing your attention here to Mrs. McPherson, have you ever seen her before?

Answer: Could I see the hat off?

I removed my hat with what I hoped was a brave flourish. The stonemason's eyes under shaggy eyebrows beat down upon me. He even leaned a little forward although he was hardly more than ten feet from me. Then he settled back in the witness chair, and his jaws came together with a click of conviction. In the death-like stillness of the room, every eye focused on him eagerly. You could have heard a pin drop. Then his voice boomed out no.

Mr. Murray appeared annoyed. He pressed the examination. "Did you see the lady that occupied that house at any time?"

"Oh, yes," Mr. McMichael replied. He described her as a lady of about thirty years of age. "Her hair seemed to be a little bit blonde."

Question: On how many occasions did you see this lady that occupied the Benedict house?

Answer: Why, six, anyway, probably more.

In his cross-examination, Mr. Gilbert pointed toward me and inquired, "As far as you are concerned, this is the first time you have ever seen this little woman in your life?" The witness replied firmly, "The first time I ever saw this lady in my life."

"The first time you ever saw this little woman in your life," my attorney repeated. "Is that plain, Brother Keyes?"

The prosecutor and his aides deflated almost with an audible bang during this testimony, while the courtroom attachés and attendant newspapermen glowered in disappointment at seeing this beautifully baited trap snap down its steel jaws upon the hand of the hunter instead of his intended prey.

One would have thought that the opposition would have leaped to their feet and rushed over to shake hands and offer congratulations warmly for this exoneration. Instead, consternation reigned in their camp! The prosecution's big gun among the "identification witnesses" had backfired. The heralded witness had become the champion of truth.

But a telegraph messenger awaited in the witness room. He had delivered a telegram to the mystery woman at the Carmel cottage, and she had signed for the message. Deputy District Attorney Dennison took his turn at questioning. He asked, "Do you see anybody in the courtroom who signed this?" He had produced the receipt for the telegram. "Do you see the lady around here anywhere?" Mr. Dennison waited, expecting the messenger, whose name was Jesse Williams, to identify me. But Mr. Williams, after looking around the courtroom, declared, "No, I don't recognize anybody here." My attorney asked only one question on cross-examination, to which the Western Union messenger replied that the woman who signed for the telegram in question had blonde hair. The prosecution's own witnesses were now supporting my case.

Wednesday and Thursday, September 28 and 29—the third and fourth days of the hearing—were occupied mostly with the reading into the record of the testimony I had given before the grand jury on July 8.

It was quite a revelation. Because this long transcript was being read by the deputy district attorneys and would continue for several sessions, and because an interruption of the reading would not inconvenience other witnesses by delaying their opportunities to testify, my attorney requested permission to put on a defense witness, Mr. August England, the city marshal of Carmel, who was in Los Angeles for the hearing but who needed to return to his duties in the north.

Deputy District Attorney Dennison leaped to his feet and objected strenuously. He announced that the reason he objected was because "I now know what his proof will be in this matter, and this defendant is a very powerful woman. She has a magnificent opportunity to herald garbled statements in relation to this witness over the radio."

I sat there, and my mouth fell open wide. I looked at this big prosecutor with distinguishing grey hair and wondered if he had a mother, a wife, or a girl with yellow curls like my girl, or a son who is growing up and expecting to face the world and who would always love to look back and speak with pride about "my mother." Why did he not want the man to testify when he knew what his testimony would be? Why should not he and all the district attorney's office and in fact the whole world want to uphold a woman's honor and reputation if the truth does uphold it? I always thought it was as much the duty of the district attorney to protect the innocent as to prosecute the guilty. Perhaps I should have realized that it was something like a game of basketball, with two opposing sides, each one trying to win for the sake of the game itself. For a long time I would be haunted by the specter of that prosecutor standing there and saying, "That's the reason we do not want this witness on this afternoon. We have found out what his testimony will be, and this is a powerful woman and we know she will send it over the radio tonight!"

After my attorney and the district attorney's camp had a heated argument, the judge ruled that Mr. England might testify. The city marshal of Carmel, who is what we would call the chief of police (he had held that office for the past ten years there), as well as the tax collector, a man of high standing in his community, walked into the courtroom.

To Mr. Gilbert's questions, Mr. England answered that he

lived at Carmel-by-the-Sea, that his occupation was that of city marshal and tax collector, and that as such he patrolled the town generally and looked after properties there. "And do you know where the Benedict cottage is?"

"Yes, sir," the witness answered.

"Have you had any instructions or any suggestions from Mr. Benedict to look after his cottage while he was away, in a general sort of way?" asked Mr. Gilbert.

"Yes, sir."

"Directing your attention to the time between May 19 and May 29 of this year, did you have occasion to patrol that street and look after and watch this particular piece of property with others?"

"Yes, sir."

"Were you at the Benedict house during that period of time? If so, how often?"

"I passed—patrolled there twice a day every day."

"Now, beginning after May 19, did you see anybody in the Benedict cottage?"

"Yes, sir," the witness declared. "I passed by and saw a gentleman and lady outside the garage door."

"How often did you see that lady around the house?" inquired my attorney.

"Well, I saw her after that in the garden one time and I met her on the lane—what they call Scenic Drive, between Benedict's house and the Ocean Avenue."

"That was three times, at least, that you saw her?"

"Yes, sir."

"How close were you when you saw her at the house? How close were you to her?"

"Eight to ten feet."

"When did you next see her?"

"A few days after I saw her walking between Ocean Avenue and Benedict's house."

"When did you see her the third time?"

"I saw her out in the garden, passing by, you know."

"You have seen Mrs. McPherson since you came down [from Carmel] this time at my suggestion?" Mr. Gilbert questioned.

"Yes, sir."

"You recognize Mrs. McPherson here in the courtroom now?"

"Yes, sir."

"Tell the court whether or not Mrs. McPherson was the woman who was there with that man at that place?"

"Positively not that woman."

Mr. Dennison did not ask any questions in cross-examination challenging Marshal England's statement that I was positively not the woman in question. Instead, he queried the witness concerning conversations he had with other parties in Carmel, especially with a man who showed him a picture of me and wanted him to identify it. Mr. England remarked that he listened to people discussing the case, stating, "A policeman listens: he don't talk very much."

Immediately after the transcript of my grand jury testimony had been read into the record, the prosecution called another witness in an effort to link me with Mr. Ormiston and Carmel. Wallace Moore, a reporter for the Santa Barbara *Morning Press,* had stopped Mr. Ormiston's car on the road near Santa Barbara at about 11 P.M. on the night of May 29. A tip had come that Mr. Ormiston and I were motoring south toward Santa Barbara, and Mr. Moore had been staked out for some hours to watch for the car. He had talked to the occupants and returned to his newspaper, reporting that the woman whom he had seen in the car was not Aimee Semple McPherson. He dictated an article to the newspaper in which he stated that the woman was not Mrs. McPherson. He had heard me preach in Fresno for a total of about twenty hours at various meetings. He had talked to me and interviewed me. So when he wrote that the woman in the car "did not resemble Mrs. McPherson, except in general build," he was well prepared to come to a conclusion.

This witness, however, appeared now to want to suit the district attorney. It took several minutes of questioning to get him to admit that he had in fact submitted the newspaper article stating that I was not the woman in the car. Yet he conceded that he had stated to the couple at the time, "Oh, well, I guess this is not Mrs. McPherson," and then left.

Three years later Mr. Moore would testify that he thought the woman in the car really was me. However, isn't it strange that he would change his mind after being so emphatic on the night in question that it was someone else? What enormous pressures must have been brought to bear upon him to cause him to change his testimony!

The district attorney's case next tried to prove I met a man at a downtown hotel on the morning of my disappearance. Fortunately, I had witnesses who could prove I was elsewhere at the time the witness stipulated. This party declared he had never seen me before, but he was sure the woman he watched was me because she carried a briefcase with "Aimee Semple McPherson" stamped in big letters on it. (I had never had such a briefcase.)

Can you imagine the absurdity of this line of thought? Can anyone seriously believe that an internationally known evangelist if planning an escapade such as this would go downtown to meet the lucky man at ten thirty in the morning in front of a hotel on Hill Street? Can you imagine the couple plotting. "Shh! Nobody must know. We are going to put over a big *coup de grace* here!" with her walking along with a bag sporting her name in big letters? Of course, I was not at that hotel. At the very time in question, I was with a saleslady in Bullock's Department Store, and she would later swear to this at the hearing.

I was, however, at the Ambassador Hotel at the times Mr. Keyes insinuated into the case, and it bothered me when he got people to imply that I was keeping a rendezvous there. Now for the first time witnesses were produced linking me to a place where I really had been. To counteract the innuendo, my attorney, Mr. Gilbert, requested me to issue a statement:

> I was at the Ambassador Hotel and in room 330, not once but many times while the school building was under course of construction, a fact known to every member of my family, many of my friends, and announced from my pulpit.
>
> This room I requested because it was at the end of the corridor and directly across the hall from the room occupied by one of my parishioners, Mrs. Florence Underwood and her patient. Therefore, it was unnecessary for me to be at any time alone. I always felt that I had company. Our doors were often left open and Mrs. Underwood and I visited back and forth.
>
> Mrs. Underwood is an elderly lady whose hair is whiter than my own dear mother's.
>
> I entered the Ambassador Hotel as any other guest, after my night meetings, registered my full name, Aimee Semple McPherson, and always insisted that this particular room should be assigned to me because of the reason just given, my church member and friend, Mrs. Underwood, being just in the room adjoining.
>
> The cashier of the Ambassador Hotel, a lady, was at that time an attendant at my church, and I do not believe I ever entered the hotel that I did not visit with her for a moment at the desk, talking with her about my work and the sermons I was preparing.

My reason for leaving the Temple was the desire to avoid the noise attendant upon construction of the school building annex. During that period of time, while preparing my sermons, I was not only at the Ambassador, but also at the Alexandria, and if I recall, two or three times at the Rosslyn, when it was inconvenient for me to go to the Ambassador, and especially when I would have business to transact in the downtown district.

The only time I ever saw Mr. Ormiston at the Ambassador Hotel was during the time that I participated in the program at the Radio Exposition, and was on the platform with "Uncle John" and with all the other prominent radio owners, officials, and announcers. Several hundred people were present and heard the banquet address which I delivered at that time.

The vile insinuations in court which necessitated that statement boomeranged to some extent. Several spectators who had never been our friends gasped with horror at the allegations and were the first to come and pat mother and me on the shoulders, put their arms around us, or shake our hands, saying, "Well, from this time on, I am for you. That was inexcusable!" Attacks of this nature led us to the conviction that a giant plot was being prosecuted to wreck Angelus Temple, the work, and its pastor. Some newspaper reporters who had been warning us that something terrible was going to happen came that night and said, "Well, Sister, the worst is now over. They have said the very worst they can possibly say." We thanked God in anticipation that the worst was over.

Before those days in 1926 I used to say often as I watched hundreds of people come to Jesus at Angelus Temple, "Why doesn't the devil fight this work more?" I said it jokingly at the time but I guess maybe he took the hint! I would never again give him any more suggestions!

Going up the steps toward the courtroom on that gruesome "hotel day" of the hearing, I looked up to Mr. Gilbert with a rather weary smile and said, "Mr. Gilbert, I believe you would have an easier time defending me if I were a murderer or just an ordinary person rather than an evangelist."

"Why," he said, "I could get you off far easier right now for murder than this that they are accusing you of. Because you are an evangelist, everybody wants to get their pictures in the paper with you. Everybody wants to climb on the bandwagon because they are making it an international case to get some notoriety out of it."

The prosecution case continued till October 19. Mr. Ryan testified. Mrs. Wiseman-Sielaff, the district attorney's "star witness" of the many confessions, was produced, repeated her latest "confession," and retired to come back another day with another "confession." One witness was subpoenaed from Douglas who voiced skepticism of the possibility of my making the desert trek I had described. His testimony, however, would be more than overshadowed by the several Douglas officials who would testify in my behalf when the turn came for the defense to present witnesses. My mother's testimony given before the grand jury on July 13 was read into the record. Miss Bernice Morris's, the secretary to the blind attorney McKinley who had been killed in an automobile accident, comments on the facts were quite the contrary. We dealt with Mr. McKinley, and, after his death, with Miss Morris in good faith. We thought they were sincere in their belief they had been in contact with the kidnappers. My mother declared, "If Mr. McKinley was wrong, he fooled Judge Hardy, because it was only after Judge Hardy had declared his belief that the man had been approached by the actual kidnappers that we retained him."

According to Miss Morris, her employer believed I had staged my disappearance and that I would identify anyone who might phone and claim he was my kidnapper. She said they engaged a man named Joe Watts to phone me and that I exclaimed when I talked to him, "My God, it's really you," or something to that effect. When the district attorney interviewed this man, he denied he had made such a call. However, I did receive a phone call on the day in question from a man purporting to be one of the kidnappers. But I did not say, "It's really you," or anything of the like. Mrs. Herbert Price, who was present during the entire phone call, indeed, who answered the phone and called me on that occasion, would later in the hearing relate my end of the conversation.

On cross-examination Deputy Attorney Murray asked Mrs. Price, "Did she [Mrs. McPherson] turn around on that occasion and say to her mother, 'My God, that is him, mother. I recognize his voice'?"

"Absolutely not," insisted Mrs. Price. "Nothing like that."

If, as several claim, Mr. McKinley actually expressed doubt about my story, he was talking out of both sides of his mouth, for his friend of twelve years, Mr. C. C. Patterson of Pomona,

California, a man who visited the lawyer at his office many times and at his request would frequently read to the blind attorney press articles, signed a statement describing a conversation shortly before the attorney's tragic death. In it Mr. Patterson declared:

> Mr. McKinley told me that he believed every word that Mrs. McPherson had said in regard to her being kidnapped. He said he was satisfied that the two men who came to see him were the real men that did the kidnapping. The reason he felt so sure of that, he said, was from their conversation—they told him things that he didn't think they could have told him had they not been the real men that did it.

At any rate, our dealings with both the attorney and the secretary were in good faith.

My secretary, Miss Emma Schaffer, was one day called as a prosecution witness. "Isn't it true that Mrs. McPherson wears a whole lot of false hair on top of her head?" the deputy district attorney inquired. Miss Schaffer denied it, but the questioner persisted. Mrs. Wiseman-Sielaff in her "confession" had insisted that I wore switches.

Finally the debate grew too much for Mr. Gilbert. My attorney turned around and said in his kindly, gruff way, "Take it down."

"Take what down?" I asked, meekly. You speak meekly to Mr. Gilbert when he lets out one of those roars of his.

"Take your hair down!"

"Why, Mr. Gilbert," I protested, "right here in the courtroom?"

"Yes, take it down."

Mr. Dennison said, "Oh, no, that isn't necessary."

But my attorney said, "Yes, it is necessary. There has been enough of the innuendo. Anything we can prove we will prove right here and now."

So I took my hair down. I guess thousands of people, all told, have said, "Why, it's a shame the amount of money Mrs. McPherson spends on her hair! She has a hair dresser come every day, and it takes two hours to comb her hair." I did my own hair in open court that day in two minutes and a half, without a mirror. I repeated the exercise that night, combing my hair for the Temple service in front of a camera at the request of newsmen.

It seemed very silly and a very trivial thing, hardly worthy of mention, but there's just as much truth in the fact that I have a hairdresser spend two hours on my hair and that it is all pinned on, and all that as there is in all the rest of those things that people were saying, and I was glad to have an opportunity to let the truth be known!

Now the tide was turning. Drifting sand dunes of innuendo and calumny that had been piled mountain high began fading away. Upon this unstable, ever-changing sand the prosecution had sought to rest a case against me on a three-legged legal stool. One leg was the contention that I was the mystery woman who had been in the cottage at Carmel. Another leg was that the account I gave of my escape on the desert was impossible and untrue. The last leg was that I had hired the "confession woman"—or "hoax woman"—as the press would come to call her more unkindly, to say that she was the mystery woman at Carmel.

The first leg was removed by the witnesses from the north who swore emphatically that the lady in the Carmel cottage was definitely not me. Mr. Benedict, Mr. England, Mr. McMichael, Mr. Horton, and Mr. Williams all had been in close contact with her and declared with conviction she was someone else.

The second leg fell when the troop of peace officers and border riders from Douglas testified that they had found evidence which convinced them that my account of my escape from the kidnappers was true.

These men from the border gave the cosmopolitan courtroom spectators an unaccustomed thrill as they stalked in attired in their wide-brimmed hats. They corroborated my account of the escape and harrowing trek over miles of sand to Agua Prieta. These men, familiar as anyone could be with every bit of that desert, testified that they had tracked my footprints and that those prints corroborated my account.

There came with them also Mr. and Mrs. Gonzales to testify in my behalf—the couple who picked me up the night I had fallen exhausted at their gate in Agua Prieta. Mr. Gilbert asked Mr. Gonzales, "What did you do with her?" He meant what did Mr. Gonzales do when he first reached my fallen form.

"I felt her pulse," he replied. It was necessary to use an interpreter to relay the questions and answers into Spanish and English. "I found her cold with very little sign of life. I said to my wife, 'I think this lady is dead.' "

His wife, when her turn came, also testified, "We thought she was dead." When they discovered faint signs of life, Mrs. Gonzales related, "I severely rubbed her forehead, the back of her neck, and arms with alcohol. When she came to, she did not know anything that was going on."

"Now what did she do when she started to recover consciousness?" Mr. Gilbert questioned, to which Mrs. Gonzales replied, "She asked for water."

"Now did you have occasion to examine Mrs. McPherson's arms or wrists to see if they had been burned with rope or something?" my attorney asked.

"Yes, sir. There was a bruise upon each of her arms as though they had been bound tightly with something—I can't say what."

"Were those plainly visible?"

Mrs. Gonzales replied, "Yes, sir."

Ambitious newspapermen had dug up someone to quote who had said it was "strange" that Mrs. McPherson could walk over the desert in the mesquite and brush without tearing her stockings or her skirt. The testimony of Douglas Police Officer G. W. Cook certainly helped dispose of that objection. He was the first officer I met at the police station there after being brought across the border. The testimony proceeded as follows:

Question: What was Mrs. McPherson's physical condition?

Answer: She was in a state of collapse—complete physical exhaustion, all in.

Q. Now what did you do?

A. I took her to the hospital.

Q. Did you observe her physical condition as she was being taken to the hospital from the car?

A. I did. Her ankles turned. People had to support her. She walked with a weak step.

Q. Did you notice any marks of violence?

A. I did. I looked at her wrists closely and found some red welts around them.

Q. Where they had apparently been bound by a rope or thong?

A. Yes. It was from friction.

Q. Did you subsequently go out and make any investigation over that country? (Mr. Gilbert was asking about the country I had described as having traversed.)

A. About ten days after she arrived in Douglas, I took my wife, daughter, and four-year-old baby. My wife and I put on hiking clothes. We went out to Niggerhead country to see what it looked like and note the surface of the ground. We went about nine miles, left our car, walked from the American side of the line, crossed the international fence, and went over behind Niggerhead Mountain for about two miles.

Q. You say you had a little baby with you?

A. Yes. A four-year-old baby.

Q. How was the baby dressed?

A. She was dressed in summer socks and little slippers.

Q. Was the baby running around over there all the time?

A. All the way around Niggerhead and back, except the last half mile, when she grew tired and I had to carry her.

Q. What was the condition of the little baby's legs with those little socks and slippers?

A. I could not notice anything on them at all—no difference at all.

Q. How far did you say you walked?

A. Four miles or more.

Q. As far as any of the territory you saw, I will ask you whether or not you walked through that territory with a pair of shoes such as those revealed in exhibit [my shoes]? Could one walk fifteen or eighteen miles and leave the shoes in the condition that those are in now?

A. Yes, sir.

Certainly the Cook family's desert hiking offered strong confirmation that a trek such as I pursued was really possible. Several other representative citizens from that desert country added the weight of their knowledge to help me. Among them I remember a well-known mining engineer and peace officer from Douglas, Mr. C. E. Cross. Mr. Cross had been quoted previously as challenging my story, but in the preliminary hearing he emphatically denied making such statements. Part of his testimony follows:

Q. Have you traveled in the desert on foot in the summer months around Agua Prieta?

A. Yes.

Q. What do you know of the ability of anyone to travel fifteen or twenty miles without water?

A. Well, it is done. I have done it. I remember one time I walked twenty-two miles when the horse fell with me on the range just a few miles west of where Mrs. McPherson was.

Q. What time did you start on this twenty-two mile walk?

A. About noon.

Q. How long did it take you to complete the twenty-two miles?
A. Sometime about ten o'clock that night.
Q. Did you have any water on that trip?
A. No, there was no water.
Q. Now will you describe your general physical condition after you had completed that twenty-two mile walk.
A. I worked the next day. Did not feel any bad effects from it.
Q. To what extent did you suffer from the lack of water?
A. Well, I wanted water, sure, but I could not get it.
Q. So you just went on without it?
A. Yes. I have gone twelve hours in the daytime several times in that country without water.
Q. Now, Mr. Cross, I hand you a pair of shoes that have been heretofore marked as people's exhibit W. Have you examined those shoes?
A. Yes, sir.
Q. Now assuming that some person would walk through the territory some twenty to twenty-two miles, what would you say as to whether or not that territory could be covered with those shoes and still be in the condition they are in now?
A. Yes, sir. I say these shoes could have been walked twenty-five miles and wouldn't scar up any more than they are there on the soles there or on the uppers in that country.

Mr. Cross was asked whether he made examination of the heat records for the area on the day I made my desert trek and subsequent days. The prosecution objected and tried to keep the witness from answering. However, the judge overruled. Mr. Cross had previously sent a statement in which he declared:

On June 22 (the day I escaped) the thermometer registered ninety-seven in Douglas, Arizona. On the twenty-third, ninety-nine. On the twenty-fourth, one hundred one, and the wind blew at the rate of six or seven miles per hour. It would probably be four or five degrees cooler where Mrs. McPherson was walking than in Douglas where these observations were taken.

It may seem unusual to some people that I, like the witness Cross, had made so long a walk and recovered so quickly. But I have spent my life from childhood days in outdoor sports and exercise. I used to tramp over miles of our Canadian farm and ride the country on horseback. I have continued to ride and swim a great deal. My endurance and stamina have amazed my friends, and a walk of fifteen miles over any kind of territory is not a hardship to me.

There followed Douglas newspaperman Harold Henry, Douglas Police Lieutenant Leslie Gatliff, and O. A. Ash, the constable of Douglas, who testified that their investigations and experience tended to confirm my account. Mr. Ash displayed the very same clothes and shoes in which he had walked over that desert more than forty-seven miles in four trips in following my tracks. They appeared but slightly worn. Judge Carlos Hardy's testimony established our good faith in dealing with Attorney McKinley and Mrs. Wiseman.

The transcript of this preliminary hearing filled 3,608 pages, so it is impossible to cover the whole range of testimony. However, I must mention the handwriting experts who inspected the photographs of the grocery slips found out in the yard at Carmel almost two months after the "mystery couple" left. (The originals, you remember, disappeared mysteriously during the grand jury hearing.) Wonderful grocery slips, unaffected by fogs, dews, or irrigation! While the prosecution's handwriting authority endeavored to link those two order slips to me, the defense handwriting expert, Douglas L. Swan, demonstrated conclusively that the originals had been "altered, patched, erased, rewritten, overwritten, and otherwise strengthened" before those photographs were made. And when the negatives of those photographs were wanted for investigation, they were suddenly destroyed in a mysterious fire!

Between the time the defense rested its case on October 28 and Judge Blake announced his decision, the district attorney and press heralded a new sensation about a "little blue trunk" and a crazy cryptographic note I was accused of writing to Mr. Ormiston. Mae Waldron, my stenographer, later confided to me that reporters admitted they had cooked up this evidence. Nothing would be gained now by naming the newsman who masterminded the scheme. Many of my friends believed that this new innuendo was launched with a view to helping influence the judge's decision whether to bind mother and me over for trial on the conspiracy charge.

The trunk in question, which Mr. Ormiston was said to have shipped about the country under an assumed name, contained a wardrobe of clothes which, it was said, could be traced to me.

When I first heard this report, I fully expected to find some of my belongings in the contents of the trunk, for our house had been ransacked in the preceding months, and many schemes were put forward to prejudice the public and the court. Reporters made themselves at home without invitation there. It was not uncommon for us to come downstairs in the morning and find a reporter sleeping on the sofa and others out in the kitchen helping themselves to breakfast!

At any rate, Emma Schaffer, my secretary, looked over the list of garments and said, "I didn't recognize a thing." The proprietor of the dry cleaning establishment in Carmel which the mystery couple had used was unable to identify any of the dresses in the trunk as those brought to his establishment by Mr. Ormiston. Two pairs of shoes in the trunk were stamped "Wetherby Keyser." Mr. H. B. Wetherby told the authorities the shoes were not my size and offered the opinion that I could not comfortably have worn them.

Somebody obviously was playing a huge hoax. There probably wasn't a woman in Los Angeles who would have bought, worn, or owned such a conglomeration of garments, makes, trimmings, and colorings as were assembled and described to a long-suffering public. Note the ridiculous, gaudy outfits which would immediately brand their wearer as a freak, circus woman, or escaped lunatic! There was a bright cerice dress with orchid under-slip and peach stockings! There was a pale green dress with salmon chemise and green stockings. There was a blue evening gown with gold lace, with your choice of peach or brown stockings and silver slippers! And then consider the colors of the fifteen or more gowns jammed and crammed into that little blue trunk: dark green, light green, dark blue, black, pink, gold, white, blue and gray, bright cerice, peach with green, purple, blue and white, trimmed with ostrich feathers, flowers, ribbon, and gold thread!

Some modest outfit! Figure your favorite combination from the list advertised!

And then the blue trunk—blue to match the blue car I reportedly had been seen in! But the bluest of all is the one who would believe that the great newspaper syndicates, nobly cooperating with the powers that be, had this evidence—this magnificent evidence which absolutely "clinched" the case, they say —in their possession from the very day the preliminary hearing began on September 27 and concealed it from the court and the public until the psychological moment when the hearing ended. And then—bang! Headlines!

The day came when Judge Blake would announce his decision whether or not the case against me would go to trial. That was the only issue to be decided by the weeks-long preliminary examination—the longest preliminary hearing in the history of California courts up to that time. The district attorney's office was represented in force. Someone told me that the office boys in Mr. Keyes's department usually attend to the preliminary hearings—that there had not been another case since he became district attorney of Los Angeles County in which he appeared personally at a preliminary hearing for one hour, let alone a month. And if he wanted to appear in person in this case, I wonder upon what theory he needed two of his top assistants—Mr. Dennison and Mr. Murray—to prosecute me in that preliminary. We were wondering about how much the hearing would cost the taxpayers until Mr. Keyes later announced that the costs were small because the newspapers footed most of the bills in investigating and locating witnesses!

Judge Blake ruled that the case go to trial. But, of course, it never did. The prosecution's key witness changed her story again and again. Asking for a dismissal of the case against my mother and me on January 10, 1927, District Attorney Keyes conceded that "without her testimony, proof of the alleged conspiracy is impossible. Since the preliminary hearing, she has changed her story almost daily, until it now contains so many contradictions and inconsistencies to the one given in court that she has become a witness for whose truth and credibility no prosecutor could vouch." The district attorney declared that the case could no longer "be prosecuted with honor or with any reasonable hope of success." The court agreed and granted the dismissal he requested.

Some people at the time felt that the dismissal of the case was a less satisfactory conclusion than would have been acquittal by a jury. But in dropping the charges, the district attorney admitted he had no possible chance of making a case before a jury. Judge Jacob F. Denny, formerly of the Fifty-eighth Judicial Circuit of Indiana and at that time a member of the California bar, wrote:

The vindication of Mrs. McPherson and Mrs. Kennedy could

not be more complete. It is infinitely stronger than if it had been determined by a jury after hearing all the evidence and resulting in an absolute acquittal. A jury passing on the case would naturally be supposed to be unbiased and to give an unprejudiced decision. But in the present case, the State of California, with all its machinery, power and prestige, spent many thousands of dollars in the investigation of the truth of the charges which it had made against these women. These charges they admitted were all false.

In addition to the ordinary investigation which is made by state officials, this case, by reason of its having excited national interest, was given special attention. For more than a half a year the entire resource of the State of California was devoted to the unearthing of evidence against them. Special agents were employed in great numbers to trace down every remote rumor that might throw light on the case.

All of this evidence collected was reviewed by the officers themselves most interested in procuring a conviction and naturally supposed to be highly hostile to the defendants. This tribunal themselves determined that there was not sufficient evidence against the defendants even to justify placing them on trial before an unprejudiced jury.

Seldom, if ever, in the history of American or English jurisprudence has so signal a vindication been achieved without a single gun being fired by the defendants in their own defense.

My attorneys had collected more evidence to use in a superior court trial if matters came to that—considerably more than was offered at the preliminary hearing. However, now it would not be needed and so was not publicized. It was interesting to note, however, that just a few days before the case was dismissed, the New York *Times* and other newspapers carried a story that the mystery woman who had occupied the Carmel cottage had been "partly identified as E. Tovey." Mr. Ormiston himself had said that his companion was a "nurse from Seattle."

Meanwhile, as headlines in Los Angeles screamed, "Mrs. McPherson Cleared," the news flashed around the world. Seas of humanity poured into Angelus Temple, wave upon wave. Such a scene certainly never took place in any church in the world as followed my appearance at the pulpit. As though jerked to their feet by a magnet, the congregation arose. Shouts of "Hallelujah!" "Praise the Lord," "God bless you," "Jesus answers prayer," resounded from everywhere in the great church which was packed to the dome, even though it was Monday night.

To God we gave all the glory, for we stood helpless except for divine intervention. But God had helped. As at the tower of

Babel, when God confused the tongues, so God confused the tongues of my accusers. The whole structure of this case against me was built like that of the ancient tower. It was rotten from the bottom. Each block, built one upon another, reached just so high, and then, like the Tower of Babel, God looked down and confused the tongues of the builders. Each one told a different story. One confused another, and thus it has ended, leaving standing only the true facts as I told them. Certainly no one would have invented a story like my ordeal. Anyone fabricating a tale could have manufactured a more outwardly credible story. But I stuck to my account because it was the truth. How often I have thought, "It was bad enough to be kidnapped, but it was far worse to have to try to prove it to an unbelieving world." Little did I realize that the prosecution would continue for years in their attempt to discredit it. Be that as it may, I was now vindicated before the law. And I could again devote my entire energies and time to the preaching of the Foursquare Gospel.

In the Center of God's Will

For four years I had devoted my energies almost exclusively to the ministry at Angelus Temple. I don't believe I was away from that work for a longer period than five consecutive days except for the periods at my kidnapping and my vacation in the Holy Land. Now, however, insistent calls were coming from all over the world, and I felt constrained to spend time on the evangelistic field. During the next ten years I would be away from Los Angeles almost as much as I would be there.

Immediately after my vindication I departed on what amounted to a barnstorming tour across the country. I wanted to preach in as many places as possible in the eighty days I would be away, so the campaigns in the various cities were necessarily very brief— only two or three days—with me speaking twice each day.

One stop on this tour was Baltimore, Maryland. Many years before I had come to the Lyric—that great, classic theater there. Here it was that the Lord brought out in a larger way his plan for me to minister his Word to the sick and afflicted. Because news reached reporters in Baltimore of healings God had performed in my meetings elsewhere, a newspaper headlined my arrival as the "Miracle Woman."

Of course, that theater was packed with sick people as a result of such publicity. I came up the stairs to the stage, peeked out at the stretchers and wheelchairs that filled the front, and exclaimed, "Oh, my goodness." I took another look and nearly fainted. I ran back down to the dressing room, dropped on my knees beside an old chair, and said, "Now, Lord, see what you have done. People up there with broken backs in casts and in wheelchairs. Oh, Lord, I can't heal them!"

There and then the Lord spoke to my heart. Here was an emergency, but I believe it was the real beginning of this Foursquare ministry. The Lord said, "If those sick people are healed and saved, who is going to save and heal them?"

"You are, Lord, of course. I couldn't save or heal one of them."

"Why are you nervous? Just go up there and open the Bible," the Lord directed. "You know the Scriptures on healing and salvation. You tell the people what I am going to do, and when you lay your hands on them, I will lay my hand on yours. And all the time you are standing there, I will be standing right back of you. And when you speak the Word, I will send the power of the Holy Ghost. You are simply the mouthpiece of the telephone. You are the key on the typewriter. You are only a mouth through which the Holy Ghost can speak. Will you go now?"

"Yes, Lord, it is wonderful. I will speak," I answered, "and if they are not healed, it is your business." When the time came, I preached. Then we prayed for the sick. Methodist, Baptist, Episcopalian, and Presbyterian preachers helped me and wept when they looked on the victims in those cots and wheelchairs. The Lord told me, "Now I lay my hand over yours. I AM the Lord that healeth."

To my surprise—and with shame I add to my shock—there were more healings that day than I had witnessed in any other place. People with broken backs—Catholics and Protestants—just ran around that theater.

After it was over, the Lord seemed to say to me, "Remember, if at any time you allow people to call you 'the Miracle Woman' and to say you heal them, you will have no power. Whatever the results, you are to say, 'The glory belongs to the Lord.' "

That was in 1919. Now, in 1927, I was back in Baltimore—this time not for three weeks as before but for just a few hours. Of this service Dr. Leech of the Franklin Memorial United Brethren Church there wired the Temple, "Great meetings. Overflow crowd. Never better spirit." He did not exaggerate in the least.

As this tour drew near its end, I learned of rumblings of criticism in Los Angeles. Toward the end of the preliminary hearing about the kidnapping, I had engaged two newspaper reporters—one from the *Times* and the other from the *Examiner*. I hoped that their expert experience in public relations would have a favorable effect on future publicity, and while the Los Angeles press remained for the most part hostile, these men, who were with my party on this nationwide tour, certainly produced good results. However, they were both worldly men making no Christian profession, and they offended some of my friends. I hoped that association with evangelism would win them to Christian living. Mother especially resented them, as they took matters into their own hands at times—both before and after I was vindicated.

In subsequent years the press would puff the idea that my mother and I separated in the work because mother doubted my story of the kidnapping. Nothing could be further from the truth. Mother never changed—even at times when the differences between us were at the worst (and they never were nearly as bad as the press publicized). She insisted that nothing could make her doubt my innocence. She denied statements attributed to her to the contrary.

Our differences were mostly of a business nature. Mother wanted me to spend most of my time in Los Angeles at Angelus Temple. I felt the call to evangelize throughout the world. And when I was absent from the Temple, little frictions between mother and some of the workers there became irritated. After some months, it seemed obviously best that either mother or I take full charge of the church. Mother chose to withdraw, and we reached an amicable property settlement. However, the newspapers would constantly keep the pot boiling—quoting mother about me or me about mother—and most of the time the statements of both of us were grossly misrepresented.

Meanwhile, the tares had been sown amid the wheat well before I returned on April 1 to Angelus Temple. Some time after this we suffered the first serious schism in our ranks when our fine choir director and bandmaster, the Rev. Gladwyn Nichols, left us and organized his own church. At first about three hundred of our singers and musicians followed Brother Nichols, but in the ensuing weeks many—probably most of them—returned. Mother at this point had an important part in contacting the dissidents and wooing them back to the Temple. I hoped Brother Nichols would return too, and eventually he did, but not for about three years. If the press had not given the incident so much coverage, it is possible he would have come back much sooner.

When I returned to Illinois for campaigns in Chicago and Alton, in July, the festering dissatisfaction at the Temple came to a head. I received an urgent message from the department heads of Angelus Temple to return home at once and assume full management of affairs.

Upon my return from Illinois, reporters pressed me for comments of the reported tension involving my mother. I stated at that time, "She is my mother, and I love her. I have the greatest respect and admiration for her and for all her invaluable services to me over the past many years. There is no trouble between us. My mother signified her intention of retiring long ago. She deserves a good rest and she shall have one."

A little more than two years later, mother returned as business manager of Angelus Temple and served briefly, again furnishing invaluable assistance at a crucial time. During the interval of her absence she had commented several times that unscrupulous schemers were taking advantage of my generous nature, and to some degree she was certainly right. Without mother's strict oversight, I became fair game for all kinds of promoters who inveigled me into lending my name and that of the church to a number of business propositions which, had they worked out, would have been wonderful. But several did not work out, and several lawsuits ensued. Indeed, almost all of the lawsuits which over the years were filed against me arose out of contracts and agreements which, not being a hardheaded business woman, I did not fully understand. It was good to have mother back. Now would-be promoters would have to do business with her, not me. And mother proved a big help in testifying before a grand jury hearing investigating Temple finances.

This hearing had been prompted by bitter charges made by our former general supervisor of Foursquare Churches, the Rev. John Goben. Several ministers on the field had warned me that Brother Goben had ambitions of taking over the leadership of the movement. Some complained that he was placing ministers loyal to him in strategic positions and sending pastors loyal to me to distant fields. Earl Dorrance was removed from Burbank to Colorado, for example. Then Harold Jefferies phoned from Portland that Mr. Goben contacted him personally and sought his support to back my ouster.

Meanwhile, Rev. Goben was having me followed by detectives. They reported that they traced me one night to the Alexander Pantages home. At a minister's meeting Brother Goben called in one of our suburban churches, he suggested something sinister was going on when this report was given.

Some people wondered whether the detectives' report was mistaken. It wasn't. I had gone to that home to visit Mrs. Pantages. She was a friend of mine who was in extreme trouble, and I went to give what comfort I could. On the night of her husband's conviction, Mrs. Pantages's adopted daughter came to me and said, "Mrs. McPherson, mother is calling for you. Will you come?" I was driven to Mrs. Pantages's home and prayed with her. It seemed strange to me that critics would make so much of a stricken woman calling for a minister and the minister responding to the call.

On another occasion I was driven to the Pantages's home in my attorney's car, but that attorney was not present. His chauffeur drove.

It became necessary to dismiss our general supervisor. Five or six churches withdrew from the Foursquare movement, but almost all of them were back very soon. Delegations from more than fifty Foursquare branches in Southern California came to the Temple and pledged their loyalty.

Mr. Goben continued making wreckless charges against me, accusing me of being a "gold-digger," and convening mass meetings whose avowed purpose was to effect changes at the Temple and in Foursquaredom. His accusations caught the attention of the authorities, and an investigation was launched. However, our accounts were found to be in order. Mother's testimony carried great weight.

Unfortunately, frictions again developed in connection with mother's management, and she again withdrew, charging that I had come under the influence of three of our workers—Harriet Jordan, Emma Schaffer, and Mae Waldron. I had just returned from the Holy Land, where I had led a pilgrimage of Foursquare members. Mother showed up in a sanitarium with a broken nose. The press reported—erroneously—that I had inflicted the injury.

I watched with distress again how degrading a disagreement or misunderstanding could look in print. I am as sorry as can be that I ever said a word about such differences, no matter who spoke unkindly about me or what was said.

While the press was busy headlining turmoils in which I was named, the Foursquare work progressed gloriously. The revival continued at Angelus Temple while I was there and when I was absent on the evangelistic field. I had never been so happy nor so eager to go for the Master in all the years that I had been preaching the gospel. Scores of churches were affiliating with the International Church of the Foursquare Gospel, which had been incorporated in 1927. The Foursquare movement was growing in America, and we were sending out missionaries overseas—to Latin America, to Africa, to the Orient. Back in Angelus Temple, I resumed my full schedule of services, plus teaching five times each week in the Bible school which now was called LIFE—Lighthouse of International Foursquare Evangelism.

By now Angelus Temple was beginning to appear a bit shabby. The carpets were especially worn. It occurred to me that many not only of the Temple people but of the *Bridal Call* family as well would covet the opportunity to donate at least one yard of this crimson carpet to be a path leading down the vast aisles to the cleansing fountain at the altars. I announced that two dollars and fifty cents would provide a yard of carpet at wholesale. Immediately people contributed.

The biggest project in the remodeling of the Temple was the installation of the beautiful proscenium arch flanked by two choir lofts. (The choir had previously sat above the stage and platform.) This change afforded greater opportunity for the presentation of my illustrated sermons and of the sacred operas the Lord gave me.

The development of this type of message came as a result of my disappointment that many left my meetings unconverted, in spite of the fact that hundreds and sometimes thousands flocked to the altars. The thought struck me that perhaps if people could see the messages as well as hear them, more would come to Jesus.

In the beginning the illustrations were quite elementary compared with their later development. My first sermon to be presented in this way was "Weighed in the Balances." A large pair of scales was erected on the platform over which a structure of wood canopied by velvet was built. Inside, a man was hidden. I placed toys representing worldly amusements on one of the scale pans—a toy automobile to represent a joyride, a little house for a dance hall, a miniature oil derrick to represent the search for worldly riches, and so forth. As each object was added, the operator inside would tip the scales further downward.

Then a tiny girl clad in white and carrying a huge family Bible came forward. With the aid of a chair and a lift, she got into the opposite pan. Because the curtain was thick, the operator inside did not know exactly when to let her down. I waited and waited. Finally, with a great shaking of the framework, a groaning of the machinery, and a general catching of breath, the pan with the girl was hastily lowered.

In spite of the timing problems, the illustration brought to the hearts of the people the assurance that the Bible, when received as a little child, outweighs the world with all its riches and amusements, no matter how high they are piled.

As time passed by, these sermons were worked out much more elaborately and effectively. Beautiful paintings and pastel lightings, planned and prepared by artists and construction experts, were brought into use, and the musical programs were coordinated with the themes of the messages. Through the years these illustrated sermons proved to be a joy to the hearts of thousands, besides a delight to the eye and ear. Through them countless souls which otherwise might not have come to Christ were born into the Kingdom of God.

Through the first half of 1930 I maintained my heavy schedule of preaching and administrative duties, ignoring warnings from friends and associates that I should slow down for my own health's sake. Six or seven years before this, William Jennings Bryan had predicted I would have a bad nervous breakdown if I continued the pace he witnessed. But through most of the ensuing years I enjoyed remarkably good health—in spite of the work load and tribulations that beset my path. I enjoyed being busy in the service of the King—preaching, lecturing, teaching, writing, traveling, planning, editing.

Then, having burned the candle at both ends, as the saying goes, almost continuously for fifteen years or more, the flames came together. Coincident with my mother's departure from Temple affairs, the newspaper headlines screamed that I was dying. This was in August, 1930.

Concern for my condition prompted a special meeting of our Foursquare Council of Angelus Temple on September 7. In the proceedings of that meeting were included stenographic reports of statements by my physician and my son.

Rolf had recently returned from an evangelistic trip throughout much of the country. He gave a glowing report of the services and announced he would be entering Bible school the next day. "I am willing to work up from the bottom, run errands, do anything, let the Lord have his way," he said. "I am glad to work in any way I can. I do not know just what the Lord will plan for me, but whatever he plans is best, and I must be prepared to fill that place. So I am glad to work anywhere I can." Then Rolf referred to me and my serious physical condition.

I hope I may be a great blessing to mother and help her. I surely appreciate the way you folks have taken care of her and helped her in every way. I believe mother is in good care with Dr. Williams.

Most of all we must trust in God to bear this load for us, and I am sure he will raise mother up and make her every whit whole in his own time. I appreciate the fact that you folks [the Temple board members] are not rushing mother back, not making her feel that she has to hurry back, because I believe if she were rushed back, it would be only a short time till she would have another breakdown. We want her fully to recover and be raised up so that she will be able to go on in the strength of the Lord. We want the Lord to have his way. He will have his way whether we want him to or not, and if we try to have our own way, it is not the best for us. Let us pray about mother that the Lord will have his own way. If it is his will to raise her up quickly, he will. We just have to trust him.

I want to thank all of you for your kind care of mother and for

your prayers and all your help in remaining back of her in everything she does. I surely appreciate everything you have done.

Dr. Williams, the nerve specialist, told the same council meeting:

> I was called to this case because I know something of nervous
> conditions. I found that Sister McPherson was suffering from ten
> times more work than anybody should do. I have never known
> anybody who was doing so much work.
> She was very ill, and a week ago Friday night she was at the
> point of death. She did not take nourishment. She could not eat.
> Her mind was working as fast as it always does, and she had the
> condition that we call acidosis, a condition that is really bodily
> starvation, where the mind is active and the body is not. She
> thought she was going, but she didn't go. She showed perfect
> resignation. The only expression she gave was that she was sorry
> to make us so much trouble.
> It wasn't trouble, I assure you. But she began to rally. I under-
> stand you were all praying over here. It surely must have helped.
> Within twenty-four hours she made the most miraculous comeback
> that I have ever seen. I have never known anyone to approach
> so close to the brink and return so quickly. It was miraculous.
> She wants to come back very soon, but that would be the great-
> est mistake that could happen. Her mind is working much too
> rapidly for her body. Her strength is coming back probably more
> rapidly than any other person's would come back, but it will take
> quite a long time. I mean two months, three months perhaps. The
> most I can do is to give advice and watch things.
> At the great crisis we did give her some help, but now it is
> mostly advice I give her, and she follows it. I think she is the best
> patient I have ever known. Her spirit is the same spirit that you
> all know. Her whole thought is to come back here, and our whole
> thought is to keep her from coming back too soon.
> It would be well in a few days to move her where there is no
> possibility of anything to annoy her. If anyone wants to see her,
> she would do anything to see them. She thinks of other folks many
> times before she thinks of herself, but at the present time that is
> not good.

At the very time I was stricken so seriously, Rev. Gladwyn N.
Nichols, who had led the first split from our church, openly returned to the Foursquare fold. He pleaded for the opportunity
to make a public confession at Angelus Temple. While the press
made headlines of his departure in 1927, it took little notice of
his return.

Toward the end of what Dr. Williams called "four terrible,

tempestuous years" though really the blessing of God far exceeded the comparably tiny tribulations—the Lord led me in the development of a talent for writing music.

Way back in high-school days I had written a bit of poetry. It came to the attention of a rather sarcastic teacher. He read the poem with this comment, "If the young lady who wrote this poem would take my advice, she would not write any more poetry until she could write a great deal better than that."

The criticism may have been well deserved, but it thoroughly discouraged me from further efforts. So it was not until near the end of the decade of the twenties that the Lord poured music through me in abundance.

Forty days before Christmas in 1929 God gave me the idea of *Regem Adorate,* my first sacred opera. I contacted Charles William Walkem, then pastoring the Foursquare church at Ventura, California, and outlined my plans.

"You're out of your mind," he told me. "You don't even have the story outlined yet. You want to compose the music, write the lyrics, train the choruses, teach the soloists, costume them, and put on a finished performance at Christmastime! It's—why, it's impossible."

"We'll do it," came back the resolution. And we did. *Regem Adorate*—"O Worship the King"—commenced with the creation and fall of man and continued to the Christmas story, concluding with the grand march of homage, "Worship the King." I sang the words and melody, and Brother Walkem transcribed and arranged them. By Christmas the presentation was ready, and the sacred opera was given eight times in Angelus Temple.

Other sacred operas followed as the years ensued—*The Iron Furnace, The Crimson Road, The Rich Man and Lazarus.* And individual songs multiplied—"The Key to Paradise," "A Leaf in the Wind," "Blue Monday," "The Song of the Weaver," "The Castle of Broken Dreams," "Together," "Calvary's Rose," to name but a few. Sometimes incidents in my ministry prompted a song, as when someone commented that I could not be sincere because I smiled so much on the platform. I then wrote "Should Christians Smile?" "In the Center of God's Will" was written on a paper sack retrieved from the floor of a railroad train when I heard newsboys hollering an extra heralding that I had been killed in an airplane crash. (I had missed that plane and taken the train.)

18

Love and Faith

"Why did you marry Dave Hutton?" "Is there any excuse for a Christian marrying again while his former husband or wife still lives?" (I would some years later insist that Foursquare bylaws prohibit such remarriage by our ministers, but in 1931 I felt differently.)

These queries were handwritten on one of a sheaf of question sheets turned in to me in response to my announcement that I would conduct a question box. Other inquiries submitted at the same time were easier to answer, like "Do you believe in eternal security—once in grace always in grace?" (I don't.) But in answer to the question about my marriage to David Hutton, I said, in part:

> People sometimes speak of me as a "much married evangelist," but I have lived with my husbands only about four and one-half years in my life. I was married only a short time when Robert Semple died. I tried to settle down again without going into God's work, but I could not do it. After a short time ministering with me, Harold McPherson went back to the business world, and after a time divorced me and married again, leaving me to preach alone.
>
> And then, after years and years, Mr. Hutton came along, and I thought I was through with loneliness, thought I was through with my name being blazed across the headlines. I thought it might be protection and home and love, but it did not work out that way, and once again I am alone, and as the old saying goes, "kiss my shoulder goodnight."

At the time I married David Hutton, I justified my course on the grounds that the Bible says that if a man put his wife away for any reason other than unfaithfulness, that constitutes a sin. But if one partner has gone out and sinned and has broken the marriage bond, they may be separated from each other and that one shall be as though dead. In the Old Testament they were stoned to death, while in the New Testament they were separated as though by death.

Few people know as I did what it is to be lonely in a crowd—to feel deserted in the midst of multitudes. Then David Hutton came across my path. He came filled with enthusiasm for the work, ready, he said, to help me carry the burden. Romance again would walk hand in hand with faith. At least, that was my silly womanly dream. That dream did not last long, but it did come, and how welcome it seemed while it lasted.

I was at the low ebb of my physical strength. The avalanche of activities and adversities had left me exhausted and utterly broken in health in 1930. My board of elders insisted that I take a long rest, and so, with my daughter, Roberta, I started a trip around the world. We were in the Orient, homeward bound, when Roberta met and married William Smythe, a purser on our ship. A few months later, after I had returned to Los Angeles, Rolf too was married to Lorna Dee Smith, a charming student in our Bible school. I performed the ceremony in Angelus Temple. It was a glorious occasion.

But now, for the first time in my life except for that brief month in China between Robert Semple's death and Roberta's birth, I was alone, with no member of my family to share a home. At the end of each day—after every wonderful service—our dear people and my children would go to their homes arm in arm, with their tender words and little caresses, while I would sit in silence, watching the last light extinguished in the big auditorium and the last happy couple disappear in the darkness.

On my return to California in 1931 my work had virtually doubled. On the ocean voyage I had finished the musical scores of a second and third sacred opera, *The Iron Furnace,* which portrays the story of Israel's oppression in Egypt and the ensuing Exodus, and *The Crimson Road,* an oratorio for the Easter season. For months I had been working on the musical scores. Now they were ready for the world.

No sooner was the wonderful homecoming reception accorded me over than I got busy on production. The first thing was to find a singer for the principal role of Pharaoh. Little did I dream that in finding him I would find a husband. Homer Rodeheaver, that great revivalist and old friend of mine and the Temple, heard about my search and brought David Hutton to the church.

At first glance I knew instinctively that I was going to like him.

He sang marvelously and was most enthusiastic about the forthcoming production. David came back several times. We worked hard on the musical arrangement and he was so competent and helpful. Love was rapidly coming to the surface, and my poor lonely heart again throbbed.

I remember the night David proposed to me. We had talked of art and beauty, and then he told me he loved me. He said he wanted to be at my side and work with me in the church. He said his heart belonged to the Lord and he wanted to work in God's vineyard.

Eventually I said yes and thought that once again joy was to be mine forever. This was not the girlish, elemental emotion of youthful love, but rather the reawakening, I thought, of a mature, tired heart. I saw in David Hutton the promise of so many things I had missed in years gone by—the protection of a man, the thoughtfulness and tenderness and devotion of a good husband, and the helping hand of a sympathetic co-worker. Meanwhile, *The Iron Furnace* had been produced and was a great success, due in large part, I am sure, to Mr. Hutton's splendid singing.

September came. We were making arrangements to take the sacred opera to the Northwest. One night while talking together, Dave and I decided we would go to Portland as Mr. and Mrs. Hutton. In the early morning of September 13 we left by plane for Yuma, Arizona. The laws of that state did not require a three-day notice as did California. We wanted a quick marriage. I dreaded the blast of publicity.

Few persons in the world could picture my emotions as we climbed into the big trimotor plane at Grand Central Airport about three o'clock that Sunday morning. My son and his wife, Rolf and Lorna Dee, accompanied us. Rev. Harriet Jordan, the dean of LIFE, had gone ahead by automobile to arrange for the license.

We arrived at Yuma at dawn. A short time later Miss Jordan performed the ceremony. I was married. My husband was at my side, and soon we were winging back to my beloved Temple, where I would preach in the morning service.

Then, the same night of our wedding, I heard rumblings of a storm. The newspaper reporter who had so kindly arranged the plane to Yuma for us casually remarked as we sat at dinner that another woman was preparing to sue David. "Her name is Myrtle

Hazel St. Pierre, and she says David promised to marry her and then broke her heart," the newsman calmly announced.

David was sitting at the head of the table. My son, Rolf, and his wife were there and other guests. My heart pounded against my ribs. I dared not look squarely at David, but out of the corner of my eye I saw him. He flustered, reddened, and then said it wasn't so. I smiled reassuringly, but within me a panic still lurked, a confusion and turmoil of emotion. Two days later the woman filed the suit, asking $200,000.

I accepted Mr. Hutton's assurances that this woman's claims were false. We traveled north to Portland, where we had wonderful meetings. En route we stopped at San Quentin penitentiary, where I visited briefly with several convicts, including Asa Keyes, the Los Angeles district attorney who had prosecuted me in 1926. Investigation of his handling of my case resulted in uncovering some alleged wrongdoing on his part in other cases, and he had been imprisoned. Here is perhaps the place where I should state that at the time Mr. Keyes was preparing his prosecution against me, California's Governor Richardson administered a harsh rebuke to the district attorney when the governor issued the sixth pardon he had found it necessary to give to convicts prosecuted by Mr. Keyes. They later had been proven innocent, having been convicted on mistaken or perjured testimony. The district attorney's excessive zeal in prosecuting defendants—whether innocent or guilty—was well known. However, I held no bitterness against him and wished him well.

After Portland we went to Boston for eight days of meetings, announcing as our slogan, "Back to the Book [the Bible] for Boston." I had organized a second Watch Tower band at Angelus Temple to be praying around the clock for this campaign. "This Watch Tower will be the motor behind the revival," I had announced.

The first night when we opened in the Boston Garden, seating some eighteen thousand people, we did not have the crowd that we expected. My manager reported, "We had about five or six thousand icicles." Now five or six thousand people is a sizable crowd at any revival meeting anywhere, especially in Boston, where faith had faded drastically from the days when that city had been the cradle of American religion. Nevertheless, five or six thousand spectators scattered through that immense Boston Garden looked like a small crowd. But wait! Some of my best-attended revivals had commenced from much smaller beginnings. One had grown from about three hundred at the first service to almost eighteen thousand. And after a few meetings Boston Garden too was crowded, and I was preaching to some of the largest audiences I had ever addressed. The closing service drew almost twenty-four thousand, and many were turned away because there was no room left inside. I was told that it was the largest audience ever assembled together under a roof up to that time for an evangelistic meeting anywhere.

It is impossible to estimate how many were converted in this Boston revival. At times two-thirds of my audience were Catholics. The Holy Spirit moved in the place, and when I gave the altar call, it made me dizzy. I could not believe that the people had heard correctly. Hands went up all over the garden, many even behind me, where some fifteen hundred people sat who could not see my face all the time I was preaching. As many as two thousand people stood signifying their desire to receive Jesus as Savior in a single service.

From Boston we went to Providence, Rhode Island, for three days and preached God's Word there in a building seating twelve thousand. And God filled that place too. The campaigns in New England were a real inspiration and uplift to me. So often when I go to a city, some journalist or reporter approaches me and says, "It is a wonderful work you are doing. We know that. But how do you know the converts last? How much of it do you think is excitement? Don't you suppose it is personal magnetism or psychology, and the moment your back is turned, the converts will go back to the world?"

"If they were converted to me," I would reply, "that would be true. But if they are converted to the Lord Jesus Christ, it lasts."

Still in my mind often lurked the haunting question, "You say it lasts, but are you sure about it?" For almost nine years in Angelus Temple I had had a chance to see the converts last. Only God could have held those people together through the storms and tests we had gone through. I know it lasts. And back in New England I discovered fresh evidence of this. When I stood on those platforms in Boston and Providence, people came up to me from every direction and said, "Do you remember me, Sister? I am from Pawtucket, don't you know. I was converted in your meeting there fifteen years ago."

"Do you still stand true?" I asked.

"Oh, yes," came the reply. "And there is a whole band of us still there who were converted in your meeting."

What a thrill it was to have people come and say, "I was converted fourteen years ago—fifteen years ago—sixteen years ago —in your meetings." Soul-winning is the one abiding work which is going to last when all else has passed away. That is the reason why when an offer of a stage career came to me while I was in the East from a well-known theatrical leader in Los Angeles, I sent word back, "Not even if it were for ten thousand dollars a night would I accept. I expect to stay in the church and preach the gospel."

While we were in Providence, an invitation came to meet the Governor of Rhode Island. He received us most graciously and explained something of the unemployment situation. He remarked that news had reached the state of what we were doing in Angelus Temple to help the poor and needy, and he wanted more information about our program. We were happy to take offerings both in Boston and in Providence to assist victims of the Great Depression. Indeed, it seemed then that wherever we went, authorities expected us to do something for the unemployed. We were glad to oblige. Our pleasure is giving other people pleasure. The greatest joy in this world is not, "Give me! Give me! Give me!" but getting something and then sharing it with somebody else.

We returned to Los Angeles, and illness soon struck me again. Early in 1932 I sailed with David on a cruise to Central America. Later in the spring we held a revival in Kansas and took another sea voyage, again for the purpose of regaining my health. My prostration, however, continued after we came back to California.

The day of the trial of Miss St. Pierre's suit against my husband came. I was too sick to be at David's side, though my heart was with him. Doctors had ordered me to my home at Lake Elsinore where there was no telephone, and there I lay. The newspapers had been snickering about the case for some time. Pictures and intimate details of this and that had appeared. But when the case came to trial, how the headlines did howl: "I Kiss Your Hand, Madam, Theme of Hutton Trial." "Girl Suing Hutton Screams in Court." "Baritone Bares All on Stand," and so on and on and on.

Early in July, 1932, the jury returned the verdict. I did not know what had happened until David arrived to tell me. "Five thousand dollars, that's all," he announced with a wave of his hand, dismissing the judgment against him as a trifle. I fainted dead away. When I regained consciousness, I was told that I had fallen and struck my head, fracturing the base of my skull. Later I learned that for weeks my life hung in the balance. I had been weakened by a dangerous intestinal malady contracted in Guatemala.

Soon after the sensation of the trial died down, we went on a few short trips, but I was unable to carry out many extensive campaigns. The fall months went by rapidly, and I was getting worse. These were dark days indeed.

After the Christmas holidays it was decided that I should sail on a trip to Europe. After I had been gone some time, David stated that I went away without his consent. That was strange, for he handled the money we raised for the trip and bought the ticket. He arranged the details, buzzing around, perturbed and anxious, to get me ready. He personally drove me to the harbor and placed my sick form into the berth in a stateroom which he had reserved on the Italian steamer *Falla* for me and my nurse, Bernice Middleton. And then he posed for pictures with me and told the reporters all about my trip.

When I was in Europe, I received clippings of Los Angeles papers telling how David left the boat crying. Certainly he never said then that I went without his consent. I was going away for a while to make a desperate fight for my life, and my husband knew it. But though the trip brought me the rest I needed, it turned out to be the end of our marriage.

I left America in January, 1933. I wrote to David, and he answered frequently. So far as I knew, all was well. He kept telling me, "Take your time, honey." "Don't hurry until you are well." "We need you here." "The church needs your strength." How could I doubt his love when reading phrases like, "I love you and miss you, and nearly die with loneliness, but you are first, and I want you a well woman"?

How embarrassed I was upon returning to the United States to see my letters to David splashed across the front pages of newspapers. Before I landed, he had moved away from the parsonage and instituted proceedings for a divorce. And he started appearing on theater stages making jokes about me and the Temple.

My romance and sorrows with Mr. Hutton would have been crushing indeed were it not for that ever-present overwhelming divine love that is ours for the asking. I had made a mistake in remarrying. Some of my friends consoled that I had just married the wrong man and urged me to accept Homer Rodeheaver's later proposal, but I could not do that. At any rate, out of the shattered, broken relationship with Mr. Hutton there was nothing for me to do but begin the reconstruction of things that were and things that are to be—for no life is ended until the heart is stilled and the spirit no longer responds to those twin emotions of love and faith.

America, Awake!

More than fifteen thousand miles! Forty-six cities in twenty-one states! Broadcasts on forty-five radio stations! Three hundred and thirty-six sermons, sometimes as many as five in a single day. Aggregate audiences in auditoriums, arenas, churches, and theaters of almost one million people! That is the summary of my whirlwind evangelistic tour in the last half of 1933.

For one hundred and fifty days I looked into the heart of America. From ocean to ocean and from border to the gulf, from the largest metropolitan city to some of the oldest little villages, I journeyed and preached and studied. I planned and pondered the heart hunger and longings of the multitudes with whom I came into personal contact. I read mountains of mail from others whom I reached over the various radio stations and networks of the nation. I came to the firm conclusion that America was starving for the Word of God.

In late 1933 America was looking to the "Blue Eagle" of

national recovery to dispel the clouds and mists of the Great Depression. I reminded the multitudes who came to our meetings that in order to fly an eagle must have two wings: "One wing is material recovery. The other is spiritual recovery. The first wing is not enough. We will just flop about helplessly. Let us get back to God! Let us turn our eyes from self and mankind and behold the Lamb of God that takes away the sin of the world."

The specter of communism and other totalitarian evils haunted the nation; indeed, they thrived on the desperate conditions which saw so many millions unemployed and in dire need. But the severest threat was in the realm of the spiritual. Atheism and modernism were rife.

It was at this time that I received a challenge from Charles Lee Smith, the founder and president of the American Association for the Advancement of Atheism. In my evangelistic itineraries my messages, he complained, had stepped on his toes, and he wanted to debate me. Mr. Smith said I would not dare meet him on any platform because I knew in my own heart that evolution was true.

My debating experience was rather limited, though it was true that in March, 1932—when the Prohibition issue was under such violent discussion—we had a debate about it at Angelus Temple in which I upheld the law of the land and Mr. Walter Huston, a famous motion picture actor, took the other side. The distinguished author, Upton Sinclair, attended, and when asked to greet the great audience, expressed his fervent opposition to liquor. But that was a debate in friendly surroundings. Mr. Smith wanted me to appear against him in public auditoriums across America, where his followers and militant collegians who belonged to groups with such blasphemous names, as "God's Black Sheep," "Circle of the Godless," "Hell's Angels," and the "Legion of the Damned" could turn out en masse to support their atheistic hero.

With fear and trepidation I accepted the challenge. But I decided to appear at the debates in conjunction with a nationwide lecture tour in which I would endeavor to alert the nation to the perils which threatened and to awaken America to its need of God. After a number of appearances on the West Coast in late January, I would be visiting areas where there were very few Foursquare churches. This would be a scouting trip. I would meet with city officials, become acquainted with new territories, speak over radio stations, line up auditoriums with a view to later extended revivals, and especially look over the field for the opening up of new churches for the graduating students of LIFE.

So I would be waving two flags. Proudly I would hail Old Glory—the finest national banner in all the world, with its red for bravery, white for purity, and blue for loyalty. Time and time again as I would preach my patriotic sermon, "America, Awake!" audiences across the country were electrified when I proclaimed, "America is not in the market for a red flag"— meaning the flag of atheistic communism, which was at that time enamoring so many, especially among the young.

The other flag I was eager to plant was a newer banner—the Foursquare flag. I had designed and sewn the first Foursquare flag in the early months of 1931. It would not be long before we could praise the Lord that the sun never sets on the Foursquare flag. But there were at this time large sections of America where there were not yet any of our churches. As a result of this lecture tour, some of these areas would soon be welcoming our graduates.

The first of the debates took place in Seattle, Washington's Municipal Auditorium. At last I met my opponent—the man without God, the man who was doing his best to pervert the minds of the youth, especially college students of America and Canada with the doctrines of atheism.

After I had once met Mr. Charles Lee Smith on a public platform, I was no longer afraid. Up to the last moment before that, a degree of nerve strain had held me rigid. I had prayed long and earnestly. I believed the promise of the Word of God with all my heart and soul, but I trembled lest I personally should fail the Lord and be insufficient to meet so seemingly formidable a foe.

People had read for years about this bold atheist—his audacity and militant tactics. He had debated the famous John Roach Stratton of New York and the president of the World Fundamentalists Association, Dr. W. B. Riley. He had debated Tingley and Oliphant, two fiery evangelists of the South. Gerald B. Winrod had written in his books and periodicals concerning him. Now I had taken the challenge which he flung out and was to meet him in an open debate. How I needed the help of God!

When first I saw the streams of people standing in line for admission, I supposed they must be going to the great auto show which was being held in the lower auditorium of the Municipal

Building. Soon I found that this mass of smartly dressed intelligentsia was bound for the debate. There were many Jews. Yes, this subject would interest them, for the debate embraced the question, "Is There a God?" and Jews believe in God. Catholics and Protestants were there. University professors, students, ministers and priests, attorneys, the lieutenant governor, and busy housewives were there. I began to realize what wide-reaching lengths and breadths the subject covered. The Christian was there to help me uphold the faith. The atheist was there to see if he could find something which would bolster his unbelief. The agnostic was there to consider which way to jump.

The question of the first debate saw Mr. Smith challenging— "There is no God, and America would be better if ridded of her churches." He sailed into his attack upon faith and hope in the hereafter.

Almost immediately I relaxed in my chair at the opposite table, for the realization swept over me that this atheist had not a leg to stand upon. The glory of the Lord swept over my soul, and a wave of reassurance and courage seemed to lift me, like a tidal lifting a vessel, and bear me along its crest. I knew my flock at home was praying for me. When it came time for me to rise and answer Mr. Smith, the words came tumbling out. I had studied for several weeks upon the subject of evolution and its conflict with God's Word. My book was filled with notes, but I scarcely glanced down at them, for my heart was so full of the message the Lord poured within.

Glory to God, the Rock of Ages still stands! There is certainly no reason to forsake the shelter of God's pavilions for the quaking quicksands of unbelief until some shred of evidence against the good Book can be presented. Mr. Smith had no such evidence.

Noting the interest which prevailed, listening to the people cheer for God's Word but groan and shudder at the atheist's propositions, I felt that it was a great pity that every American citizen—and especially every parent—could not hear that series of debates. The evolution Mr. Smith championed is just what is taught in our schools and universities worked out to its final analysis—the ripened flower of atheism. On the easel behind me was a lovely portrait of the Savior, while behind Mr. Smith stood a huge cardboard cutout of an immense gorilla. Above us a sign challenged, "God or Gorilla?"

Here in part is how a reporter described the encounter:

Mr. Smith seemed to be making rather good headway. I was almost ready to vote for the gorilla.

Then Sister Aimee stood up to speak. Well, if you have ever heard her speak, I do not need to describe to you the mental somersault I did. She pierced the wall of Mr. Smith's sarcasm and showed an utter emptiness behind it. She snatched the false robe of "science" from his gorilla theory and left it standing naked and without substantiation. She kicked the props from under the basic theories of evolution. And when she lifted her white Bible triumphantly and declared that it was the inspired Word of the Living God, I don't believe there was anyone in that audience who doubted her assertion. If applause is any criterion, they were with her to a man.

My vote went back to the white side of that overhead sign. As far as I was concerned, the gorilla was all washed up. I hadn't intended to make any such decision. I had not come for that. I resented that sign jumping out at me and shouting, "God or Gorilla?" It demanded an answer. Well, by the grace of Sister's preaching, the question was answered.

It was a little amusing to follow the mentions of time made by the debators. Mr. Smith flipped off millions of years without a flicker of an eye. Sister Aimee complained that evolution began in a mist and ended in a fog—that when the evolutionist is cornered, he takes to the wilds of eternity, where he is difficult to follow.

But according to Mr. Smith, the eternity of years of which he speaks is behind us. We came from a brute and to a brute we shall return, and death is the end.

Sister Aimee also dealt with an eternity of years—an eternity that is before us beyond the grave where we will meet the God who made us. Somehow, I believe that I prefer this idea of eternity. It is not half as difficult to believe God created the world as it is to believe that we came from a germ in some scum in a pond.

Yes, God has my vote. Down with the gorilla!

The debates in other West Coast cities toward the end of January (including Los Angeles, where we used the Shrine Auditorium) likewise proved to be triumphs for God's Word.

Continuous Revival

For ten years—from 1926 to 1936—I had been away from Angelus Temple as much or more than I had been present. My first vacation to the Holy Land, the weeks of my captivity during the kidnapping, the many evangelistic tours in America and abroad, plus the illnesses made it expedient for me to be away considerably longer than I liked. Angelus Temple is my life—my past, my present, and my future. And now conditions there dictated that I devote to that church almost my entire attention for a considerable time to come.

At the beginning of 1936 I had little idea that the coming year would bring both dreadful heartbreaks and glorious blessings. Relationships which had flourished for years would begin to rupture, while a wave of revival perhaps greater than I had ever witnessed would sweep the Temple. There were so many problems, but the Lord marvelously proved himself more than equal to every emergency. Surely he did help us.

I became aware of a serious financial emergency. Although Angelus Temple had been built and dedicated debt free, the operating expenses during the years of depression had put the church in a severe monetary bind, and the report reached me that the indebtedness had skyrocketed to what I considered to be the astronomical figure of $66,500.

Part of this severe deficit had been occasioned by expenses of operating the famed Angelus Temple Commissary, which the Lord led me to organize in 1927 to help the needy with food and clothing. The outbreak of the depression in 1929 greatly multiplied the scope of this work. From time to time, as new emergencies occasioned by the depression arose, the Temple was called upon to respond sacrificially to pressing needs.

Help from our commissary was offered without regard to creed. No questions were asked except as to the nature of the need. By the time of the outbreak of World War II, we would help with feeding or clothing about one and a half million people. We tried to operate the commissary off the donations of food and clothing from Temple members and friends and from a number of businesses who contributed commodities regularly. However, outgo almost always exceeded income, and the commissary expenses contributed to the accumulation of the large debt which burdened the Temple early in 1936. Rumors reached us of an impending action by our creditors to foreclose on some lots right down through the center of Angelus Temple.

Obviously the business manager, Sister Harriet Jordan, who was also dean of the Bible college, needed help. I appointed my daughter, Roberta, as associate business manager and Rev. Giles N. Knight as assistant business manager. Mr. Knight's policies later led to friction with Miss Jordan and Roberta and also with Rheba Crawford, who had been serving as associate pastor for several years. Because of the desperate financial plight, it soon seemed advisable for the good of the church to put the business management completely in Brother Knight's hands. Roberta felt she could not work with Mr. Knight and so withdrew from church activities, much to my sorrow. However, because Angelus Temple faced insolvency and Giles Knight seemed to be the man to cope with the problems, I felt I had to put the Temple's welfare even ahead of my family. As I told the Temple congregation, "I feel that God placed Brother Knight here and called him just in time to save this Temple from bankruptcy." We can prove this from the books.

There were spiritual problems as well as financial. The revival spirit which had surged for years had waned by the spring of 1936. Attendances when I was not in the pulpit had dropped somewhat, though they were still probably by far the best in the city. Miss Crawford, our associate pastor, had been attacking the city administration over the radio, much to my distress, for I never felt a church should participate actively in politics. And when I returned to the Temple after some evangelistic meetings in the spring of 1936, Miss Crawford preferred not to appear if I were there. She stated that there was not room for two stars on the platform at one time. I suggested that the star ought to be Jesus.

For months rumors were rife. Charges flew. My attorney, Willedd Andrews, made comments which provoked a lawsuit in which I had to testify at length. Angelus Temple's board of elders requested termination of Miss Crawford's contract. Dr. Knight agreed. Months later Miss Crawford sued me for slander, asking $1,080,000 and alleging I made statements which I certainly did not make. At any rate, on an August morning painters climbed ladders in front of Angelus Temple and replaced the name of the associate pastor with the words *Continuous Revival* —words which would remain on that sign as long as it occupied its place there over the main entrance.

A mighty revival had swept in upon the church about three months earlier. Mere words fail utterly to describe that outpouring. Angelus Temple, which in early 1936 was the mother church to three hundred eighty-seven branches, was shaken to its very foundations! Conviction hung like a cloud over record audiences, and hundreds rushed to the altars in ever-recurrent waves, crying, "God, be merciful to me, a sinner." No less than three altar calls marked some of the services, especially the divine healing services each Wednesday afternoon and Saturday night. Deaf mutes commenced to speak and hear the Word of God, and lines of beds were carried out empty as joyous patients rose and walked. Moreover, hundreds of people at a time were sometimes slain under the power of God, many receiving the baptism with the Holy Ghost. It was as though a scythe had passed over a wheat field and left the stalks piled three deep. Strong men wept for joy and went down like trees of a forest before a hurricane. Upon women and children came the Spirit like dew on the mown grass. Frequently the tarrying services ran until dawn.

This revival had started out as a one-week effort, but it continued for months. And even after the revivalists departed, the glorious outpouring of God's Spirit continued marvelously. How providentially God directed in this respect. Just at the time when the Temple most needed a spiritual refreshing, some colored saints who had participated in the great Azusa Street outpouring of 1906, from which a twentieth-century Pentecost spread round the world, came to the offices and inquired about conducting in Angelus Temple in the month of April a one-week celebration of the thirtieth anniversary of the Azusa Street revival. We welcomed with open arms the opportunity to host such a gathering.

One of the continuing outgrowths of this thirtieth anniversary celebration of the 1906 Azusa Street outpouring was the launching of the Holy Ghost rallies. May 29 set a new record in Pentecostalism. For eighteen consecutive hours thousands were swept by divine fires of unbelievable fervor. For eighteen consecutive hours saints laughed, cried, sang, shouted, danced, and prayed. During those eighteen hours twenty sermons were delivered, one after another like a hammer drives a nail in a sure place.

These rallies attracted worldwide attention. Letters, cables, and telegrams came pouring in from the ends of the earth. The revival spirit which pervaded the Temple made me more reluctant than ever to be away on lengthy evangelistic itineraries. While I did hold meetings in many places in the following years, I never absented myself long from Angelus Temple and LIFE, which had now become a Bible college authorized to confer both honorary and scholastic degrees. The first ministers to be honored as doctors of divinity were William Black and Giles Knight.

While revival fires flamed in the church, my own personal sorrows mounted. Remarks assertedly made by the corporation attorney against my daughter resulted in a heartbreaking lawsuit between them. This caused a division within the family that indeed prostrated me physically for a time. I well remember the Sunday morning when the Lord lifted the load of distress off my heart. It seemed that in the preceding two weeks I had been passing through the valley of the shadow of death. I thought my heart was broken. But the Lord raised me up and filled my heart with courage.

It had always been understood in my family that if Jesus tarried and my hands would grow weak, I would pass the work on to Roberta. She was to be my successor. Rolf understood this and went to a radio technicians' school, where he graduated with high honors. But now Roberta had withdrawn. In the past she had occasionally told me, "Mother, I don't want to work like you work. I have seen you come home wringing wet with perspiration from your meetings. I never want to have to do that." And who is to say that she should?

At any rate, when Roberta moved, my son, Rolf, forgetting his technical training, stood in the gap, squared his shoulders back, and took this whole burden. For my dear little star of hope, my love is unchanged. And though I carried on and bawled about losing her from the work, I finally came to the good understanding with the Lord and cast this care upon him.

Rolf assumed the position of assistant business manager of Angelus Temple, working with Dr. Knight, and later became managing editor of the *Foursquare Crusader*. He escorted me down the rampart to the platform at almost every service and sat by my side. His presence was a wonderful comfort and strength.

The Lord not only blessed Angelus Temple with a glorious spiritual revival in the aftermath of the celebration of the thirtieth anniversary of the Azusa Street outpouring in 1936 and of the thirty-third anniversary in 1939; he also marvelously met the material needs. Dr. Knight put the church on a cash basis, and although many disliked his lengthy appeals for offerings, by the end of 1938 the entire indebtedness of Angelus Temple was paid off. While three billion candlepower of lights bathed the front walls and the dome of the church, at one point in our Watchnight service I climbed to the top of the dome and there burned each and every note, representing over $66,000 of former indebtedness. Once again, as when the church was dedicated, Angelus Temple stood debt free! And the great revival continued.

21

Around the World with the Foursquare Gospel

"I will never rest until the gospel is preached around the world," I told reporters in Dayton, Ohio, when I arrived to speak at a Great Lakes district conference in the summer of 1938. "Ours is a colossal task but not an impossible one." I pointed out to the newsmen that at that time Foursquaredom supported one hundred eighty-eight foreign mission stations.

Then came World War II. The outbreak of the war and America's subsequent involvement hindered several plans of the missionary department to spread the Word to untouched regions. But it also afforded us an opportunity to minister to thousands of servicemen who would pass through Los Angeles. Each Sunday hundreds of men in uniform attended services at Angelus Temple. The overwhelming majority of these had never been in a Foursquare or Pentecostal church before. Many of them had no religious affiliation and did not own Bibles. What a privilege it was to invite the servicemen present in every Sunday night meeting to come to the platform, where I greeted them, gave each one a New Testament, and knelt in prayer with them for their spiritual needs and God's guidance and protection on their lives. Later, when the altar call would be given, many of these same servicemen would make another trip to the platform publicly to receive Jesus Christ as their personal Savior.

Travel within the United States was not curtailed until after the attack on Pearl Harbor, when gasoline and tire rationing was instituted. It was possible for me to conduct a twenty-five thousand mile evangelistic tour in the summer of 1940 and another less ambitious itinerary the following year. After December 7, 1941, I was able to conduct individual meetings from time to time in selected cities, including Nashville, Tennessee; Vancouver, B.C.; Joplin, Missouri; and Portland, Oregon. In these services God confirmed his Word mightily with signs following. But most of my time was devoted to Angelus Temple and the Bible college.

The war had its effect on the Temple program. At the time Hitler's forces were overrunning France, Belgium, and Holland, we instituted a series of all-night prayer meetings every Friday night. After a message constituting a call to prayer at 10 P.M., the people fell on their knees to ask God's help for the nation, the church, and for souls. President Franklin D. Roosevelt, through his secretary, Mr. Stephen Early, expressed appreciation for these efforts, as did the governor of California and other public officials.

To dramatize pleas by national leaders that people use their automobiles sparingly in order to conserve on gasoline and tires, I drove to the Temple in a horse and buggy one Sunday night in

May, 1942. "Drive slowly and use less rubber," I advised the congregation in the service which followed. When some expressed surprise that I would attempt to travel in such a conveyance, I replied, "Certainly I can drive a horse and carriage. I haven't forgotten my farm days."

Government regulations that public buildings prepare for blackouts made it necessary for a thorough and painstaking job to be done on every door, window, or other outlet for light. Even the stained-glass windows had to be covered, and the dome was painted black. As for dousing the lights throughout the huge plant, our nightwatchman conducted a test for a possible alert and blacked out both Angelus Temple and the LIFE Bible College building in a record twenty-eight seconds! Moreover, my son Rolf announced publicly that we were prepared to convert the edifice into an air-raid shelter if grave emergency made this necessary.

We also instituted first-aid classes and on one Sunday evening simulated an air-raid emergency to test the knowledge of the students and to give them practical experience. A number of serious "casualties" were handled in the test, and the realism, with tape, bandages, and other emergency accessories supplied made the test highly successful.

The war had its effect on our radio station also. Because transmitter tubes could not be easily replaced, it was deemed necessary to cease broadcasting at 11 P.M. No longer could my Sunday morning and evening services be rebroadcast between midnight and 3 A.M., reaching radio fans from coast to coast.

We determined to comply strictly to the wartime regulations set up by the Office of Censorship in Washington, D.C. Our radio manager explained that the granting of telephone requests had been definitely forbidden. While it was still permissible to make dedications and grant request numbers, these could be done only if no definite time were designated. A person might ask for a favorite singer to present, say, "The Old Rugged Cross," on some future program. However, if he asked for it on Monday night, June 12, for example, the request could not be granted. In the matter of reading letters over the air, it was necessary to change the wording in order to break the original succession of letters and their numerical value in case a code message might be contained in that letter. We were also discouraged from permitting messages in tongues and interpretations to be aired.

As loyal Americans, we cooperated as best we could with the war effort, and several citations of appreciation from government agencies were received. We also sent *Foursquare Crusader* magazines to army camps and helped certain companies to obtain furniture for their day rooms.

It was a privilege to make war bonds and stamps available to the public at Angelus Temple. And I took our musical department to Victory House in Pershing Square in downtown Los Angeles, where we conducted a program to encourage the sale of bonds and prayer for the war effort. Entertainers had been performing their songs and dances there, and I announced that if some could dance for victory, others could pray for victory. The press reported that record crowds gathered for the occasion and estimated that upwards of $150,000 was subscribed in the sale of bonds and stamps on June 20, 1942. Two years later, on July 4, we returned for a similar effort.

During a vacation in Mexico in the summer of 1943, I contracted a tropical fever which prostrated me intermittently for weeks at a time. How I regretted the protracted absences from my pulpit and the college classrooms! When my health improved slightly after the beginning of 1944, I decided it was time that Rolf assume the office of vice-president of the International Church of the Foursquare Gospel. The convention body had earlier written into the bylaws the provision that he be my successor as president of the church. Several years before, Dr. Knight had told the Temple congregation, "Rolf McPherson is a man of real judgment, and someday he is going to step forward and turn things up for God in Angelus Temple." Much as I appreciated Dr. Knight's outstanding management, I chafed at the restrictions he insisted on putting on my activities. They had certainly worked to a large extent for my own good, for the adverse press publicity had been almost completely muzzled, and lawsuits no longer plagued me as they had for years. However, I longed for closer contact with my people. Dr. Knight resigned, and Rolf assumed his several capacities. I cannot begin to express the thrill I experienced as my son so capably performed his responsibilities. I know he will carry on my work.

Actually, I feel that I have done so very little, though I have preached around the world and seen thousands of people saved. I feel I've done virtually nothing. If I were a man, I could do a lot more. But I'm only a woman who yielded herself for God to use. All the glory for anything accomplished belongs completely and only to the Lord I love and to whom I surrendered my whole life when I uttered the sinner's prayer in the cutter on that snowy Canadian road as a girl of seventeen.

People sometimes voice sympathy to me, saying, "Sister Mc-Pherson, you've suffered a little bit of persecution." Oh, well, if you have time to think about it, I suppose I have. People say this about me and say that about me. I haven't time to deny it or to affirm it. All I have time to do is to keep on preaching Jesus. Often friends suggest, "Why don't you ever get up and defend yourself?" Well, maybe I'll get a chance to do that sometime. But right now I'm too busy preaching the gospel. There has been no church federation back of us, but just by the grace and power of God, we've rolled the old chariot along. And we haven't got started yet—glory to God! My prayer is ever, "O God, keep me preaching Jesus until millions have heard the story of the Savior, Baptizer, Healer, and Coming King." My chief ambition has always been to move under God's guidance, much as a leaf is swayed by the wind.

As a leaf swayed in the breezes
    On a windswept hill—
As a leaf swayed in the breezes,
    Of Thy perfect will,
Swept and swayed by the Spirit,
    Moved at Thy command,
Let me be, Lord Jesus,
    Yielded in Thy hand.

A leaf in the wind, would my soul forever be,
A leaf in the wind, swayed ever Lord by Thee;
Swept by Thy Spirit through eternity,
Wonderful Savior, more than life to me.

Once my heart struggled and trembled,
    And I feared Thy will,
But I rest now in Thy promise,
    Trusting, yielding, still.
Perfumed breeze born of Springtide,
    Tempest dark and drear,
Bring me blest assurance,
    That my Lord is near.

Come, thou South Wind and blow softly,
    Rock me to and fro,

Wake, thou North wind in Thy fury,
   Rise and fiercely blow;
Rains of tears, skies of sable,
   Oft' though be my lot,
I know my Father sent them,
   And shall question not.

O'er the hills soon brightest Autumn,
   Multi colors weaves,
And fierce fingers of Winter
   Rend the frightened leaves;
But when death shall then loosen,
   Life's so fragile hold,
Take me to Thy bosom,
   Sweep me to Thy Fold.

EPILOGUE

On the evening of September 26, 1944, Aimee Semple Mc-Pherson preached her last sermon. It was a soul-stirring message delivered before a packed crowd in the Civic Auditorium in Oakland, California. This was the same city where twenty-two years earlier she had received the vision of the Foursquare gospel. And the words she spoke this night were vivid reminders that for this handmaiden of the Lord, Jesus Christ truly was the same yesterday, today, and forever. She expounded Jesus the Savior, Jesus the Baptizer with the Holy Spirit, Jesus the Healer, and Jesus the Coming King, and then she retired to her hotel room for the night.

The earthly ministry of Aimee Semple McPherson ended tirelessly just as it had begun. She often commented during the latter years of her life that she wanted "to wear out—not rust out," and when her son, Rolf, found her the next morning, he knew that her desire had been granted.

No sooner had the news of Sister McPherson's passing flashed around the world than skeptics commenced predicting that the far-flung Foursquare organization would now "come apart at the seams." But it didn't! All forces rallied immediately around Dr. Rolf K. McPherson, whose own deeply personal loss was transformed into confirmation that what his mother had begun was the Lord's work, and that the Lord would indeed continue to carry it out.

At the time of Sister's passing over three thousand had graduated from LIFE Bible College and had been ordained as Foursquare ministers, missionaries, and evangelists. Since her passing the number of Foursquare churches in the United States and Canada has risen from four hundred to seven hundred eighty-three; the foreign mission stations from two hundred to over two thousand with two thousand two hundred ninety-two missionaries and national workers registered. There are thirty day schools, thirty-two Bible schools, and two orphanages on foreign shores, plus one hundred seventeen radio broadcasts daily and weekly in twenty-seven countries outside the United States and Canada. Foursquare churches on the home field raise over one million dollars annually to support the world-wide missionary program.

Foursquare membership has risen to two hundred twenty-five thousand.

God gave Aimee Semple McPherson a remarkable ministry. She did not shirk her specific and divinely appointed task, but rather did the seemingly impossible for a woman in establishing an organization which continues pressing forward victoriously into the frontiers of this world. She insisted, "Nothing I could have done could have built up this marvelous work. All I had to offer was a yielded life. For everything that has been accomplished we give God all the glory."

DATE DUE

JAN 31 '78		
NOV 26 1984		
NOV 11 1986		
DEC 04 1986		
30 505 JOSTEN'S		